OBITUARIES

from

Barbour County, Alabama Newspapers

1890-1905

Compiled by
Helen S. Foley

Southern Historical Press, Inc.
Greenville, South Carolina

Copyright 1976
By: Helen S. Foley

Copyright Transferred 1983
To: Southern Historical Press, Inc.

All rights reserved. No part of this publication may be reproduced, stored in a retrieval system, transmitted in any form, posted on to the web in any form or by any means without the prior written permission of the publisher.

Please direct all correspondence and orders to:

www.southernhistoricalpress.com
or
SOUTHERN HISTORICAL PRESS, Inc.
PO BOX 1267
375 West Broad Street
Greenville, SC   29601
southernhistoricalpress@gmail.com

ISBN #0-89308-182-5

Printed in the United States of America

The Clayton Courier
1890

Sat. Jan. 11, 1890
Died last week, Mrs. McKee, the wife of Mr. D. J. McKee.
Mr. Frank Watkins, age 72, died last Monday. He lived about six miles from Clayton. He leaves a family.

Sat. Jan. 18, 1890
Mr. R. G. Hall, an aged citizen of Midway, (Ala.) died on the 6th inst.- Union Springs (Ala.) Herald.

Sat. Mar. 15, 1890
Died on Friday at the home of Dr. W. F. Wright, Mr. Thos.C. Wright. He was a young man and a brother of Dr. W. F. Wright.

Sat. Mar. 29, 1890
Died at the home of Mr. James E. Fenn on Wednesday, Mrs. Glover, the mother of Mrs. J. E. Fenn.

Sat. Apr. 19, 1890
Mrs. Thomas, the wife of Elder P. L. Thomas, died Tuesday.

Sat. Apr. 26, 1890
Dr. Henry Blair, after a long and painful illness, died at Louisville, (Ala.) last Sunday.

Sat. May 17, 1890
Mr. J. W. Smoot, living near Mt. Andrew (Barbour Co.) died on the 8th of May.

Sat. June 7, 1890
Josiah Bass, age 88, of Barbour County, died May 6th, 1890. He was born in Sampson County, N. C. on July 8th, 1802.

Sat. June 14, 1890
Mr. Robert Bradley, age 81 years, of near Clayton, (Ala.) died on Tuesday.

Sat. Nov. 29, 1890
Mr. John Bell, age 84 years on the 13th of January next, died at his home five miles from Clayton on Friday. Burial at Beasley's Burial Ground.

Sat. Dec. 6, 1890
Mr. Burrell Price, age 80 years old, died at the home of his son-in-law, Mr. D. J. Tomberlin last week.

Eufaula Times & News
1890

Thurs. Jan. 2, 1890
Mrs. C. C. Wells, age 72 years old, mother of Mrs. N. M. Bray, died at Mr. Bray's home Tuesday. Up to two years ago, until the death of Mr. Wells, she lived at Macon (Ga.). Burial in Macon.

Prof. Van Houton, age 54, died at his home on Colby Street in Eufaula on Wednesday. He left a widow and two sons and three daughters. His wife is a daughter of Mr. John McNab. Burial from the Baptist Church.

Mr. M. J. Hollis, a former resident of Quitman Co., Ga., died

Eufaula Times & News
1890

at Perote in Pike Co., (Ala.) on Tuesday. Burial at his old home.

Thurs. Feb. 20, 1890
  Mr. Jack Hilliard of Coleman, Ga., was shot and killed on Tuesday morning.

  Sidney, the ten year old son of Mr. F. M. Johnson of Ozark (Ala.) died last Wed. of dropsy and was buried near his mother who has gone on before.-Ozark (Ala.) Star.

Thurs. Apr. 3, 1890
  Miss Mamie Spann, daughter of Mr. & Mrs. J. E. Spann, died yesterday. Burial from the Methodist Church this morning.

Thurs. May 8, 1890
  Mr. Edwin O'Neal of Florence, Georgia, died recently.

  Miss Minnie Walker's clothing caught fire in Atlanta while she was cooking on a gas stove. She was 17 years old. She died of her injuries.

  Mrs. B. H. Hill, Jr., who was recently on a visit to the family of Dr. Copeland (in Eufaula), died at her home in Atlanta Sunday. Burial in Atlanta.

Thurs. May 29, 1890
  Mr. S. A. Woods, formerly of Eufaula, but had been a resident of Savannah for many years, recently moved to Anniston, (Ala.) where he was president of a bank, died yesterday. He will be buried today in Bonaventure by the side of his wife who died a year ago, after a married life of only one year. Mr. Woods has two sisters living in Eufaula, Mrs. Bloodworth and Mrs. Tullis. He was a brother of R. J. Woods and Mrs. J. M. McKleroy and Mrs. (Jos. Asbury) Sylvester. The last two of Anniston, (Ala.).

  Jackson, Miss. May 27,- A. M. Kimball, an old and highly respected citizen, was murdered while on his way home from the midnight train where he went to meet his son that night. It is supposed the crime was committed for the purpose of robbery. Mr. Kimball was receiver of public moneys.

Thurs. June 19, 1890
  Ada Richards, age 12, daughter of Mr. Dallas Richards, died Sunday at the home of her grandmother in Lawrenceville, (Ala.).

Thurs. June 26, 1890
  Mr. John Price, age 27, died at the home of his brother, Andrew Price, near White Pond (Barbour Co.) of Bright's disease. Burial at Kelley's grave yard today.

Thurs. July 3, 1890
  Mrs. Mollie Freeman, age about 50 years, died in Maryland. She was a sister to Messrs. S. H., George H., and Warren F. Dent, of Eufaula.

  Col. C. H. Wooten, of Americus, (Ga.) was found dead in his room Monday. It is believed he died from apoplexy.

Thurs. July 17, 1890
  Mrs. Wade Helms, age 35, of Lawrenceville, (Henry Co., Ala.)

Eufaula Times & News
1890

died Thursday of typhoid fever. She was the daughter of Mr. Wright Flowers. Survivors are her husband and five small children. Burial at County Line Church.

Thurs. July 24, 1890
  Atlanta, July 20.- Dr. R. C. Word, prominent physician of Decatur, Georgia, died this monring.

  The remains of W. A. Fry, who drowned near St. Vincent's Island recently, were found at West Gap. Burial in the city cemetery. - Apalachicola (Fla.) Times.

  Charles Peacock, age 15, son of Mr. T. M. Peacock, of Aberfoil (Bullock Co., Ala.) was killed by lightning recently.

  Lieutenant John U. Rhodes died in New Orleans yesterday. He was a nephew of our townsman Mr. C. Rhodes.

Thurs. July 29, 1890
  Hartselle, (Ala.) July 29.- Mrs. L. A. Woodall, age 57, living two miles from this place, committed suicide today by jumping off a bluff 45 feet high. Survivors are her husband and five children.

  Jacksonville, Fla., July 23.- The death of G. Tate Carr occurred at Romeo, (Fla.). He was from Ocala, (Fla.) where he had been living for the last five years. He was originally from Chicago, Ill.

Thurs. Aug. 7, 1890
  Granger, Ala., July 28,- Mr. G. G. Williams living two miles east of this place, committed suicide yesterday by the use of his pocket knife. He cut his throat from ear to ear. Survivors are his wife and children.

  Mrs. J. T. Tyre, of Bumbleton district died with pneumonia last Friday. Burial in the family grave yard. Georgetown (Ga.) Correspondence & Cuthbert (Ga.) Enterprise.

Thurs. Aug. 21, 1890
  Mrs. Henry Cummings died yesterday. She was accidently shot.

Thurs. Oct. 2, 1890
  Mrs. Thomas Reaves, between 60 and 70 years old, died at her place eight miles south of Eufaula, recently.

  Mr. John D. Glass, age about 45, died yesterday at his home ten miles out on the old Daleville road.

Thurs. Oct. 23, 1890
  Tuskaloosa, Oct. 16.- F. R. M. Williamson, age about 75, a resident of Monroe County, Georgia, died suddenly of heart disease on the train Tuesday.

Thurs. Nov. 13, 1890
  Frank S. Butler, general yard master of the Georgia Pacific R. R. in Anniston, Ala., was run over and killed by a train in that city on Thursday.

Eufaula Times & News
1891

Thurs, Jan. 1, 1891

Col. John M. Thornton, age about 75, died on the 30th ult., at his home at Batesville, Ala. (Barbour Co.). He was born in Elbert Co., Ga., on 6 March 1816. At an early age he came to Russell Co., Ala., and in 1849 removed to Barbour County. He was married three times and was the father of twenty children. His last wife (nee Frances Sylvester) and eleven children still survive him. His living children are: Mrs. M. Cody, Dozier Thornton, H. C. Thornton, Mrs. Geo. Boyer, J. M. Thornton, Jr., Mrs. Marion Ansley, Mrs. J. B. Davie, Fred Thornton, Mrs. R. I. Fields, Miss Mollie Thornton and Mr. Nat Thornton.

Near Gadsden, (Ala.), on the 25th, Mr. James W. Lester died while on a visit to his sister. He died from heart trouble. He was one of Etowah's oldest citizens.

Thurs. Jan. 8, 1891

Richland, Ga., Jan. 1.- Dr. Chas. N. Alston, Sr., age about 70 and for forty years a prominent physician of this section, was found dead in his bed yesterday. He was originally from Colloden, Ga.

Mrs. McGehee, widow of the late Alfred McGehee, died yesterday at the home of her son-in-law, Mr. Jesse Whitehurst, at White Pond (Barbour Co.). She was born in the year 1807 and was a little over ninety years of age.

Mr. W. I. Baxter, age about 50, of Lamar Co., Texas, died suddenly at the depot. He was known to several of our citizens and was on his way to Henry Co., (Ala.) to visit his brother, Mr. Sol. Baxter. His remains will be sent to Paris, Texas.

Mrs. Sarah Robertson, aged 87 years, mother of Dr. S. G. Robertson, died yesterday.

Thurs. Jan. 15, 1891

Henry W. Venable, of Talladega, (Ala.) who was a conductor on the East and West R. R., was killed at Ragland, (Ala.) last Tuesday by being struck by a pipe which had been left on the road way.

Rev. George W. Mills, one of the oldest Baptist ministers in Alabama, died a few days ago at Plantersville, (Ala.).

Dr. Nathan D. Bussey, a prominent manufacturer and capitalist of Columbus, Ga., died at Lithia Springs on Saturday.

Mrs. Florence, wife of Mr. Monroe N. Phillips, of Union, in Quitman, Co., Ga., died of typhoid fever Saturday. Burial at Spring Vale. She was the daughter of Dr. C. C. Willis, of Morris Station.

Mrs. Brinson, wife of Capt. S. S. Brinson, of Russell Co., (Ala.) died last Monday.

Mr. J. L. Adams, age 70, of Tuskegee, (Ala.) died Monday. He had been express agent for forty years. He was one of the oldest Masons in the state and was a member of the highest order.

Eufaula Times & News
1891

Thurs. Jan. 15, 1891

Mr. Alex McKinnon, age 65 or 70, a former citizen of Eufaula, died last week in Wadesboro, N. C.

Monroeville, Ala., Jan. 12.- As the result of an old feud a fatal shooting occurred here yesterday when John L. Stallsworth was killed. He was a prominent citizen, being a brother to Hon. N. J. Stallsworth, member of the legislature.

Mrs. Alice Peters and little daughter, Agnes, were found burned to death in their dwelling in Cordele, Georgia, on Thursday last.

Thurs. Jan. 22, 1891

Mr. John V. Woodson, an aged and helpless Confederate Veteran, burned to death at the home of Mr. John S. Davis in Covington, Georgia recently.

Mr. Will O. Baldwin died of pneumonia near Fort Gaines, Ga. on Sunday. He was the son of Dr. Baldwin of Cuthbert, Georgia.

Mrs. Moses Sanders, over 60 years old, living on the road to Abbeville, Ala., died last Sunday. She had been a great sufferer from some chronic disease. Her husband was killed in the war between the states. She leaves five children, all of whom are grown.

Shorterville, Ala., Jan. 15, '91.- Mrs. Huldah Henden, (Herndon) died Monday and her husband, Mr. Benjamin Henden, (Herndon) died the next day. They raised six sons and one daughter to be grown. Mr. Henden (Herndon) was an ordained Missionary Baptist. They were between the ages of 70 and 80. Burial at Shorterville Cemetery in the same grave.

Miss Sarah Elizabeth Harrell, age 17, daughter of Mr. and Mrs. Elisha Harrell, died at the home of her parents in Quitman Co., Ga. on the 13th inst. She suffered from consumption.

Mr. R. F. Rish, living near Otho, Ala., (Henry Co.) died Tuesday of typhoid fever.- _Abbeville_ (Ala.) _Times_.

Mr. Rhynehold, of Prussian descent, was murdered at his home in Columbia Thursday as he sat reading. He married only a short time ago to Miss Laura Godfrey, daughter of Mr. Enoch Godfrey and a niece to Mr. W. T. Peters.-_Abbeville_ (Ala.) _Times_.

Thurs. Jan. 29, 1891

Mrs. M. B. Graham, of Montgomery, died in that city last Thursday.

Mr. John C. Woolfolk, of Montgomery, died in that city last Thursday.

Mrs. Anna Pruett, wife of Maj. W. H. Pruett, died at her home in Eufaula on Sunday. Pall bears were her six brothers: Noah W. Roberts, Mac Roberts, Will H. Roberts, Clarence P. Roberts, Oliver T. Roberts and Ed Roberts.

Mrs. B. F. Lokey, who lived just on the line of Clay Co.,

Eufaula Times & News
1891

(Ga.) died Friday with heart disease. She left seven children. Georgetown (Ga.) Correspondence.

Hon. Americus C. Mitchell, Sr., age 73, died of dropsy at his home in Glennville, (Russell Co., Ala.). He was the father of Dr. W. A. Mitchell and A. C. Mitchell, Jr., of Eufaula.

Mr. Chas. Chestnut, pioneer citizen of Stewart Co., (Ga.) died at his home near Florence, (Ga.) on Jan. 22nd. His years numbered four score and three. He will be buried with Masonic honors.- Lumpkin (Ga.) Independent, 24th.

Capt. Thomas Swanson, aged about 57, died at his home at Cowikee, (Barbour Co.) Friday. He leaves a wife and five children. Mr. W. C. Swanson, of Eufaula and Mrs. W. C. Thornton being the oldest.

Mrs. Mollie E. Lucas, wife of W. C. Lucas in Henry Co., (Ala.) died on the 13th inst. She was born Oct. 3rd, 1869, and was the daughter of John and Jane Davis. She married Mr. Lucas Dec. 12th, 1889.

Thurs. Feb. 5, 1891

Mrs. W. A. Cary died Wednesday last, also Mrs. B. W. Ball, died in Montgomery, Ala.

Capt. Herman Kenneworth, aged 65 years, died in Montgomery on Wednesday. He had been a resident of that city for 40 years.

Mr. Jack Johnson, for many years a citizen of Henry Co., (Ala.) living near Abbeville, but removed to Dale Co., not long since, died at Daleville on Sunday. Burial yesterday at Ozark. He was the father of Mrs. S. E. Sheehan, of Eufaula.

Mrs. Thos. J. Reynolds, age about 24, died at her mother's in Glennville on Sunday. She was the daughter of Col. A. C. Mitchell. She was a bride of a year or two.

Mr. John M. Dewitt died at his home at Geneva, (Ala.) of heart disease yesterday. He lived in Eufaula before the war. He was brother-in-law to Capt. John C. McNab, of Eufaula. He leaves a wife and three children.

Joseph Hillman, aged 35 or 40, of Oak Grove, Quitman Co., (Ga) died Friday of congestion of the bowels. He had married the second time. He leaves a wife and seven children and two brothers.

Mr. Seab Ramsey, merchant of Union Springs, (Ala.) died within the last few days.

Mrs. R. J. Price, of Belcher, (Barbour Co.) died yesterday of typhoid pneumonia. She leaves a husband and four children.

Mrs. R. W. Flowers died at Dothan, (Ala.) Thursday of pneumonia. She had just moved to that town. She leaves a husband and five children. Burial in Lawrenceville, her old home.

Thurs. Feb. 12, 1891

Mr. William Barry, age 65, died with pneumonia at his home in Barbour County, Alabama.

Eufaula Times & News
1891

Mr. Samuel Beall died at his home at Lumpkin, (Ga.) Sunday. He was once a merchant in Eufaula, but for the last few years devoted himself to farming. His widow is a sister to Mrs. C. C. Skillman and Mrs. Frank Hart, of Eufaula.

Mrs. Dock Rollins died at her home in Dothan on Sunday last and was buried at County Line Church. She leaves a husband and several small children.

Mr. John Williams, of Eufaula, died at his home Wednesday. Burial in Clayton. He was a brother of Hon. J. N. Williams of Clayton, Mr. Richard Williams, of Birmingham, and Mrs. J. C. McEachern, of Eufaula.

Mrs. J. T. Coker, of Clayton, who for so long sick with consumption, died recently.

Mrs. Fannie Rollins, age 26, wife of Prof. J. W. Rollins, died at her home in Dothan, (Ala.) Feb. 1st. She was born and raised near County Line Church in Barbour County. She was the daughter of Mr. G. W. Richards.

Hon. James B. Mitchell, brother to Dr. W. A. Mitchell of Eufaula, died recently at his home in Russell County, Ala.

Mrs. R. E. Stokes, of Abbeville, died last week. She was the second daughter of Dr. Lee of Abbeville. She leaves two small children.

Mrs. Hildreth, an aged lady living with her son at Enterprise, Coffee Co., died Monday. She was the mother of Rev. T. Z. Hildreth, who lives near Haw Ridge.

Thurs. Mar. 5, 1891
Mrs. Anna Long, age 83, of Louisville, (Ala.) died yesterday. She was an aunt of Mrs. R. Q. Edmonson, of Eufaula. She leaves one daughter, Mrs. Kate McRae, of Louisville.

Mrs. Rebecca Hartzog, of Spio, died last week of old age.

Thurs. Mar. 19, 1891
Mrs. Dorman, age 79, mother of Mr. Alex Dorman, died at her home in Louisville on Friday last.

Mr. S. S. Singleton, age 64, living six miles from Clayton, died Wednesday. He leaves a wife and two children.

Thurs. Apr. 23, 1891
Mr. B. R. Kaigler, of Georgetown, Ga., died at his home on Monday. He had had a long illness from paralysis and pneumonia.

Jackson E. Long died yesterday. He was born April 8, 1865. He was the eldest and last surviving son of Mr. and Mrs. N. W. E. Long, of Hurtsboro, Ala. In 1887 he married Miss Nellie Beall Dent.

Thurs. Apr. 30, 1891
Mr. S. R. Foy died at the home of his mother in Eufaula yesterday. He was born in this county on May 13th, 1857. In his earlier years he lived at Batesville, (Barbour Co.). He leaves a wife and two children.

Eufaula Times & News
1891

Thurs. May 28, 1891
Mrs. R. P. Tatum died at her home near Clio, Barbour, Co., on the 21st inst. She leaves a husband and four children.

Thurs. June 4, 1891
Judge M. B. Green died at his home in Ft. Gaines, Ga., on the 23rd, ult. He was born and raised in Burke Co., Ga. He settled in Henry Co., (Ala.) about 1843. Soon afterwards he married Miss Elizabeth Chambers. His wife died in 1887.

Thurs. June 11, 1891
Miss Martha B. Davis, age 80, died at the home of her brother-in-law, Mr. John Marks, in Macon, Ga. Burial in Eufaula yesterday.

Mr. Richard Bishop, about 60 years old, of Spring Hill in Barbour County, (Ala.) died Sunday. He was a brother to the late Boland Bishop.

Mrs. W. F. Wilkerson died at Midway, (Ala.) after a long illness and was buried today.

Mr. Joseph S. Powell, aged 76, died at his home near Hurtsboro, (Ala.) on Monday. He has two living children, Mr. Sid Powell and Mrs. S. T. Margart.

Mrs. Junius Flewellen, daughter of Capt. John H. Bass, died at her home at Orange Lake, Fla. last Friday. Deceased was raised at Glennville, Ala.

Mrs. E. W. Roquemore, age 77, of Howe, (Barbour Co.) died yesterday. She was the mother of Mr. J. W. Roquemore, Mrs. G. W. Stovall and Mrs. T. R. Freeman and grandmother of Mr. Orbie Spurlock. Burial at Howe.

Thurs. June 18, 1891
Mrs. Bradley, relict of Henry Bradley, died at her home in Clayton last Sunday with Cholera morbus. She leaves five children.

Mrs. Jennie Davis Reed died recently at her home in Atlanta. She was the youngest daughter of Benj. B. Davis, of Eufaula. Mrs. Reed had been married eighteen months.

Mrs. J. B. Mainor died at her home near Cuthbert, Ga., from pneumonia on Monday. Burial at Shellman, (Ga.).
Cuthbert (Ga.) Leader.

Mrs. Margaret Wood, age 60, died at the old homestead in Quitman County, seven miles east of Georgetown, (Ga.) She had suffered with consumption. She was buried at the family burial grounds.

Thurs. June 25, 1891
Cuthbert, Ga., June 20.- Mr. Arthur E. Barlett died yesterday. He leaves a wife and a large family of children.

Mrs. S. E. McNeill, mother of Mrs. Thomas W. Givens, died Friday in Jacksonville, Fla. Burial in Eufaula.

Thurs. July 2, 1891
Mrs. Glover, wife of Ed. Glover, died at her home nine miles

Eufaula Times & News
1891

southeast of Clayton on Thursday last. Clayton (Ala.) Courier.

Mrs. Annie W. Wells, wife of Mr. Louis Wells, died in Eufaula yesterday. She leaves a husband and three children.

Mrs. A. J. Galloway, who lived in Henry Co. near Cureton's bridge, died recently.

Thurs. July 9, 1891
The remains of Mr. Alex McLeod, aged 81, passed through Eufaula on the way from Terrill Co., Ga., to his old home at White Oak, (Barbour County).

Thurs. July 23, 1891
Mr. C. W. Beale, brother-in-law to Mr. R. S. Roddenberry of Eufaula, died in Nashville, Tenn., on July 17th. He leaves a wife.

Mr. W. C. Espy, of Columbia, (Ala.) died recently. He leaves a wife, six daughters and five brothers.

Thurs. July 30, 1891
Mr. J. A. Wright, aged 65, died last Saturday. He was the father of Dr. W. F. Wright. Clayton (Ala.) Courier.

Mr. Thos. M. Borland, age 67, died at his home near Newton, (Dale Co.) Saturday. He came to Dale County from Jones County, Georgia in 1855.-Ozark (Ala.) Star.

Mrs. W. H. Stantifer died at her home in Eufaula yesterday. She leaves a husband and four children.

Thurs. Aug. 6, 1891
Mrs. H. M. Wilson, wife of the editor of the Opelika (Ala) Industrial News, died recently.

Mrs. N. K. Keyton died at Keyton Hotel in Dothan, (Ala.) on Monday. Burial in Arlington, Ga., her former home. She leaves a husband, J. T. Keyton, postmaster, and six children.- Dothan (Ala.) News.

Miss Maggie Quillin, aged 18, daughter of E. R. and M. M. Quillin, of Clayton, (Ala.) died July 27th, 1891.

Thurs. Aug. 13, 1891
Mr. Andrew Bates died in Atlanta yesterday. He was a son of Maj. W. M. Bates, of Ft. Browder, near Batesville, Ala.

Mr. Amos Parker, one of the first settlers of Ozark, died at the home of his son there last Friday.

Miss Willie Croft, age 17, daughter of Mr. John Croff, died at his home at Hatcher's Station Friday.

Mrs. Sandy Martin of Clayton died recently.

Master John Quincy Rutland, age 14, youngest son of Mr. W. W. and Martha Jane Rutland of White Oak, (Barbour Co.) died recently.

Mr. John C. Thomas, aged 49, died in Eufaula last Tuesday. He

Eufaula Times & News
1891

leaves a wife and two daughters, Mrs. Wm. Tully and Miss Mattie, and three sons, John C., Jr., and Hubbard and a baby boy.

Louisville, Ala., Aug. 13.-Mr. John Helms, aged 80, one of Barbour County's oldest citizens died at his home near town yesterday.

Thurs. Aug. 27, 1891
Mrs. M. P. LeGrand, of Montgomery, died at Blount Springs on Sunday, where she had gone for her health.

Montgomery, Ala., Aug. 22.- Mr. Joseph Silvas died here last night. He was a native of Portugal and came to Montgomery many years ago. His wife died about four years ago.

Miss Viney Stokes died at the home of her mother near Louisville, (Ala.) last Saturday. Burial in Louisville Cemetery.

Mr. G. W. Stovall, age about 51, living near Eufaula died last Saturday. He leaves a wife and six children.

Thurs. Sept. 3, 1891
Mr. Chas. G. Meriwether died last Saturday in Atlanta. He was born in Petersburg, Va. in 1838 and in 1856 began his career in telegraph work in Mobile, Ala. Burial in Mobile. He leaves a family.

Miss Janie E. Borders, formerly of Eufaula, a sister of Mrs. J. D. Andrews, of Eufaula, died at Charlotte Harbor, Fla. recently.

Mr. James Dykes of near Clopton in Dale County, died Friday. Ozark (Ala.) Star.

Mrs. Susan Parker, wife of Mr. Joel Parker, died at her home in Ozark last Wednesday. She leaves a husband and 5 little girls. Ozark (Ala.) Star.

Thurs. Sept. 10, 1891
Mr. J. C. Bryan died in Rome, Ga., recently, at an advanced age. He was one of the early settlers of Eufaula. He moved to Rome 22 years ago. He was an uncle to W. T., H. J., and L. C. McLeod, of Eufaula.

Mr. John McGhee, of Coffee Co., (Ala.) died at his home near Clintonville on the 28th inst. He was for many years County Supt. of Education in Coffee Co. Ozark (Ala.) Star.

Mr. Thomas H. Ferrell, age about 90, died at his home near Clayhatchee in this county (Dale), last Thursday.- Ozark (Ala.) Star.

Thurs. Sept. 17, 1891
Salem, Mass. Sept. 14.- Hon. George B. Loring, age 74, died here this morning.

Mrs. D. Martin, age 76, died at her home near Clio, (Ala.) last Sunday. Survivors are Mr. Murdock Martin, Mr. Sandy Martin, and Dr. J. P. Martin, of Birmingham, Ala.

Mr. Franklin Buchanan, formerly of Baltimore, but recently of Savannah, Ga., died Saturday at the home of his mother near Miles River, Md. He was the son of Admiral Franklin Buchanan.

Eufaula Times & News
1891

Thurs. Sept. 24, 1891

Mrs. Kate Logan, aged 103, of Pleasant Grove in Walker Co., Alabama, died recently. She went to that county 60 years ago from Georgia. She leaves a large number of descendants.

Mrs. M. M. Tye of Ozark, Ala., died at her home last Monday. She was a member of the M. E. Church. Burial in the Ozark cemetery. Survivers are her husband and several children. Ozark (Ala.) Star.

Nevada City, Calif., Sept. 7.- S. Gallavotti, supt. of the Derbec mine, was murdered by highwaymen this morning near this city.

Union Springs, (Ala.) Sept. 17.- Mr. Sidney Strickland died at the home of his father, Capt. A. B. Strickland, this morning.

Mr. John M. Thornton, age 39, died in Eufaula on Sunday last. He was a brother to Mr. Dozier Thornton and Mr. N. Thornton, of Montgomery.

Mrs. William Thornton, age 73, died at her home near Union Springs, (Ala.) recently.- Union Springs (Ala.) Herald.

Capt. C. A. Redd, of Columbus, Ga., died recently. His sons, Messrs. W. A. and L. D. Redd, lived in Bullock Co., (Ala.) Union Springs (Ala.) Herald.

Mrs. Jordan Peacock, aged about 50, of Hilliardsville, (Henry Co.) died recently.

Mrs. J. L. Skipper, wife of Rev. Skipper, living at Newberne, Ala., died at her home on the 20th of Aug.-Ozark (Ala.) Star.

Miss May Roquemore, age 17, daughter of Hon. John D. Roquemore, died at the home of her father in Montgomery last Sunday. Burial in Montgomery.

Thurs. Oct. 8, 1891

Hon. Harvey M. Watterson, of the Louisville Courier Journal, died last week in Louisville, Ky. He was born in Bedford County, Tenn. on Nov, 23, 1811.

Gen. Alpheus Baker died in Louisville Ky. last Friday. He was a native of Abbeville, S. C., born in 1828 and went to Eufaula, (Ala.) when a boy. He practiced law in Eufaula in 1864-1878, when he moved to Louisville, Ky. He married Miss Ricks, of Quitman Co., Ga. He leaves a wife, two daughters and two sons.

Mrs George H. Thompson died at her home in Glennville, (Ala.) on last Thursday.

Mr. Quin Searcy died at his home in Skipperville (Henry Co.), yesterday. He was a brother to Messrs. J. B. and E. J. Searcy of Eufaula. He leaves a wife and five children.

Thurs. Oct. 15, 1891

Mr. Frank Boykin, age 81, died at the home of his son, Mr. J. W. Boykin, near Villula, (Russell Co., Ala.) on Thursday. He was once treasurer of Bullock Co. (Ala.) where he formerly lived.

Eufaula Times and News
1891

Mrs. Thomas Hardeman, of Macon, Ga., died yesterday. She was a sister to Mrs. B. D. Lumsden, of Eufaula.

Newton, (Ala.) Oct. 14.- Conductor Jesse McDonald was accidently killed here this morning by a train.

Mrs. G. W. Butler, nee Miss Nan Hudson, sister to Mr. E. A. Hudson, of Eufaula, died at her home near Montezuma, Ga., on Thursday. Sne was married in Eufaula last February.

Mrs. W. J. Cox, of Ozark, (Ala.) died last week. She was the daughter of Mr. H. Z. Parker. She leaves a husband and several small children.- Ozark (Ala.) Star.

Thurs. Oct. 22, 1891

Mobile, (Ala.) Oct. 15.- Dr. Seymour Bullock was shot at Navy Cove and died soon afterwards. He was a northern man who settled in this city after the war, marrying here.

Alex Johnson, an old citizen of Barbour Co., died at his home near Louisville on Thursday. He settled near Louisville about 1820 and has lived there all his life.

Thurs. Oct. 29, 1891

Mrs. William Richardson, wife of Judge Richardson, died at Huntsville, (Ala.) on Saturday.

Mrs. Junius Jordan, wife of Rev. Jordan, aged about 65, died at her home near Eufaula. Burial in the Wilson plot in Eufaula. She leaves a husband and several children.

Mr. William A. McKay, age 47, machinist in the DeBardeleben Coal Co. at Bessemer, (Ala.) was killed at the furnace yesterday by being caught in the machinery. Burial in Autauga Co., (Ala.) his former home. He leaves three children. His wife died some years ago.-Birminghan (Ala.) News.

Thurs. Nov. 5, 1891

Mr. C. Ward, of Henry Co., (Ala.) died at his home near Abbeville on the 30th of October.

Georgiana, Ala., Nov. 2.--- Mr. and Mrs. Thomas Sheppard, of near Georgiana (Butler Co., Ala.) ages about 65 or 70 were murdered last night at their home.

Thurs. Nov. 12, 1891

Mr. Constantine Newton, the oldest man in Henry Co., (Ala.) died near Dothan on Oct. 31st, aged 104 years. Abbeville (Ala.) Times.

Thurs. Nov. 19, 1891

Mrs. Caroline R. Hogue, age 89, died at the home of her grand-son, Mr. L. E. Irby, in Eufaula on yesterday. She came from Inverness (Bullock Co., Ala.) about two months to reside with Mr. Irby.

Miss Annie Morgan, age about 18, died at the home of her mother in Eufaula yesterday.

Thurs. Nov. 26, 1891

Mr. Cyrus Oates, an old citizen, died at his home near Ozark (Ala.) last week.-Ozark (Ala.) Star.

Eufaula Times & News
1891

Thurs. Nov. 26, 1891

Capt. Daniel Martin, aged 67 years, died at the home of his nephew, Mr. M. Martin this morning, at Clio, Barbour Co., Ala. He was an elder in the Presbyterian Church.

Mrs. A. W. Faulk, aged 74, died at her home near Louisville, (Barbour Co., Ala.) on Monday. Burial at Faulk's Church. She was a member of the M. E. Church. Clayton (Ala.) Courier.

Thurs. Nov. 29, 1891

Jacksonville, Fla., Nov. 29.-W. O. O'Brien of Jacksonville, Fla., was killed in a train wreck last night.

Thurs. Dec. 3, 1891

The death of Felix Blancho occurred at the Odd Fellow's building in Savannah, Ga., on Monday. He was the first Knight of Pythias initiated in Georgia.

Thurs. Dec. 10, 1891

Mrs. L. Manassas, of Clayton, died recently. Burial in Montgomery. Survivors are her husband and two children.

Mrs. Seney Powell, aged 83, of Russell County, (Ala.) died Tuesday. She was the grandmother of Mr. R. D. Powell, also Mr. Powell's niece, Georgia Mays, aged 5 years, daughter of Mr. John Mays, died in Russell Co. on Wednesday of typhoid fever.

Thurs. Dec. 17, 1891

Mr. John Q. Baldree, a citizen of Dale Co., Ala., died at his home near Newton last Tuesday.

Mrs. Henry Bernstein died at Louisville, Ky., last Saturday. Burial in Eufaula from the home of Mr. Phil Bernstein. Survivors are Mr. Henry Bernstein and his seven children: Messrs. Ben and Theodore, Misses Melinda, Minnie and Henrietta Bernstein, Mrs. Kaufman, of Columbus, and Mrs. Lowenstein, of Cuthbert, (Ga.).

Mr. William J. Ross, age about 30, a native of Eufaula, and son of Mr. James Ross, died at Macon, Ga., on Monday. Burial in Eufaula.

Col. E. G. Simmons died suddenly at his home in Americus, Georgia on Thursday.

Mr. W. T. Peters, of near Columbia, (Ala.) died yesterday. Columbia (Ala.) Recorder, 10th.

Mr. Reuben Brown, aged 66, died at his home near Clayton, (Ala.) last Monday. Survivors are his wife and several children. Clayton (Ala.) Courier.

Thurs. Dec. 24, 1891

Washington, Dec. 20.-Senator Preston B. Plumb, representative from Kansas, died today. Survivors are his wife and two children in Kansas.

Troy, (Ala.) Dec. 22.-Mr. A. T. Lockard, business man of Troy, died today. Also, Mr. Abe Culver, of Troy.

Eufaula Times & News
1891

Mr. E. E. Glover, age 70, died near Rocky Mount Church on Thursday. Burial at New Hope Church. He was the father of Mr. E. M. and Mr. E. Glover.

Thurs. Dec. 31, 1891
Mr. Robert Cherry, age about 57, of Eufaula, died yesterday. Survivors are his wife and a daughter.

The Clayton Courier
1891

Sat. Jan. 10, 1891
Died on Monday last at the home of her father, Mr. W. L. Kennedy, Miss Annie Kennedy.

Sat. Jan. 24, 1891
Miss Strada Reynolds, age about 16, died of pneumonia on Monday. She was the daughter of A. L. Reynolds.

Died on Wednesday at Louisville, Ala., Mr. D. D. Stephens. He was a very old man, and had lived in this county for many years. He leaves a number of children, all of whom are grown and married.

Mrs. Grubbs, wife of Mr. James W. Grubbs, died with consumption Thursday. She leaves a husband and children.

Mrs. Pruett, wife of Maj. W. H. Pruett, died at Eufaula on Sunday last. She was the daughter of Capt. G. A. Roberts.

Sat. Feb. 14, 1891
Died on Wednesday last near Oateston, Ala. (Barbour Co.), Mr. William Berry, aged 60 years. He was a consistent member of the Methodist Church.

Sat. Feb. 28, 1891
Dr. J. G. Armstrong died at his home in Atlanta last Sunday from a stroke of apoplexy.

Sat. Mar. 7, 1891
Mr. G. Raley, an old and respected citizen, living six miles from Clayton, died on Wednesday. He had been living in the county over fifty years.

Mrs. Ann Long, age about 81, died on the 2d of Mar. in Louisville, (Ala.). She was one of the daughters of John McNeill, who came to this state from North Carolina in 1821 or 1822 and settled three or four miles beyond the site of Pea River Church. John McNeill died the first or second year after coming to Alabama, leaving one son and a family of daughters. He was the first white man buried in Barbour County. His son became Dr. J. C. McNeill who died in Clayton in 1875. The daughters married while this was a frontier region, except the youngest who married Dr. E. M. Herron in 1841. The others were Mrs. John Windham, Mrs Currie, Mrs. Emanuel Cox, Mrs. Harrel Hobdy and Mrs. J. S. Williams.

Mrs. Long married Lemuel Long who lost his life by service

The Clayton Courier
1891

in the Indian War of 1837. Mrs. Long is buried at the Presbyterian Church.

Sat. Mar. 14, 1891

Ex-senator Jashua Hill died at his home in Madison, Ga., on Friday last.

Josiah Morris, age 73, the oldest and best known banker of the south, died suddenly at his home in Montgomery, Ala., on Monday.

Sat. Mar. 28, 1891

Major B. J. Duncan died a few days ago at his home at Lakeview, (Ala.), Few men in Alabama were so well known as Major Duncan. He was reared at Talladega, (Ala.) and at various times lived in Selma, Mobile, New Orleans, Montgomery, and for the last few years in Birmingham.

Henry, age about 16 years, the third son of Mr. J. T. Watkins, died on Monday last.

Recently Mrs. Jane Johnson died near Roswell, (Ga.). She would have been ninety years of age on the 8th of next Nov. She had over one hundred grand and great-grand children, and six great-great-grand children.

Sat. Apr. 4, 1891

Capt. Richard Williams who recently went to New York to have an operation for a tumor died. Burial in Eufaula. He was born near Louisville in Barbour Co., Ala. about 1837.

Mrs. H. M. Weedon, age 47, wife of Dr. Weedon, died in Eufaula on Monday last. She leaves a husband and six children.

Sat. May 16, 1891

Mr. E. Jacobs died at his home on Dale Road in Eufaula on Saturday and was buried at Epworth Church. He was 82 years old.

Sat. June 6, 1891

Mr. Jason Cooper, living a few miles from Clayton, died on Monday.

Mrs. N. A. Petty died Wednesday. She was the widow of Mr. Allen Petty, who died a few years ago. Her father was Victor Norton, one of the pioneers of Barbour County.

Sat. June 20, 1891

Mr. David Appling, age 82, died at the home of his son ten miles from Clayton. He was receiving a pension for services in the Indian War.

Sat. July 4, 1891

Died at his home one mile west of Zeigler, Barbour Co., Ala., on the 29th of June 1891, B. F. Emerson. He was born in Jones Co., Ga., Oct. 17, 1809, and was married to Narcissa Ball Oct. 17th, 1833, and soon after moved to Barbour County, Ala., where he has since resided. He was a member of the Missionary Baptist Church for about 45 years.

The Clayton Courier
1891-1892

Dr. T. B. Ligon, physician of Montgomery, (Ala.) died on Friday.

Sat. Sept. 19, 1891

Dr. John A. Reynolds, age 74, died at his home a few miles west of Clio, (Barbour Co., Ala.). He leaves a wife and several grown children.

Mrs. James Hurst, age about 40, died at her home six miles from town on the Louisville road last Wednesday. She leaves a husband and three children.

Sat. Oct. 17, 1891

Union Springs, (Ala.) Oct. 11.-The body of John McNair, a farmer living five miles from Union Springs, was found murdered this morning along the side of the railroad. He had been to town and sold a bale of cotton.

Lorenzo M. Wilson, age 82, died at Mobile, (Ala.) Wednesday. He was a native of Maryland and came here in 1836. He had once been vice president of the Mobile & Montgomery R. R.

Sat. Oct. 31, 1891

Miss Ann Cox died at her home on the 25th inst. Her only sister, Elizabeth, died before the war. Three brothers and her father died a few years later.

Sat. Nov. 7, 1891

Mr. Alex Wright, living abour ten miles from Clayton, died on Monday.

Sat. Jan. 2, 1892

Mr. Hillard White, age 70, died at the home of his brother John C. White, in the northwestern part of town on Saturday.

Mr. Robert Cherry died at his home in Eufaula on Tuesday. He leaves a wife and one child.

Sat. Jan. 16, 1892

Mr. James Ventress, age 74, died at his home near Mt. Andrew, (Barbour Co.) on Wednesday.

Sat. Jan. 30, 1892

Mr. William Seabon died suddenly from heart disease at Lodi, (Barbour Co., Ala.) on Wednesday.

Dr. J. B. Smith, age 80, died on Monday at Anniston, Ala., at the home of his son-in-law, D. C. Blackwell, Esqr. Dr. Smith was the father of Mrs. H. W. B. Price.

Phil McKay, age 11 years, son of Mr. Farquhar McKay, of Eufaula, died Sunday of hydrophobia. Burial at Pea River Church.

Sat. Feb. 6, 1892

Died at Clio on Friday last, Mr. I. H. Chambers, age about 80. He had been a resident of Barbour County for a long time. He had 17 children, 10 of which are now living.

Mrs. I. M. Valentine died at the home of her father, J. F. McDonald, Esqr., (in Ozark, Ala.). She married Mr. I. M. Valentine about three years ago. She leaves a husband and a babe only a few

The Clayton Courier
1892

days old.-Ozark (Ala.) Star.

Sat. Feb. 27, 1892

Died on the 23rd inst., Mrs. Annie Andrews of near Clayton. She was the wife of Mr. S. A. Andrews. She leaves her husband and two girls and one boy. Burial at Mt. Pleasant Church.

Miss Lizzie Ward, age about 20 years, sister of Mr. E. D. Ward, died at his home near Clayton on last Wednesday.

Sat. Mar. 12, 1892

Mrs. H. J. Carter, age about 60 years, living near Lawrenceville, (Henry Co., Ala.) dropped dead yesterday.

Sat. Mar. 19, 1892

Mr. Henry Simms, living near Star Hill, (Barbour County, Ala.) died on Wednesday last.

Mr. C. W. Hagler died at his home near Mt. Andrew, (Barbour Co., Ala.) on Thursday. He was an old man and was confined to his bed nearly twelve months before his death.

Mrs. Smitha Price, age 79, of Clayton, died at her home Tuesday. She had been living in town for over 45 years.

Sat. Apr. 2, 1892

Mrs. Watkins, wife of West Watkins, died on last Tuesday.

Died last Saturday at his home in Clayton, Mr. H. Oppert, aged 76 years. On Monday Miss Mattie, one of his daughters died, and on Wednesday Miss Gussie, another daughter died, making three out of the family in less than a week.

Died at his home near Mt. Andrew, (Barbour Co.) on Tuesday, Mr. Obadiah Whittington. He was quite an old man and had been living in Barbour County for many years.

Eufaula Times & News
1891 & 1892

Thurs. July 23, 1891

Col. C. W. Beal died in Nashville, Tenn., recently. He was brother-in-law to Mr. R. S. Roddenberry.

Thurs. Jan, 14, 1892

Miss Hattie Peacock, age 17, daughter of Mr. O. H. Peacock, died in Ozark where she was visiting her uncle. Burial in Eufaula on Thursday.

Mr. Perry Spencer, of Columbus, died suddenly Wednesday from a stroke of apoplexy.

Thurs. Jan. 28, 1892

Mrs. Eloise Buford Jessup died in Decatur, Ala. on Dec. 23rd.

Mr. Edward C. Doughtie, age about 41, formerly of Eufaula, died at Opelika from pneumonia recently. He leaves a wife.

<u>Eufaula Times & News</u>
1892

Thurs. Feb. 4, 1892
    Mr. J. H. Chambers, of Louisville, (Ala.) died on Friday last.

    Mrs. Mary Smith died at the home of her daughter, Mrs. Robert Lee, near Lodi (Barbour Co.) yesterday of typhoid fever. Burial at Bethel at White Pond.

    Judge Elias M. Keils died recently in Washington city where he held a clerkship in one of the departments.

Thurs. Feb. 11, 1892
    A. J. Floyd, age 68, died recently in Columbus, Ga.

Thurs. Feb. 18, 1892
    Mr. Jesse Cobb, age 54, died at his home in Eufaula on Monday. He was born in Muscogee Co., Ga., and lived in Cuthbert, Ga. until eight years ago when he moved to Eufaula. About five years ago he married Miss Garrett, of Eufaula. Besides Mrs. Cobb, he leaves two grown children by his first wife, namely: Mrs. J. W. Speight and Jesse Cobb, Jr., of Cuthbert.

    Mrs. J. W. Crawford, wife of Treasurer Crawford, of Henry Co., (Ala.) died suddenly at her home in Abbeville, (Ala.).

Thurs. Mar. 3, 1892
    Mr. T. G. Whigham, formerly of Barbour Co., but for the last five or six years, died at his home near Belton, Texas, on the 5th of Feb. last.

Thurs. Mar. 10, 1892
    Mrs. H. J. Carter, age about 60, living near Lawrenceville, died today.

Thurs. Mar. 17, 1892
    Mrs. Robert Braswell died at her home on the Dale Road in Eufaula on Wednesday from typhoid fever. She leaves a husband and four small children.

    Mrs. Louisa A. Cargile, relict of Mr. Thomas Cargile, aged 82 years, died while on a visit to her grand-son, Mr. Reuben Kolb. She was born in Georgia Oct. 1st, 1810. Burial in Eufaula at Shorter Cemetery.

Thurs. Mar. 24, 1892
    Mrs. B. F. Petty, age about 60, of Clayton died Sunday. Mrs. John M. Edmonson, of Eufaula, and Mrs. J. W. Foster, of Abbeville are daughters of Mrs. Petty.

    Mr. Hatcher Vickers, Sr., age 72, died from injuries he received when his horse ran away. Burial at Lawrenceville, (Ala.)

    Mrs. Steve Brown died of consumption at her home near Clopton last Thursday. Survivors are her husband and one child.

Thurs. Apr. 14, 1892
    Dr. R. W. Flowers died suddenly at his home at Lawrenceville, Henry Co., Ala., on Mar. 31st. He leaves a wife and two small children.

    Mr. S. O. Cureton, of Cureton's Bridge died suddenly on

The Clayton Courier
1892

yesterday. He leaves a large family. (This item taken from the Eufaula Times & News, Thurs. Jan. 8, 1891).

Sat. Apr. 23, 1892

Mrs. Mann, wife of Mr. Jube Mann, living near Star Hill in Barbour County, died suddenly on Tuesday.

Rev. J. D. Burkhead, pastor of the First Presbyterian Church in Montgomery, died of heart trouble in that city on Monday last.

Mr. John Barefield died suddenly in Eufaula on Tuesday at Holt's Drug Store where he was clerking.

Mrs. Edith McCraney, age 60, wife of Mr. Norman McCraney, died at her home Monday. She leaves eight children.

Sat. Apr. 30, 1892

Maj. James F. Waddell, of Seale, Ala., (Russell Co.,) died recently.

Mr. Hilliard Crew, of near Louisville, (Ala.) died last Friday.

Mr. H. H. Caraway, (Barbour Co., Ala.) died Monday. He was a brother of county commissioner Caraway.

Sat. May 7, 1892

Mr. Simon Baxley, aged about 70, died at his home near Louisville, (Ala.) last Wednesday. He had lived in Barbour County for 50 years.

Sat. May 28, 1892

Dr. James H. Randolph, age 83 years, died on Monday in Tallahassee (Fla.).

Mr. Norman McCraney, of Clayton, (Ala.) died on Monday. Burial Tuesday with masonic honors.

Sat. June 4, 1892

Mrs. Fletcher McCraney, living in the McGilvary neighborhood, Barbour County, (Ala.), died last Tuesday.

Mrs. Oates, age 86, the mother of Hon W. C. Oates, died at her home in Abbeville last Sunday.

Sat. June 25, 1892

Mr. Benjamin Manley, age 72, died at his home near Eufaula on Saturday. He leaves three daughters, Mrs. N. H. Miller, of Eufaula, Mrs. Moore of Batesville,(Ala.) Mrs. J. M. Helms, of Fla., and one son, Mr. Albert Manley. Burial at Mt. Pleasant Church in Henry County. Eufaula Times.

Sat. July 9, 1892

Mrs. Sophia Williams, aged about 82, died in Clayton on 5th inst. In Oct. 1830 she married Osborne J. Williams, who died in 1854. Two of her children survive her.

Sat. July 30, 1892

Daniel M. Grissitt, aged 82½ years, died Saturday at his in Henry County. He had been living in Barbour County for 60 years, with the exception of six years, which has been spent in Henry County, (Ala.).

The Clayton Courier
1892

Dr. W. B. Stewart, formerly a dentist at Clayton, died at the home of his sister, Mrs. M. E. McCracken, in Phenix City, (Ala.) Saturday. He leaves a wife and two grown sons.

Mrs. A. P. Jones, wife of Mr. Harrison Jones, of Rocky Mount, died on the 26th. She was a sister to Mrs. A. A. Crews, Messrs. D. K., W. H. and Carter Thomas. (Note - Aug. 6, 1892: Mrs. A. P. Jones left ten children, among them twins about three weeks old. Mr. Carter Thomas and Mrs. A. A. Crews have adopted one each of the twins).

Mr. W. M. (Mike) Efurd, of Louisville, (Ala.) a young man, died on last Saturday.

Sat. Aug. 27, 1892

Mrs. Frank Watkins, age 67 years, died Monday at the home of Mr. W. H. Nix, in Clayton.

Mr. Craft. Cox was buried in Eufaula yesterday. He leaves a widowed mother, a wife and a sister. -Eufaula Times.

Sat. Sept. 24, 1892

Hon. Thomas H. Watts died Sept. 16th, 1892.

Sat. Oct. 8, 1892

Macy L. Davis died September 20th, 1892.

John R. McNab, only son of Capt. John C. McNab, died recently.

Sat. Nov. 5, 1892

Senator Reuben Jones died Monday in Atlanta. His home was in Newton, Baker County, Ga. The late Primus Jones, of Georgia, was one of his brothers. He was a consistent member of the Methodist Church.

Sat. Nov. 19, 1892

Mr. A. B. Harris, age about 50, died suddenly in Eufaula yesterday. He came to Eufaula from Glennville about a year ago. He is survived by his wife, he had no children.

Sat. Nov. 26, 1892

Mrs. Ann Dyches, wife of Mr. Z. W. Dyches, of Columbus, died in Clayton last week. Burial in Clayton on Wednesday. Survivors are her husband, one son and two daughters and a sister.

Sat. Dec. 3, 1892

Mr. Wilson Deshazo, aged 89, died at his home near Cotton Hill last Sunday. He had lived in Barbour and Dale Counties for 66 years.

Sat. Dec. 24, 1892

Miss Rose Lewis, of White Pond, (Barbour Co.) died at the home of her brother, Quinn Lewis, on Sunday.-Eufaula Times.

Mrs. Jane Lassiter, age 62, member of the Baptist Church, died suddenly at the home of her son-in-law, Mr. James Moore, in Clayton on last Sunday.

Mr. S. A. Sims died at his residence near Mt. Andrew on Friday. Burial at Bethlehem Church (Barbour Co.) with Masonic honors.

The Clayton Courier
1893

Sat. Jan. 14, 1893
Dr. J. P. Chazel, aged 79 years, of Charleston, S. C., died at his home on Sunday.

Mrs. Dr. Bennett, widow of Dr. Bennett, formerly Tax Collector of Barbour Co., died at Louisville, (Ala.) on Tuesday last.

Sat. Feb. 11, 1893
The Mobile (Ala.) Register reports the death yesterday of Hon. John M. Foster, chancellor of the southeast division of the State of Alabama. In 1876 he was elected to the legislature from Barbour County.

Sat. Feb. 25, 1892
The remains of Mr. James Lewis, who was burned to death Sunday in a flour mill in Birmingham, were shipped to Spring Hill, (Barbour Co.) and conveyed from there to his father's home near Belcher.

Sat. Apr. 29, 1893
Dr. C. R. Duncan, one of the oldest physicians of Montgomery, Ala., died on Sunday.

Sat. May 13, 1893
Mr. William Efurd, age 67, of Clayton, died Tuesday.

Sat. May 27, 1893
The Eufaula (Ala.) Advertiser reports the death of Capt. J. J. Kaigler, who died in Eufaula on Tuesday.

Mrs. Jane Stewart, age 83, died at the home of her son, Mr. C. F. Stewart, near White Oak (Barbour Co.). She had been a member of the Presbyterian Church for a long time. She leaves four daughters and three sons, among them is Mrs. W. H. Snipes, of Clayton.

Sat. June 3, 1893
Mr. Tom McRae died at his home in Louisville, Barbour Co., Friday of last week.

Sat. June 10, 1893
Mrs. Willie Glover, age 124, "it is said by those who know", died Friday at the residence of her son-in-law, Mr. Seth Herring, near Louisville, Ala. She was a member of the Bethlehem Baptist Church.

Mrs. E. H. Fitzpatrick, of Eufaula, died at the home of her mother in Midway, (Ala.). She was a sister of Judge W. H. Pruett, of Barbour County, Ala., and Messrs. S. G. and Oscar Pruett, of Montgomery, and Judge J. W. Pruett, of Midway. She leaves several children, one only a few months old.

Sat. June 17, 1893
Reuben C. Shorter died at his home in Montgomery on Sunday. He was the son of Reuben C. and Carrie A. Shorter.

Rev. O. R. Blue, Methodist minister, died at his home in Montgomery last week.

Col. W. C. Dawson died in Eufaula recently.

The Clayton Courier
1893

Sat. July 1, 1893
    Rev. J. R. Graves, D. D., age 73, Baptist minister, editor and author, died at his home near Memphis, Tenn., on last Monday.

    Mr. Ben Jones of Montgomery, brother-in-law of Mrs. Lucinda Fryer (of Clayton), died suddenly with apoplexy.

    Mr. James Spradley, of Crenshaw County, (Ala.) died from injuries he received when he was struck by a train at Patsburg, Ala., recently.

    Mr. Horry D. Clark was buried in Eufaula on Sunday. Rev. I. O. Adams, rector of the Eufaula Episcopal Church officiated.

    Mr. T. F. Jones died suddenly at his home in Eufaula on Sunday.

Sat. July 8, 1893
    Mittie, age 7, daughter of Mr. Willie Butts, died and was buried at Antioch Church last Monday.

Sat. July 15, 1893
    Daisy Lee Long, age 7, daughter of Mr. and Mrs. W. O. Long, died at Abbeville, Ala., on last Saturday.

Sat. July 22, 1893
    Mrs. John Will Roquemore died at the residence of Mr. C. H. Bishop, at Harris (later Comer, Ala.) on Tuesday. She was a sister to Mrs. C. H. Bishop, and Messrs. B. F. and J. H. Long.

Sat. Aug. 5, 1893
    Mrs. Needham Lee died at Louisville, (Ala.) on Wednesday. She had been married about 15 months.

Sat. Aug. 12, 1893
    Miss Mary Godwin died in Eufaula on Tuesday.

    Mr. Lem Passmore, age between 93 and 94 years, died at his home near Louisville on Friday of last week.

    Mr. Felix Meadows died recently at Caddo, Indian Territory. He was a brother of Mr. Jule Meadows.

Sat. Aug. 19, 1893
    Mr. S. Q. Mullins was killed by lightning at his home near Newton on last Thursday.-Ozark (Ala.) Star.

Sat. Aug. 26, 1893
    Mr. Will Andrews committed suicide at his home in Montgomery on Sat. last, by shooting himself. He kept a family grocery. He was a native of Eufaula and had been living in Montgomery with his sisters for ten or twelve years.

    Ryan Bush, the six year old son of Mr. R. O. Bush, died yesterday of slow fever. Burial at County Line Church.

Sat. Sept. 2, 1893
    Mrs. Civil Steverson, mother of Mr. Charley Steverson, of near Clayton, died Tuesday night.

Sat. Sept. 23, 1893

The Clayton Courier
1893

Mr. Wyat Reed, age 50 years, died at his home near White Oak, (Barbour Co.) on Monday. He leaves a wife and five children.

Sat. Sept. 30, 1893

Mrs. Arabella McCraney, age about 84 years, died Wednesday at the home of her son-in-law, Mr. W. N. McRae, of near Clayton. She leaves a number of children, among whom are Mrs. W. H. Thomas and Mrs. W. N. McRae.

Hon. Alex H. Thomas, age nearly 42, died on Monday. He was born in Henry County near Otho. He came to Clayton in 1872 where he has lived and practiced law ever since.

Sat. Oct. 7, 1893

Mr. W. P. Stokes, age 36 years, one month and 26 days, died at his home in Clayton last Thursday. He was born near Louisville. Survivors are his wife and adopted child, a number of brothers and sisters. Burial in Clayton Cemetery, by the Knights of Pythias.

Mrs. R. B. Lee, wife of Rev. R. B. Lee, died at her home in Belcher (Barbour Co.) Wednesday. She leaves five children, the youngest being only a few hours old at the time of her death.

Mrs. Jennie Mills, aged 52 years, died of heart disease at the residence of her husband, Mr. Enoch Mills, near Louisville, on Saturday. Survivors are her husband and a number of children. She was a sister of our townsman, Mr. John T. Britt and Mr. M. W. Britt, of Midway.

Mr. Haywood Pipkin, age 80 years, died at his home in Midway on Monday last. He had lived in Barbour and Bullock Counties for about 55 years. At one time he represented Barbour County in the legislature.

Sat. Oct. 14, 1893

Mr. Thomas H. Harrison, age 66 years, died at his home near Clayton on Friday. He came from Georgetown, Ga., at the age of 9 years and had been living in this county 57 years. He has a large family. Burial at Bethlehem Church near Louisville.

Mr. C. H. Spencer, an old citizen living near Clayton, died Monday. He had been engaged in the saw mill business ever since he came to the county, and was for a number of years bridge inspector. He was a native of New Hampshire, and had been living in Alabama over forty years. Survivors are his wife and step-son. Funeral from the Baptist Church at Clayton and burial in the Masonic Cemetery.

Sat. Oct. 21, 1893

Mrs. Annie Dawson died at the home of Mr. A. C. Mitchell yesterday. Her daughter, Mrs. Dr. W. A. Mitchell, survives her. Burial at Glennville.- Eufaula Times.

Mrs. A. L. Martin, age about 70, died at Abbeville on last Thursday.- Ozark Star.

Sat. Nov. 4, 1893

Mrs. W. A. Doughtie died yesterday at her home on Sanford Street in Eufaula.- Eufaula (Ala.) Times.

The Clayton Courier
1893

Mr. Thomas Malone died at his residence near Judson Church last Wednesday. Survivors are his wife and four children.- Eufaula Advertiser.

Fred Sauter, a young man from Germany, who had been living in this country about two months, and a tailor, died in Eufaula yesterday. He has a sister in New York.- Eufaula Times.

Mrs. Viccie Baxter, age about 40, wife of Mr. Dan Baxter, living near Clio, died on Thursday last. She was a member of the Presbyterian Church. Survivors are her husband and two children.

Sat. Nov. 11, 1893

Mr. James Richards, age 82 years, of Richards Cross Roads, died recently. He had been living in Barbour County over 63 years. He leaves six grown children.

Sat. Nov. 18, 1893

Mrs. F. J. Strickland, age 65, died at her home near Clopton on Sunday. She was a member of the Methodist Church for 50 years. Survivors are her husband and eleven children.

The body of Wiley Hartzog was found near Robert's Mill in Barbour Co., on Friday. He had said he would take strychnine. He had threaten to take his life and had told his wife where his body would be found.

Sat. Nov. 25, 1893

Mrs. Bowden, wife of Mr. Jesse Bowden, living a few miles east of Clayton, died on Monday.

Mr. John D. Perkins, who was so brutally murdered at his store in the suburbs of Montgomery on last Saturday, was a native of Barbour County and has relatives living between White Oak and Fort Browder.

Mr. Calvin Wright, formerly of Clopton, was cut on his face and throat while on an excursion train returning from Ozark to Headland last Sunday, and died afterwards.

Mr. Thomas Weathers, of Batesville, (Ala.) was killed by his horse running away and throwing him against a tree.

Sat. Dec. 2, 1893

Miss Mary Simms, age about 60, died at her home near Clayton last Tuesday. She had been a member of the Baptist Church over 40 years.

Mr. A. Bush, brother of Mr. A. B. Bush, of Cotton Hill, died at Thorpe Springs, Texas on Friday of last week. He was a former citizen of Barbour county, and moved to Texas about twelve years ago.

Sat. Dec. 9, 1893

Rev. Junius Jordan, age 82, Methodist minister, died suddenly recently. He was born in Luenburg County, Va. He moved to Florida in 1829 and came to Eufaula in the fifties. His first wife died many years ago and his second wife about three or four years since. He leaves seven living children, two daughters, Mrs. R. H.

The Clayton Courier
1893

Simonton, of Dothan, and Mrs. H. E. Jordan, of Eufaula, and five sons, Mr. H. C. Jordan, Rev. J. S. Jordan, of South Georgia Conference, Prof. Junius Jordan, of Arkansas, Mr. Adrian P. Jordan, of Florida, and Mr. A. B. Jordan, of Dothan.-Eufaula Times.

Died at his residence near Solomon's Mill on Wednesday, Mr. A. K. McRae, an old citizen.

Sat. Dec. 16, 1893
Hon. John W. Dowling died at his home in Ozark, (Ala.) on Thursday.

Sat. Dec. 23, 1893
Mr. Joe Nix, well known in Clayton and a distant relative to the Nixes living in this section, died suddenly at Pitt's House in Covington, Ga., on Tuesday last.

Eufaula Times & News
1893

Thurs. Aug. 3, 1893
Mrs. Archie McLeod died at her home in Barbour County on Saturday. Burial at Palmyra Church near White Oak.

Thurs. Aug. 17, 1893
Wyatt B. Walker died in Warwick County, Va., on July 11, 1893. He was born in Charles County on Jan. 5, 1836. He was a brother of R. C. Walker, of Eufaula.

Mrs. R. S. Roddenbery, age 26, died at the home of her father, Dr. A. Ogletree, in Eufaula.

Thurs. Aug. 31, 1893
Mr. H. L. Deshazo, an old resident of Headland, Ala., died recently.

Thurs. Sept. 7, 1893
Mr. James H. Durham, age 63, a resident of Eufaula for thirty years, died at his home here yesterday. He leaves five children, Messrs. Alonzo and Jeff Durham; Mrs. W. T. Sheets, Mrs. Rosana Burdett and Miss Mary Durham.

Mrs. Henry E. Williamson died at her home in Atlanta, (Ga.) on Tuesday.

Thurs. Sept. 14, 1893
Mrs. Charles I. McLaughlin, nee Miss Leila Ricks, died recently. She leaves a husband and three sisters, Mrs. Alpheus Baker, Mrs. A. J. Locke and Mrs. H. H. Way. Burial in Eufaula.

Mr. Fred (F. J.) Hartung, age about 40, died at his home in Eufaula yesterday. He came to Eufaula with his two brothers, Messrs. Joe and John Hartung in 1859. He leaves a wife, a brother and a niece.

Mr. James Ross died in Eufaula yesterday. He came from Quebec, Canada and engaged in the manufacture of buggies and

Eufaula Times & News
1893

wagons. He leaves a wife and eight children, Mrs. Frank Bloodworth, Mr. Charles R. Ross, Mr. James L. Ross, Mr. Edward H. Ross, Misses Clara and Clifford Ross. Burial from the Episcopal Church.

Thurs. Sept. 21, 1893
    Mrs. J. M. Barr, age about 50, died in Eufaula on Sunday at the home of her son, Capt. J. R. Barr. She leaves, beside her son, her husband, a brother, Mr. Ben Seay and sisters, Mrs. R. D. Thornton and Mrs. Wallace Comer.

Thurs. Sept. 28, 1893
    Mr. Austin C. Cargill, age 68, died at his home in Eufaula on Sunday. He was born in Little Rock, Ark., and came to Eufaula in early manhood. He leaves a wife and ten children.

    Mr. William C. Gunn, editor of the Cuthbert Liberal died Sunday.

Thurs. Oct. 5, 1893
    Mr. O. H. Peacock, age about 45, died at his old home in Clopton, (Ala.). He leaves a wife and several children. Burial from the M. E. Church in Eufaula.

Thurs. Oct. 19, 1893
    Richmond, Oct. 14.-Mr. Hugh A. Walker, of Farmville, Va., died today from injuries received when he was thrown from a horse.

    Hon. Raphael J. Moses, over four score years old, of Columbus, (Ga.) died recently.

Thurs. Oct. 26, 1893
    Mr. George C. Price, of Macon, (Ga.) died recently.

Thurs. Nov. 2, 1893
    Charleston, Oct. 27.-Gen. W. L. Prince, lawyer of the Pee Dee section, died Wednesday at Cheraw.

    The funeral of Mrs. H. T. Cobb, of Eufaula took place yesterday. She died at the home of her daughter, Mrs. Turner. She was the mother of the late Mr. Jesse Cobb.

    Mrs. Dave Lore, aged 88, wife of Capt. Lore, died at her home near Eufaula Tuesday. She was Miss Gibhard, and had been a resident of Barbour County nearly all her life, having been a member of the M. E. Church in Eufaula about 70 years. She married Capt. Lore 25 years ago. Burial in Eufaula.

Thurs. Nov. 9, 1893
    Miss Missouri Clark, sister to Messrs Warren and Lint Clark, died at the home of her brother-in-law, John James, last Saturday. Burial at Rocky Mount, (Barbour Co.).

    Mr. F. Strauss, of Eufaula, died at his home yesterday. His wife died nine years ago and since that time he has lived with his two daughters and his son, Mr. Meyer Strauss.

    Mrs. J. W. Burdeshaw died recently at her home near Skipperville on Wednesday.- Ozark (Ala.) Star.

Thurs. Nov. 16, 1893
    Mr. Andrew C. Fulmore, planter, died at his home near

Eufaula Times & News
1893

Columbia, (Ala.) on Saturday last.

Thurs. Nov. 23, 1893
Montgomery, Ala., Nov. 18.-Mrs. H. M. Jackson, wife of Bishop Jackson, of Alabama, died recently at the home of her father, J. B. Pace, in Richmond, Va. Burial in Richmond.

Thurs. Nov. 30, 1893
Dr. E. W. Warren, Baptist minister, died at his home in Macon, Ga., on Sunday last.

Mrs. Jesse B. Bowen, age 76, living near Clayton, died last week. She was a member of the Baptist Church for 36 years. She leaves six grown children.

Thurs. Dec. 7, 1893
Mrs. N. S. Kendrick, formerly and for many years of Eufaula, died on Dec. 3d in Birmingham at the home of Capt. Walker. Burial at Chunnenuggee Ridge at Mt. Zion.

Mrs. Mary Garland, age 73, died Tuesday at her home near Howe, (Barbour Co.). She leaves several children, among them being J. B. and E. H. Garland and Mrs. Calhoun and Mrs. Wellborn.

The death of Mr. F. M. Fredrickson occurred at Vine Hill, in Autauga County, (Ala.) on Dec. 1st.

Thurs. Dec. 14, 1893
Roanoke, Va., Dec. 8.-A. Barlow, manager of the Elkhorn Coal & Coke Co., died here today of pneumonia. He was a native of New Philadelphia, Penn.

Mrs. Annie Hart, formerly of Eufaula, died in Montgomery yesterday. She was a sister of Mr. H. B. McGough and Mrs. W. M. Bray, of Eufaula, and Mr. Thomas McGough, of Montgomery. Burial at Glennville, Ala.

Thurs. Dec. 21, 1893
Dr. J. W. Mercer, of Georgetown, (Ga.) died Sunday at Dawson, (Ga.) while attending the South Georgia Conference. He leaves a wife and two children, Mrs. Addie Barnett and Mr. Charles G. Mercer. Burial at Georgetown.

Thurs. Dec. 28, 1893
Mrs. Jim Roberts, of near Clopton, (Ala.) died Sunday. She leaves a husband and seven children. Burial at Bersheba Church.

New Orleans, Dec. 21,- The death of George B. Prechaska, president of a rice milling company, occurred this morning.

The Clayton Courier
1894

Sat. Jan. 6, 1894
Capt. J. C. Ainsworth, age 71, an 1849 pioneer to Calif. and Oregon, died Saturday at his home in Oakland, Calif. He was three times a millionaire.

Mrs. Sallie Butt, of near Cox's mill (Barbour Co.) died

The Clayton Courier
1894

of pneumonia on Friday last. Survivors are three children, all grown.

Mr. Council Bush died at his home Friday of last week. He was born in Houston Co., Ga., in 1817, and at the age of four his father moved to Barbour County. Had he lived until the 4th of next May, he would have been 77. He was a member of the Primitive Baptist Church.

Mr. Beauregard Thomas, of near Midway, died Tuesday. He leaves a mother.

Mrs. W. H. Russell, of Tuskegee, Ala., died Dec. 22nd at the home of her son-in-law, Mr. Charles Valentine, where she was visiting. (Barbour Co.).

Died on Wednesday of last week, Mr. Isham Phillips, age 81, at his home near Cook's Ford. He had been living in Barbour and Bullock Counties many years.

Sat. Jan. 13, 1894
The death of Dr. John H. Blue occurred in Montgomery on Monday.

Mr. Samuel Roach, son of Mr. Ed. Roach, of near Geneva, Ala., was accidently shot and killed during Christmas holidays.-Geneva (Ala.) Mirror.

Mr. Jess Fillingame, an old citizen of near Texasville, (Barbour Co.) died at his home Tuesday.

Mr. Rance Godwin, of Eufaula, died at his home Sunday.

Sat. Jan. 20, 1894
Gen. William H. Forney died at his home at Jacksonville, Ala., last Tuesday.

Mrs. M. A. Watson died Friday last near Judson Church, in Barbour County.

Mr. Gideon Carlton Nix, son of Mr. Gideon Nix, of Clayton, died Jan. 15, 1894.

The five year old daughter of Mr. John T. Bell, Jr., died Thursday. Burial in Louisville.-Ozark (Ala.) Star.

Sat. Jan. 27, 1894
Mrs. Gilbert McCall, age 66, died at her home near Louisville on Thursday. Burial at Warren grave yard in Clayton.

Mrs. Lizzie Johnston Oliver, teacher, died at her home in Eufaula Jan. 23rd. She was the daughter of the late L. F. Johnston, and relict of Clayton W. Oliver, who died at Lancaster, Texas in 1887.

Mr. Stephen T. Gibbons, age 85, died at his home near Belcher yesterday. He had resided in Barbour County for 62 years. He was the father of Hon. J. W. T. Gibbons.-Eufaula Times.

Sat. Feb. 3, 1894
Col. James Walton Mabry, age 68 years, 10 months and 7 days,

The Clayton Courier
1894

died Jan. 26th. He had resided in Clayton for more than 45 years. He was a senator from Barbour in 1874.

Sat. Feb. 10, 1894

Hugh McGough died at his home in Eufaula on the 6th inst.

Sat. Feb. 17, 1894

Gen. Lucien B. Northrup, CSA, age 83, died Friday at the Confederate Soldier's Home, at Pikesville, Md. He was a native of South Carolina.

Maj. Henry C. Semple, age 72, lawyer, died at his home in Montgomery on the 12th inst. He had resided in Montgomery since 1845.

Sat. Feb. 24, 1894

Died on Saturday last, Mrs. Warren Baker, of near Hagler's mill. Survivors are her husband and three children. Burial at Salem Church in Dale County.

Mrs. Annie Merrick, widow of Col. John Merrick, who left this place about two years ago to make her home with relatives in Miss., died Jan. 29th ult.

Sat. Mar. 10, 1894

Gen. Jubal Anderson Early died at his home in Lynchburg, Va., on Friday. He was born in Franklin Co., Va. on Nov. 3, 1816.

Mrs. Mary Whitlock, age 79, mother of Mr. J. H. and Mr. George Whitlock, died in Eufaula on 3rd inst. She was a native of Connecticut and had been living with her sons for the past ten years.-Eufaula Advertiser.

Mrs. Clara Adams, nee Miss Clara Wright, of Midway, Ala., died Sunday.

Sat. Mar. 17, 1894

Mrs. Mary A. Walls, age about 76 years, died near Clayton on Thursday.

Judge George W. Stone, chief Justice of the Supreme Court of Alabama, died at his home in Montgomery on Sunday.

Sat. Mar. 24, 1894

Mrs. A. M. Brannon died at her home in Columbus yesterday. She joined St. Luke's M. E. Church in 1857. She was Miss Julia Fuller, daughter of the late Col. Hiram Fuller, of Chattahoochee County, (Ga.) and was born Feb. 22, 1831. She married on Sept. 20, 1855, at the family home in Chattahoohee County and lived in Columbus since that time. Four Children survive her, Mrs. R. A. Carson, Columbus, Mrs. F. A. Norman, Clayton and Messrs. W. H. Brannon, Jr., and R. Means Brannon, of Columbus. She also leaves four sisters and three brothers.- Enquirer (Ga.) Sun.

Mr. Daniel McEachern, age 73 years died at his home near Clayton last Sunday. He was a member and elder of the Pleasant View Presbyterian Church. Burial at Miller's Church with Masonic honors.

The Clayton Courier
1894

Sat. Mar. 31, 1894

Senator Alfred H. Colquitt, age 70, died at his home in Washington, D. C. In 1876 he was elected Gov. of Georgia and served six years. He was born in Walton Co., Ga. in 1824, the son of Hon. Walter T. Colquitt.

Sat. Apr. 14, 1894

An explosion in the fireworks factory of Romaine & Bro., in Blandford, Va., Saturday took the lives of: Charles N. Romaine, Capt. James T. Tosh, John B. Bland, James Rowland, Robert Rowland, William Traylor, Edward Traylor, James Bryant, Quincey Livesay, James W. Perkins, and Thomas Woolfolk.

Sat. May 5, 1894

Mrs. Cornelia G. Weir Morgan, wife of Alabama Senator John T. Morgan, died at her home in Washington Saturday.

The infant of Mr. T. H. Ventress died Tuesday.

Mary, oldest daughter of Mr. Floyd Land, died at her home near Dothan on the 1st inst.

George Abell, proprietor of the Baltimore Sun, died Tuesday.

Sat. May 12, 1894

Judge W. Green Smith, age about 64, died at Staunton, Virginia recently.

The death of Mr. J. H. Jordan, of Mobile, occurred recently.

Sat. May 26, 1894

Gen. Phil Cook, secretary of the state, died Monday at the home of his daughter, Mrs. W. L. Peel, in Atlanta.

Col. Fred G. Sinner, age 82, Colonel of the old First Regiment during the war, died at Charlottesville, Va., on Monday. He was born in Maryland and educated at West Point.

Sat. June 2, 1894

Mrs. Nannie Andrews, the wife of Mr. James Andrews, died at her home near Clayton on Sunday.

Mr. Ben Deloach, of near Clio, died last Wednesday.

Sat. June 9, 1894

Mr. Joe Danford, age 82, of near Elamville, died last Monday. He had been a resident of Barbour all his life.

Sat. June 16, 1894

The accidental death of G. A. Ferrel, of Eufaula, occurred last night.-Eufaula Advertiser.

Miss Lutie Feagin of Clayton died Thursday.

Sat. June 30, 1894

Mr. Daniel Hartzog, living near White Pond (Barbour Co.) died Thursday. He had passed his three score and ten years mark.

Mr. J. M. Duffell, age over 90 years, died in Eufaula on Tuesday.- Eufaula Times.

Mr. John W. Thomas died Sunday at his home in Ozark. Burial

The Clayton Courier
1894

in Clayton. He is survived by his wife, children, his mother, brothers and sisters.

Sat. July 7, 1894

Mrs. Mollie Avery died at her home near Brownville, Ga., Wednesday. Burial in Clio, Ala. She was a sister of L. A. Hunt, of Clio.

Sat. July 14, 1894

Mrs. W. F. Gregory died at her home in Dothan on the 4th inst. Survivors are her husband and six children.

Sat. July 21, 1894

Col. S. J. Doster, former school teacher in Clayton, died at his home at Ariosta, in Dale Co., (Ala.) on Thursday last.

Sat. Aug. 18, 1894

Luther C. Challis died recently at his home in Atchison, Mo.

Nine men and boys were killed near DeKalb, Texas on Friday by lightning. There were: John Jacobs, Walter Atchley, Tom Blanchard, Will Hentley, John Jackson, Chris Petty, and Will Walsh.

Sat. Aug. 25, 1894

Mr. W. R. Andrews, age about 60, the engineer of the Eufaula cotton mills, died in Eufaula recently.

Mr. William Smitha, age over 80, died at his home in Eufaula last Sunday. He had been engaged in the livery stable business and dealing in stock for many years.

Sat. Sept. 8, 1894

Mrs. M. L. Campbell, age 71, died at her home in Clayton on last Monday. She was born in Brunswick County, N. C. in 1823, and married in 1848 to Rev. A. D. Campbell, who removed from N. C. before the war to this section for the benefit of his health, being a sufferer from lung affection. He bought a plantation on Pea River and was called as pastor to the Pea River Church. He moved to Clayton during war and died a short time after the close of the war. Mrs. Campbell had been a member of the Presbyterian Church for over 50 years. She made her home in Eufaula with her daughter, Mrs. McTyer, for several years before moving back to Clayton. She leaves two daughters and two sons.

Sat. Sept. 29, 1894

Mrs. Geraldine Hunter, close to 70 years of age, died at the home of her son, Dr. Z. W. Williams, in Glennville on Saturday. She was the daughter of Judge William Carter of Stewart Co., Ga. She was married twice, first to Dr. Robert Williams, physician of Russell Co. (Ala.), and second to Dr. H. M. Hunter, of Eufaula. Burial in Eufaula.-Eufaula Times.

Mr. Simpson Bryan, age over 80, died at his home in Washington Co., Fla., a few weeks ago. He was the father of Mr. George Bryan, living in Beat 10 in Barbour Co. He had been married for 57 years and had 15 children, 8 boys and 7 girls.

Sat. Oct. 20, 1894

Mr. J. F. Allison, of Jasper, Ala., died Monday.

The Clayton Courier
1894

Mr. James McBryde, late of Barbour Co., reared at Clio, drowned in Geneva County last week.-Brundidge (Ala.) News.

Sat. Oct. 27, 1894
Robert Copes, age about 50, Treasurer of Orangeburg County, South Carolina, died Saturday.

Sat. Nov. 10, 1894
William R. Leeds, for nearly thirty years a prominent figure in Philadelphia, Pa., died in that city Monday.

Sat. Nov. 17, 1894
Rev. Thomas M. Beckham, Methodist minister, died at the retrea for the sick at Richmond, Va., Sunday. He was born in Lexington, Davidson Co., N. C., on March 21, 1835.

Mrs. Green Grubbs, of Star Hill, (Barbour Co.) died on Tuesday last. She leaves one son, Dr. Grubbs, of Enterprise, Coffee Co.

Sat. Nov. 24, 1894
Mrs. Levi Wilkerson, of near Clopton, (Ala.) died last Wednesday. She leaves a husband and three children.

Sat. Dec. 1. 1894
Mrs. McKinnon, nee Miss Katie Petty, who was married about a year ago, died at her home in Inverness, Bullock County, (Ala.) last Sunday. She was born and reared in Clayton.

B. M. Stevens, ex-Probate Judge of Coffee County, Ala., died at his home in Elba last week.

The Clayton Courier
1895

Sat. Jan. 5, 1895
Dr. J. H. Card, a traveling dentist of Birmingham, was robbed and murdered near Roanoke, Randolph Co., (Ala.) on the 20th.

Mrs. R. G. Wright, mother of the editor of the Eufaula Times, died at Ocala, Fla., last Sunday.

Mrs. Ollin Whittington, of near Mt. Andrew, died on the 19th of Dec. She was the daughter of Mr. T. E. Warren.

Mrs. Charles Capels died at her home in Louisville last Sunday. She leaves a husband.

Miss Mollie Blair, daughter of Mike Blair, deceased, died at Louisville on Wednesday.

Sat. Jan. 19, 1895
Maj. J. C. Bryant, a half brother of Maj. H. B. Price, of Clayton, died at his home at Wewachitchee, Fla., on Tuesday last. He formerly lived in Eufaula.

The death of Mr. John McDonald, age between 70 and 75, of near Clio, (Ala.) occurred at that place on Thursday. He leaves a wife, but no children. He was a member of the Presbyterian Church.

The Clayton Courier
1895

Sat. Jan. 26, 1895

The death of Mr. Jeremiah Walker, of Geneva County, (Ala.) occurred Wednesday last at his relative's in Barbour Co. He leaves a wife and two children.

Mrs. Martha Tew, age 84 years, died at her home in Reeder's Mill Beat (Barbour Co.) on Sunday. She leaves one daughter and four sons, all grown and married.

Sat. Feb. 2, 1895

A little son of Mr. George Fuquary, of Cox's Mill Beat, (Barbour Co.) died on Monday last.

Mr. Thomas Morgan, an old citizen of Eufaula, died recently.

Mr. J. R. Simonton, age 47, died at his home in Clayton on Tuesday. He was born in Hancock County, Ga., and when a child his father and family moved to Henry County, Ala., where they resided for many years. He was a brother to Mr. J. H. Simonton, of Dothan, and Mr. J. B. Simonton, of Louisville. He leaves a wife, who is the daughter of Mr. J. E. Parish, Sr., of Clayton. Burial in the Masonic Cemetery.

Mrs. N. C. Dowling age about 20, living near Mt. Andrew, in Barbour Co., died Friday. She was a bride of 11 months. Burial in the Masonic Cemetery at Clayton.

Miss Vivie Vinson, daughter of Mr. N. W. Vinson, died Friday.

Sat. Feb. 9, 1895

Elder John R. Respess, noted Primitive Baptist preacher, died at his home in Butler, Taylor Co., Ga., on the 4th inst.

Col. N. H. R. Dawson died at his home in Selma, (Ala.) on Friday last.

Mr. Julie Hargrove, formerly of Clayton, died at his home at Mt. Pleasant, Texas, in November.

Mrs. Sophornia Warren, wife of Mr. Thomas E. Warren, living near Mt. Andrew, died Friday last.

Sat. Feb. 16, 1895

Mr. N. H. Hyatt died at his home in Eufaula yesterday. He was born in Westchester County, N. Y., Feb. 15th, 1812, and moved to St. Joseph's Fla., when a young man and from thence to Eufaula in 1842. He was married twice and had by his first wife four children, only one of whom Mrs. William Petry of this city survives him. By his second wife he also had four children, two of whom died young, the others are: Mrs. G. B. Burbanks, of Buffalo, N. Y., and Mr. Meltrose Hyatt of Montgomery. His widow survives him.-_Eufaula Times_.

Sat. Feb. 23, 1895

Mrs. Sarah A. Toney, age 75, died yesterday at her home at "Roseland", near Eufaula. Her husband, Col. Washington Toney, died about 16 years ago. Surviving are seven children, Judge Sterling Toney, of Louisville, Mr. T. W. Toney, of Eufaula, Mrs. J. T. Flournoy, Mrs. C. H. Bradford, Mrs. S. A. Holt, Mrs. R. L. Houston and Mrs. W. C. Oats.-_Eufaula Times_.

The Clayton Courier
1895

Mrs. Miles, age over 80, mother of Mr. Abram Miles, died at Louisville, (Ala.) on Tuesday last.

Sat. Mar. 23, 1895
Rev. John Albert Broadus, D.D., LL.D., president of the Southern Baptist Theological Seminary, died at his home in Louisville, Ky., Saturday. He was of Welsh ancestry, born in Culpepper Co., Va., Jan. 27, 1824.

Mr. R. J. Richards, Sr., age 69, died at his home near Clayton on Sunday last.

Sat. Mar. 30, 1895
Mrs. E. C. Newton, age 32, died at her home in Marlboro Co., S. C. She was Miss Fanny McNab, daughter of Mr. and Mrs. J. C. McNab. She was born in Clayton and had been married twice - Master Robert and Miss Mary Phelps, her children of her first marriage reside in Eufaula with their grandparents.-Eufaula Times.

Sat. Apr. 6, 1895
Mrs. James Richards, age 87, of near Clayton, died at her home Monday last. Her husband died last year and was about the same age of his life.

Sat. May 25, 1895
Mr. Hanford Dowling, age 78, died at his residence near White Oak (Barbour Co.) on Saturday last.

Sat. June 8, 1895
Mrs. J. W. Phillips, age 53, died at her home near Hempstead, Tex., on May 22d, 1895. She was born 20 miles north of Atlanta, Ga. Her father, Mr. Snow, moved from to Dale Co., Ala. During her residence in Dale She married Mr. Phillips, son of R. Phillips. She has lived in Texas for 22 years. She was sister to Mrs. J. W. Chambers and Mrs. G. W. Knight. She leaves a husband and nine children. Member of the Missionary Baptist Church.

Sat. June 22, 1895
Mr. J. E. Parish, Sr., age 78, of Clayton, died Monday. Burial in Clayton. He leaves a wife and eight children, among them are Mrs. Britt, Mrs. Graves, Mrs. Simonton, Miss Ida, T. R., J. E., and M. H. Parish.

Sat. July 6, 1895
Mrs. Hosea Bailey, age 74, died at the home of her son-in-law, Prof. P. P. Anderson, near White Oak last Wednesday. Burial in Clayton.

Sat. July 20, 1895
Mr. C. W. Guice died last week in New York. Burial in Eufaula on Monday last.

Sat. July 27, 1895
Mrs. Tudse McLeod, living between Fort Browder and Spring Hill (Barbour Co.) died on Tuesday last.

Mrs. Buena V. Dow, age 26, died in Atlanta on the 16th inst. She is the wife of C. Q. Dow. She was a native of Georgia, but moved to Pensalcola, Fla., at the time of her marriage about eight

The Clayton Courier
1895

years ago. She leaves a husband and children, and her father, Prof. J. W. Kenderick, of Clayton. Burial in St. John's Cemetery.-Pensacola (Fla.) Times.

Sat. Aug. 3, 1895
   Mrs. Frank Bush, of Rocky Mount (Barbour Co.) neighborhood died last Sunday.

Sat. Aug. 17, 1895
   Mr. John Glover, age 39, died at his home near Louisville, (Ala.) last Saturday. He leaves a wife and six children.

   Miss Sallie K. Raleigh died in Eufaula last Sunday at the home of Mr. Hol. Harrell. She was born in Washington, Ga., in 1815 and in her infancy was brought to Alabama where she has resided ever since. She joined the Baptist Church in 1843. She was a sister of Mr. A. A. Raleigh of Eufaula. Burial in Eufaula.-Eufaula Times.

   Mrs. Hiram Hawkins, wife of Hon. Hawkins, of Hawkinsville, Barbour County, died at her home last Saturday. (See page 40).

Sat. Aug. 24, 1895
   Mr. J. B. Doriety, of Mt. Andrew (Barbour Co.) died last Monday.

   Miss Eunice, 8½ year old daughter of Mr. R. H. Stephens, died at her home near Clayton Wednesday.

Sat. Aug. 31, 1895
   Mrs. George Hartzog, of Cox's Mill, (Barbour Co.) died last week.

   Dr. Benjamin S. James died in Clayton on Aug. 19th, 1895. He was born in Edgefield, S. C., Nov. 26th, 1823, the son of John Stobo James, a lawyer, and the grandson of Benjamin James, senator from Lawrens (Laurens). He was brother of the late Lieut. Col. George Strother James. He attended Medical University at N. Y. and after graduation, returned to S. C. and married Miss Lavinia Martin. Two of their four children survive him - Mary, now Mrs. W. F. Wright and Fannie, now Mrs. L. T. Stalnaker. In 1889 he moved to Clayton to live with his daughter, Mrs. Wright. He was a member of the Presbyterian Church. (Note: He was evidently survived by his wife, as in the next column is a poem dedicated to Mrs. James on the death of her husband).

   Mrs. William Bickley died Monday at her home in Clio. Burial in Midway. Survivors are her husband, W. M., and four children.

Sat. Sept. 7, 1895
   Mr. Marshall McDonald, of West Virginia, and commissioner of U.S. Fisheries, died Sunday at his home in Washington.

Sat. Sept. 21, 1895
   Mr. B. H. Jennings, of Clayton, died Tuesday. He leaves a

The Clayton Courier
1895

wife and four children. Burial in Clayton with Masonic honors.

Mr. John Lewis, age 25, of Alston in Barbour County, died on the 12th inst. Burial at Bethel Church near White Pond.

Sat. Sept. 28, 1895
Mr. Charley S. Anderson, formerly of Clayton, then of Union Springs, (Ala.) died in Montgomery last Saturday where he has been living for eight years.

Dr. C. W. Lee, age 22, died last Thursday at the home of his father, Capt. A. V. Lee, in Clayton. He married Miss Nettie Passmore in 1893 and has one child.

Mr. Chauncey Rhodes died yesterday in Eufaula. Survivors are Jamie Rhodes, Mrs. Florence Dickerson of Waldo, Fla., a son on the Pacific Coast, Mrs. E. T. Long, Mrs. W. Y. Dent and his wife. He was born in Weatherfield, Conn., Dec. 12th, 1826. He came to Eufaula in 1847 and married Miss Elizabeth Daniel.-Eufaula Times.

Sat. Oct. 5, 1895
The deaths of Mr. G. W. Rollins and his son-in-law, Mr. John C. Williams, occurred last Friday near Ozark by a train. Both men were from Belcher, in Barbour County.

Col. D. S. Troy died at his home in Montgomery last Saturday.

Sat. Oct. 12, 1895
Mrs. Annie McDonald died at her home in Enterprise, Ala., on on the 26th of last month. She was the daughter of Mr. and Mrs. Buckner Williams, of Clayton. Survivors are her husband, her aged mother, and a brother, W. H. Williams, of Clayton.

Sat. Oct. 19. 1895
Gen. William Mahone died Tuesday in Chamberlain's hotel in Washington. Burial at his home at Petersburg, Va. Survivors are his wife, two sons, Butler and William Mahone, Jr., a daughter, Mrs. McGilt.

Sat. Oct. 26, 1895
Mr. Morgan Williams, age 34, died Monday at his home near Baker Hill, (Barbour Co.). He was a brother of N. T. Williams, Esqr. Survivors are his wife and five children.

Sat. Nov. 2, 1895
Mr. Abe Dean, an old citizen, died in Dale County last week.

Mr. Neal McKinnon Morrison, age 28, died at the home of his father, Mr. N. Morrison, at Clayton last Sunday.

Mr. Hanse Lewis, age over 70, died at his home near Clio on Saturday.

The Clayton Courier
1895

Mr. Jehus Wilkerson, age nearly 75, died at his home below Louisville, Ala., last week.

Mrs. H. M. Sessions died at Ozark last Sunday.

Sat. Nov. 16, 1895

Dr. Robert Battey died at his home in Rome, Ga., Friday. He was born in Augusta, Ga., Nov. 26th, 1828.

Sat. Nov. 23, 1895

Mr. Alex Tomberlin, of near Clayton, died last Friday.

Miss Louise Shorter, daughter of Maj. H. R. Shorter, of Eufaula, died last Tuesday.

Mr. Jack McRae, who moved back to Barbour County from Texas about two weeks ago, died from injuries he received from a kick of a mule. Burial near Clio. Survivors are his wife and several children.

Sat. Dec. 7, 1895

Mr. J. D. Bloodworth, formerly of Barbour County, and the father of W. D. Bloodworth of Spencer's Mill, died in Coffee County, (Ala.) last week.

Mr. Thomas E. Warren died at his home near Mt. Andrew last Tuesday.

Sat. Dec. 14, 1895

Mrs. H. H. McGilvary died at her home near Clayton on last Tuesday.

Mrs. Louisa Pruett, age 77, died at her home in Midway on Dec. 8th. Survivors are six sons and one daughter. She had lived at her home in Midway over 50 years and had been a consistant member of the M. E. Church for all that time.

Sat. Dec. 21, 1895

Mrs. T. L. Dowling, the wife of Prof. Dowling of Louisville, Ala., died at the home of her father, Dr. J. R. Thomasson at Aberfoil (Bullock Co., Ala.).-Union Springs (Ala.) Herald.

Eufaula Times & News
1895

Thurs. Jan. 3, 1895

Mr. Davis Berry who died recently in Jackson County, Ala., was 99 years old and was a soldier in the Florida war.

Thurs. Jan. 10, 1895

Mrs. Sallie Miller Venable, wife of Hon. William H. Venable, died Tuesday at her home in Atlanta.

Dr. J. W. Drewry received notice yesterday of the death of his sister, Mrs. Corine Ethridge, at Eatonton. She was the widow of the late Dr. Ethridge of that place. Her clothes caught fire and the burns were so terrible that she died from the effects.

Mrs. Mary McDonald, an aged woman, died at the home of her son, Mr. Harris McDonald near Ozark (Ala.) on the 24th of Dec. She

Eufaula Times & News
1895

was the mother of Mrs. J. W. Parker and of Mr. A. C. McDonald, of Ozark.

Mr. J. D. Mancill committed suicide on the 23rd of Dec., by drowning himself in a pond near Newton, (Ala.).

Capt. M. M. Tye died at his home in Ozark, (Ala.) last Monday.

Thurs. Jan. 24, 1895

On the 2nd of Jan. 1895 Mrs. Jane Goodrum Wright was buried at Union Springs, Ala. She was born of Thomas G. and Martha Frazer in Putnam Co., Ga., on 15th Sept. 1831. She died 30th Dec. 1894. She was married twice - on the 17th Aug. 1847 she married W. D. Jelks (Eufaula) and she lived with him 21 years. Four children were born to them. On 27th Jan. 1865 she married Maj. R. G. Wright. They had one daughter, Mrs. E. C. Hood, of Columbus, Ga.

Mr. Amzi Beach died at his home in Columbia (Ala.) Sunday, after a long illness of consumption. He leaves a wife and one or two children, besides a father, mother, brothers and sisters. His wife was Miss Lelia Stow, of Eufaula.

Mrs. R. J. Clendinen, of Abbeville (Ala.) died in Columbia, Ala., while on a visit to her daughter.

Mrs. Jesse B. Garner, age 66, died at the home of her son in Henry County, (Ala.) on Monday.

Thurs. Feb. 21, 1895

Charleston, S. C. Feb. 15.- Henry M. Bruns, LL.D., age 87, died at Summerville yesterday. He was the father of the late Dr. John Dickson Bruns, of New Orleans.

Thurs. Feb. 28, 1895

Frankfort, Ky., Feb. 20.-Col. R. P. Pepper, one of the wealthiest stock breeders in Ky., died at his home at Frankfort yesterday.

Clio, Ala., Feb. 22.-Died at her home of typhoid pneumonia, Mrs. Sarah A. McInnis, age 69. She was the widow of Mr. Miles McInnis. Burial at Pea River (Presbyterian) Church, Barbour Co.

Thurs. Mar. 7, 1895

J. A. Raleigh, of Columbia (Ala.) died Saturday from apoplexy. Burial from the Baptist Church. The Knights of Honor also performed their beautiful burial rite at the grave.

Thurs. Mar. 21, 1895

Mr. Richard Ryals, age 35, died at his home in Charlton on Thursday. He was born in Eufaula and lived here the greater portion of his life. He was a brother of James Ryals, of Eufaula. He leaves a wife and six small children.

Thurs. Apr. 4, 1895

Mr. A. J. Veal, for many years a tailor in Eufaula, died at his home on Mar. 20th in Paducah, Ky., of apoplexy. He was buried at Metroplis, Ill., where his son Charley now lives.

Cuthbert, Ga.- March. Col. Solomon D. Belton, age 89, died at the home of his daughter, Mrs. D. Phelps, in this city. He

Eufaula Times & News
1895

was the father of Mrs. Howard, of Oelasco, Tex., and the late Mrs. Lucinda B. Armstrong, of New Orleans.

Thurs. Apr. 11, 1895
Capt. James Jackson, of Montgomery, formerly of Union Springs, died yesterday. He leave a wife and three children, Mrs. A. S. Cowan of Birmingham, Mrs. Hudson of Eufaula and Mr. Jim Jackson, of Montgomery.

Thurs. Apr. 18, 1895
Mr. W. A. Harrison, age 70, died at his home at Belcher on Wednesday. He was married twice and leaves a wife and five children.

Thurs. May 2, 1895
Mr. John A. Christian, of Oxford, (Ala.) died recently.

Mr. Jasper Brazwell, an old citizen of Dale Co., died recently.

Mrs. J. P. Hutchinson, of Coffee Co., (Ala.) died recently.

Thurs. May 23, 1895
The funeral of Mrs. John D. Billings, age 65, was held yesterday at the home of Mr. E. J. Black in Eufaula. She died at her home in Columbus. She was a former resident of Eufaula. She leaves a husband and four children.

Mrs. M. J. Verner, age 67, mother of Mr. S. T. Rice of this city, died at the home of Mr. Rice yesterday. The funeral will take place this morning and burial at Georgetown, (Ga.).

Funeral services for Mrs. Carrie Bradford (Note: Nee Toney, of "Roseland", near Eufaula) were held yesterday at St. James Church in Eufaula.

The funeral services for Mrs. James Tansey were held yesterday at St. James Church in Eufaula. She leaves a husband.

Thurs. June 20, 1895
New York, June 13.-Dr. Alexander Pope died at his home on yesterday. He was born in Washington, Ga. He was a graduate of the University of Athens and the University of Virginia.

Mr. J. E. Parish, Sr., an old citizen of Barbour Co., died at his home near Clayton on Tuesday.

Mrs. M. M. Cariker, age 89, died at the home of her grand daughter, Mrs. W. A. Hill at Batesville, Ala., on Tuesday.

Thurs. July 4, 1895
Mrs. Mary Ridley, of LaGrange, Ga., died at her home yesterday.

Thurs. July 11, 1895
Mrs. A. C. Mitchell, Sr., died in Eufaula Sunday at the home of her son, Mr. A. C. Mitchell. Burial at Glennville, her old home.

Mrs. Bailey, age 74, died at the home of her son-in-law, Prof. P. P. Anderson, of White Oak.-Clayton Courier.

Thurs. July 18, 1895
Mr. James Miller died of consumption at his home at Baker Hill (Barbour Co.) on last Sunday.

Eufaula Times & News
1895

Thurs. Aug. 1, 1895

Mrs. Gus Hudspeth, living near Abbeville, a bride of eleven months and daughter of Mr. W. J. Hutto, of Henry Co., died last Saturday.

Mrs. B. F. Calhoun, of Otho (Henry County, Ala.) died yesterday at her home of consumption. Burial at Chester burying ground.

Mrs. W. E. McLeod, age 26, died at her home near White Oak, (Barbour Co.) Tuesday of typhoid fever. She had been married about eight years. She was Miss Angie Sparks. She leaves a husband and three young children. Burial at Batesville.

Thurs. Aug. 8, 1895

The death of S. M. Sullivan, of Covington, Ga., occurred at Charlotte, N. C. on Aug. 6th. He was postmaster at Covington. He leaves a family.

Mrs. Mary A. Causey died over in Georgia yesterday. Burial at Union Church beyond Georgetown, Ga.

Thursday Aug. 15, 1895

Norfolk, Va., Aug. 8.-Mr. Thomas Moberly, of Richmond, Ky., was drowned at Virginia Beach yesterday while endeavoring to save his daughter's life who went out beyond her depth while bathing. The young lady was saved by Mr. Greenwood, of Norfolk.

The remains of Mrs. Hiram Hawkins, of Hawkinsville, Barbour Co., was brought to Eufaula for burial on Sunday. She was Miss Louisa Anna Nuckols, born in Elbert Co., Ga. During her childhood her parents moved to Columbus, Ga. At the age of 17 she married Mr. Frank Boykin. A few years after his death she married Mr. Hiram Hawkins, of Ky. and they made their home near Eufaula.

Mr. Edward Johnson, Treasurer of Dale Co., (Ala.) died at his home near Ozark on Tuesday.

Thurs. Aug. 22, 1895

Tuskegee, Ala., Aug. 12.-George Pearson, a young business man, was shot by Hines Reid, a good friend. Reid escaped, the wound of George Pearson is believed to be fatal.

Thurs. Sept. 5, 1895

Mrs. Sarah Bates died at her home yesterday. She was born to Mary B. and Col. Reuben C. Shorter Sept. 4th 1819. She was married at Eufaula to James Lingard Hunter. He died in 1846. Some years later she married Maj. Bates. She had three children, Mrs. Sallie B. Battle, Mrs. Mary L. Roquemore and Annie, who died in infancy. Burial in the Hunter burying ground two miles south of Eufaula.

The death of Walter L. Pou occurred in Columbus Tuesday. He was a young business man.

Mrs. G. T. Cartledge, of Midway, Ala., died Wednesday.

Thurs. Sept. 19, 1895

Mrs. Lizzie Robinson died yesterday at the home of her uncle, Mr. Sears, on Union Street (Eufaula).

Thurs. Sept. 26, 1895

Eufaula Times & News
1895

Montgomery, Ala., Sept. 27.-Col. Daniel S. Troy, of Montgomery, died suddenly at his home here today.

Thurs. Oct. 10, 1895

Mrs. Susan Jones, age about 75, died Friday at the home of her son-in-law, Henry Scarbrough in the Judson neighborhood.

Thurs. Oct. 17, 1895

Col. B. H. Richardson, editor of the <u>Columbus</u> (Ga.) <u>Enquirer Sun</u>, died at his home Thursday. He was a native of Maryland, his ancestors immigrated from England in 1636 and settled in Harford County.

Mr. James Watson died at his home twelve miles north of Eufaula on Sunday. Survivors are his wife and four children.

Thurs. Oct. 24, 1895

Mrs. P. J. Ludwig died at her home in Eufaula yesterday. She was a member of the Catholic Church. She was born in Columbus, Georgia 33 years ago and resided there until about nine years ago when she moved to Eufaula. Survivors are her husband and six children. Burial in Columbus.

Thurs. Nov. 7, 1895

Mrs. Nancy Miller, wife of A. J. Miller, died Tuesday. She had been confined to her bed and chair for twenty years or more with rheumatism. She was the daughter of Mr. Daniel Snead, of Dothan and sister of B. F. Snead and S. J. Snead of Baker Hill in Barbour Co. She leaves a husband, two daughters and a son, Mr. Joe Miller who resides in Texas.

Thurs. Nov. 14, 1895

Mr. Nathan Baker, an aged citizen living in Beat 10, died on October 10th.

Mrs. Mary Eley, age about 50, died at her home above Cowikee (Barbour Co.) on Thursday. She was the mother of Mr. Will Eley, of Eufaula and of Mrs. Alice Smith and Mrs. Lizzie Adams, who lived with her. Burial in Eufaula.

Mr. Hanson Lewis died at his home near Clio in Barbour Co., a few days ago. He was the brother of Mr. W. A. Lewis.

Thurs. Nov. 21, 1895

At China Grove, Pike County, Ala., Prof. J. W. Roquemore was killed Sunday by his nephew, William Alexander. It was believed he was "crazed from drink".

Mrs. Odum age 60, of Albany, Ga., died yesterday. She was the sister of Mr. J. W. Ryals, of Eufaula.

Thurs. Nov. 28, 1895

Mrs. James Wardsworth, of Otho (Henry Co., Ala.) died at the home of her son-in-law, Mr. E. E. Grace, on Nov. 25th.

Mr. R. Alex Tomberlin died at his home near Louisville, Ala., recently. He was a brother of Mr. Dave J. Tomberlin.

Last Monday at Dallas, Texas, Mrs. Lem Craddock blew her brains out with a pistol. Mr. Craddock was a one time resident

Eufaula Times & News
1895

of Eufaula. The dead woman was his second wife and had been married to him about three years.

Dr. S. A. Holt, age 57, died Thursday. He was born in Monroe, Ga. He moved to Eufaula about sixteen years ago. Survivors are his wife and two married daughters, Mrs. Parker, of Anniston, and Mrs. Hulsey, of Atlanta, and one son, Master Syd Holt.

Thurs. Dec. 12, 1895

Mr. Fred W. Bray, formerly of Eufaula, died Dec. 3rd at San Antonio, Tex. He was brother to Mr. Charley Bray of San Antonio, and Mr. John W. Bray, of Eufaula.

Capt. J. C. Guilford, of Quitman Co., Ga., died at Milledgeville, Ga., on Sunday. Burial near Georgetown, Ga.

Mrs. T. M. Espy, of Dothan, Ala., died there Thursday. She was Miss Farmer and formerly lived at Shorterville, Ala.

Miss Jessie Rulterford (Rutherford), age 18, daughter of Mr. Foy Rulterford (Rutherford), of Quitman Co., Ga., died Friday. She had been an invalid a number of years. Burial at her father's near the Cross Roads.

Thurs. Dec. 19, 1895

Col. James T. Norman, of Union Springs, Ala., died recently. He moved to Union Springs thirty-odd years ago. He served two terms in the state senate.

Mr. Roscoe C. Andrews, editor of The Troy (Ala.) Democrat, died at his father's home in Troy Wednesday of diabetes.

Mrs. Louisa Feagin Pruett, age 77, died at Midway recently. Survivors are seven children, six sons and one daughter. Judge W. H. Pruett, of Barbour County, is one of her sons.

Col. T. L. Guerry, age 83, died at his home in Georgetown Thursday. He leaves four children: Judge Jim Guerry, of Dawson, and Messrs. Sam and LeGrand and Mrs. Morris, of Georgetown, Ga.

Thurs. Jan. 9, 1896

Mr. Alvin Thomas, one of the oldest residents of Thompson Station (Bullock Co., Ala.), died on the 20th of December.

Mrs. John C. Craig, age 67, died at her home at Jernigan (Russell Co., Ala.) on Monday. She was the mother of Mr. M. L., C. C. and Miss Craig.

The Clayton Courier
1896

Sat. Jan. 11, 1896

Mr. & Mrs. J. B. Fryer were called to Perote (Bullock Co.) recently due to the death of a brother-in-law, Mr. John Smith, who was stricken with paralysis.

Mrs. Nix, age 81, wife of Mr. David E. Nix, died at her home at Clayton on Dec. 26th. She joined the M. E. Church when she was eight years old. She was a sister of Dr. Thomasson, of Aberfoil (Bullock Co.) and mother of our townsmen Messrs. J. M., Gideon, W. H. and David Nix.

The Clayton Courier
1896

Sat. Jan. 18, 1896

Mrs. Weston, wife of Mr. Henry Weston, died at her home in Louisville, (Ala.) last Wednesday.

Mr. John Dansby, age 102, the oldest citizen in Barbour Co., died at his home near Elamville.

Sat. Feb. 1, 1896

Col. Augustus R. McCurdy died suddenly at his home in Montgomery last Sunday.

Sat. Mar. 7, 1896

The remains of Mr. Bob Dykes were brought to Clayton from Rome, Ga., where he died on last Monday.

Died of consumption at his home near Rocky Mount (Barbour Co.) on last Monday, Mr. Benny Price, age 23, son of Mr. Jemsey Price. He leaves a wife and two children.

Sat. Mar. 14, 1896

Mr. D. B. Bishop, age 31, died recently at his home in Alacia, Ark. He leaves a wife and one child. He was a brother of Mr. Fred Bishop.

John Parmer was drowned at Blackman's mill on the Choctawhatchie while seining last Saturday. He was a young man, the son of the late Jake Parmer who was killed some years ago near Echo, (Dale Co., Ala.) and was the only support of his mother.-Brundidge (Ala.) News.

Sat. Apr. 4, 1896

R. F. Wilks of Batesville died of paralysis yesterday.

Mrs. Mary Barnett, age about 75, formerly of Eufaula, died at the home of her son, Mr. Jule C. Barnett, in Montgomery. Burial in Eufaula.

Mr. Jeff (Jefferson) Buford, age 57, died in Birmingham yesterday. He was the son of Maj. Jefferson Buford who died when he was a resident of Clayton during the war. Miss Annie Buford, a sister of Jeff, died three weeks ago at the home of her brother-in-law, Capt. R. L. Hobdy, of Union Springs.

Sat. Apr. 18, 1896

Mrs. M. M. Strickland died on Friday of last week. She leaves a husband and children.

Sat. May 30, 1896

Mr. George A. Calder died near Ozark, Ala., recently. He has made his home with Mr. J. B. Andrews for the past six years.

Miss Euna, daughter of Mr. W. S. Bishop, died at her home at Spring Hill (Barbour Co.) on Sunday.

Sat. June 6, 1896

Mrs. Emeline Green, age 76, wife of T. G. Green, died at her home near Clayton on 20th of May. She leaves a husband who is 80 old years and eight children.

The Clayton Courier
1896

Mr. Randolph Fuquay, age 80, died at his home near Cox's mill last Wednesday. He leaves a wife, age 60, and ten children.

Mr. Jesse T. Davis, age between 45 and 50, died with measles at his home near Alston (Barbour Co.). He leaves a wife and three children.

Mrs. Mary A. Brannon, age over 70, died at the home of her son, Dr. H. L. Brannon, on Sunday in Eufaula. She was Miss Mary A. Kaigler and married Mr. W. B. Brannon in 1858. Her husband died in 1873 and Mrs. Brannon moved to Fla. where she lived about a year, and where two of her sons reside.

Mrs. Florence Kendal Ross, wife of C. R. Ross, died at her mother's in Eufaula on Sunday. Burial in Eufaula.

Sat. June 13, 1896

Mrs. Alex Johnson, age 60, died at the home of Mr. Willie Butts, nine miles southeast of Clayton on last Wednesday.

Maj. Lovard Lee, age 79, died suddenly at his home last Monday. He was born in Augusta, Ga., Nov. 17, 1817 and moved to Barbour County in 1833. He married Susan Emeline Lovelace on Oct. 24, 1844, who died some years ago.

Sat. July 4, 1896

Mrs. J. E. Warr, Jr., died at her home in Prospect settlement seven miles south of Clayton on Friday. She leaves a husband and four children.

Mr. Thomas A. Hightower, age 92, an old settler of Barbour County, died at the home of Judge H. C. Russell, near Eufaula on last Tuesday.

Sat. July 11, 1896

Mrs. W. M. Miller, age between 40 and 50, of Rocky Mount (Barbour Co.) died yesterday. She leaves a husband and several children.

Sat. July 25, 1896

Mr. Gilbert Helms, age about 48, living five miles west of Clayton was struck by lightning and killed last Wednesday. He leaves a wife and six children.

Sat. Aug. 1, 1896

Mrs. Mary Jordan, age 92, mother of our townsman, Daniel Feagin and Col. Ike Feagin, of Union Springs, died in that city last Sunday.

Mrs. William Jernigan died at her home at Belcher Saturday. She leaves a husband, children and grand-children.-Eufaula Times.

Sat. Aug. 15, 1896

Mrs. S. J. Cummings died at the home of her son-in-law, A. A. McDonald, Esqr., at Louisville on last Tuesday. She had been an invalid for a long time. She leaves one son, Rev. S. J. Cummings, who is president of a female college at East Lake, near Birmingham, a daughter and an aged husband.

Sat. Sept. 19, 1896

The Clayton Courier
1897

Mrs. Archy Bryant died at her home in Reeder's mill beat (Barbour Co.) on Tuesday.

Sat. Nov. 14, 1896

Miss Jennie Ellison Petty died Wednesday. Burial from the Methodist Church in Clayton.

Sat. Dec. 5, 1896

Mrs. M. E. Laseter, age about 76, died at the home of her daughter, Mrs. Nan Williams, on last Sunday. She leaves a large family of grown children.

The Barbour Journal *
1897

Fri. Apr. 30, 1897

At Birmingham Dr. J. J. Clapp was found dead in the hall of the Southern Railway building on Saturday.

Mrs. Caller, mother of Miss Pearla Caller died recently.

Mrs. Lucinda Fryer, age 69, died Monday at the home of her daughter, Mrs. Carrie Jennings. She was born in 1828 and was reared in Clayton and lived here all her life. On 25th of July 1848 she married Dr. Fryer, who died many years ago. She leaves two children, Mrs. Jennings and Mr. R. D. Fryer, one sister, Mrs. Sallie Jones, of Montgomery, and three brothers, Messrs. C. W., J. E., and Cullis Fenn.

Fri. May 7, 1897

The Rev. Mr. Thompson, age 79, pastor of the Presbyterian church at Mobile died recently. He was the father of Mrs. E. H. Gregory, wife of Rev. Gregory, of Clayton.

Mr. Tyron Carr, age 80, who had been living in Elamville (Barbour Co.) for 50 years, died at his home Saturday.

Fri. May 14, 1897

The Apalachicola (Fla.) Times announce the death of Judge H. McD. Boylston, age 58, a former Clayton citizen. He was born in Barbour County. Twenty-six years ago he moved to Apalachicola. He moved back to Alabama, but returned to Fla. eight years ago. Survivors are his wife, two daughters and two sons.

Mrs. Grubbs, age 70, wife of Mr. Britt Grubbs, living west of Louisville, died at her home Monday.

Mr. E. L. Davis, age 28, died at his home in Clayton Friday. He leaves a wife and three children.

Mrs. T. H. Stout died at her home in Thomason, Ga. last week. She was the wife of Rev. Stout. Burial from her brother's home, Mr. F. S. Wood and interment at Shiloh near Troy, Ala.

Fri. May 21, 1897

Mrs. D. L. Blair, age about 38, died Tuesday at her home in Clayton. She was a dau. of Dr. Turner, of White Oak (Barbour Co.). Survivors are her husband and six children, one only five weeks old.

* Published at Clayton, Alabama by Edgar R. Quillin.

The Barbour Journal
1897

Mr. F. J. Dehoney, age 68, died at his home in Montgomery on Monday. He was a well known stock dealer.-Montgomery Advertiser.

Mrs. J. F. George, age about 60, of Eufaula, died in Columbus (Ga.) while on a visit to her son, Mr. Chas. George. She leaves a husband and three children.

Mrs. T. J. Irby, nee Sallie Flournoy, died at her father's home in Eufaula. She was the dau. of Capt. S. J. Flournoy and grand-dau. to the late Col. and Mrs. Washington Toney. She married Mr. Thomas J. Irby, then of Anniston, about eight years ago. Survivors are her husband and two children.

Fri. June 4, 1897

Mrs. C. B. Wellborn died at her home at Howe (Barbour Co.) on Thursday.

Mr. Henry Harrison died at his home at Rockdale, Texas, on May 26th. He was the son of the late Mr. Thomas Harrison, and nephew of our townsman, Mr. A. A. Dorman. He leaves a wife and several children.

Fri. June 18, 1897

Mrs. Elizabeth Burlison, age 83, living near White Oak, fell last Saturday and broke her neck. She leaves five children. She was buried in the Bishop and Blair grave yard.

Mrs. Bena Slosson, dau. of Mr. N. W. Boyd, died at her home at Texasville (Barbour Co.) last Saturday. She was a bride of only three months. Burial at Pleasant Plains, south of Clayton.

Mrs. Annie Morrison, age about 65, living near Orr's store, died Friday. She left three sons and one daughter. Mr. George Burlison, at whose house Mrs. Elizabeth Burlison died, was a son-in-law of Mrs. Morrison.

Fri. July 9, 1897

Mrs. J. W. Harp, age nearly 70 years, died at her home at Perote (Bullock Co.) on Monday.

Fri. July 30, 1897

Mr. Fleming Law, of Union Springs, died on Monday at the home of his daughter in Gainesville, Ga.

Fri. Aug. 13, 1897

Mrs. Fletcher McCraney died at a hospital in Montgomery last Friday. Her remains were brought home for burial at Mt. Airy Church. Survivors are her husband and four step children.

Fri. Aug. 20, 1897

Mr. H. F. Dawson, city Marshal of Union Springs, died recently.

The death of Rev. James Yeates, age 65, Baptist minister at Sheffield, Ala., occurred recently. He was a native of Detroit, Mich.

Fri. Sept. 3, 1897

Mrs. Sussie Phillips, age about 45, postmistress at Lawrenceville, dropped dead at her home last Monday. She leaves three daus.

The Barbour Journal
1897

Mr. J. M. White died in Montgomery on last Tuesday. He was born in Barbour County on Apr. 20, 1846 and began his law practice in Clayton. He was a brother of State Auditor W. S. White. He married first Miss Cowart, of Barbour County, and his last wife, who survives him, was Miss Margaret Peet, of this city. He leaves four children - two from each marriage. He was in partnership with his son, P. W. White.

Miss Lucy Oliver died suddenly at the home of her sister, Mrs. Ellison, in Clayton recently.

Fri. Aug. 27, 1897

Mr. F. B. Loyd, of Montgomery, a humorous writer and lecturer (under the name of Rufus Sanders) was assassinated in the road three miles from his home on Wednesday.

Dr. Louis C. Pynchon, age 67, physician of Huntsville, Ala., died last Friday of apoplexy. He moved to Huntsville from Savannah, Ga., forty years ago. His wife survives him.

Fri. Sept. 17, 1897

Mr. Hart McCall, age over 80, died at his home in Clio on last Tuesday.

Mrs. Katie McKinnon, age 85, mother of Messrs. Daniel and John McKinnon, died at the home of her son, John, near Clio on last Saturday. Mrs. McKinnon was the only one, with the exception of Mrs. Nancy Stephens, of the hardy North Carolina Scotch pioneers who first settled in the section lying between Louisville and Clio.

Mr. Charley Vinson, age 44, died Thursday of typhoid fever. He was reared in Barbour County. He leaves one brother, Mr. N. W. Vinson, and a sister, but no wife and children. His wife preceded him to the grave several months ago.

Mr. Seaborn J. Cummings, age 78, died suddenly at the depot in Eufaula while waiting for the train for his home in Louisville. He had been to East Lake (B'ham.) on a visit to his son. He leaves two children, Mrs. A. A. McDonald and Rev. J. B. Cummings.

The Louisville Journal *
1897

Fri. Oct. 8, 1897

Mrs. Charley Cunningham, living near Barr's Mill, died on last Sunday.

Miss Lou Farrior died at her home in Clayton on Thursday. She was a sister of Mrs. M. C. Bell, of Louisville.

Mrs. G. Raley, age 74, died at her home near Louisville on Monday.

Mr. H. Strickland, age 78, father of Mr. C. H. Strickland, died at his home at Clio today.

* Published at Louisville, Alabama, by Edgar R. Quillin.

The Barbour Journal
1897

Fri. Dec. 17, 1897
    Mrs. J. M. Grant, age 63 (?) died at her home in Louisville last Monday.

The Barbour Herald *
1897

Fri. Mar. 5, 1897
    Dr. J. D. Adair died in Birmingham, being too sick to proceed on his journey to Chattanooga for medical treatment. He was born at Perote (Bullock Co.) 5th Nov. 1869; graduated in dentistry in 1892, and married at Louisville Aug. 5th 1894 to Miss Carrie, daughter of Dr. B. F. Bennett. He leaves a family.

Fri. Mar. 19, 1897
    Mr. L. G. Dawson, living at Perote (Bullock Co.), committed suicide at Louisville, Ky., on Thursday by shooting himself. He was the son of Mr. George Dawson, dec'd. He leaves a mother and two sisters.

Fri. Mar. 26, 1897
    Mrs. R. A. Timmons, wife of Dr. Timmons, Presiding Elder of the LaFayette (Ala.) Dist., died at LaFayette recently.

Fri. Apr. 2, 1897
    Birmingham, Mar. 29.-George L. Morris, a wealthy mine developer and property holder, died tonight of Bright's disease after an illness of two years.

Fri. Apr. 16, 1897
    Mrs. T. R. Ventress, age 39, born and reared near Clayton, died Monday. She leaves a husband and seven children, one only six weeks old.

Eufaula Times & News
1897

Thurs. Jan. 7, 1897
    Mr. Marvin Merritt, of Midway, son of Mr. M. C. Merritt, died there last week of fever.

Thurs. Jan. 14, 1897
    Mr. L. D. Hatcher died at his home in Dawson, Ga., last Saturday. He was born and spent much of his childhood here. Some years ago he married Miss Lucy Gorsuch, of this county.- Quitman (Ga.) Cor., Cuthbert (Ga.) Leader.

    Mr. W. H. Harrell died at his home on Dale Road in Eufaula this morning of pneumonia. For several years he served on the police force of this city.

    Mr. Daniel Gilchrist, age 83, of White Oak died recently. He leaves seven or eight children.

    Mrs. Doughtie, the aged mother of Mr. John and Mr. Tom Doughtie, died at her home below the city yesterday.

* Published at Louisville, Ala., by Edgar R. Quillin.

Eufaula Times & News
1897

Mrs. John M. Alston, age about 35, of Cowikee (Barbour Co.) died Monday. She was a dau. of Rev. Briggs. Survivors are her husband and five children.

Mr. F. M. Knowles, of Columbia, (Ala.) died suddenly of apoplexy today. He had been a resident of Columbia for many years.-Columbia Breeze.

Mrs. Otho Appling, of Columbia, died Sunday following a long illness. Had she lived until the 6th Feb. she would have been 45 years old. Survivors are her husband, three sons and a daughter.- Columbia (Ala.) Breeze.

Thurs. Jan. 28, 1897

Mr. John J. Thornton, an old citizen of Bullock County, died at his home at Midway on last Saturday.

Annie Sue, the twelve year old dau. of Mr. and Mrs. G. W. Bragan, died of pneumonia recently.-Quitman (Ga.) Cor. Liberal.

Died near Georgetown, Ga., Saturday, Mr. L. L. (Jack) Oliver, in the prime of life. Survivors are his wife and three little tots.

Athens, Jan. 19.-Died at his home this morning, Mr. Charles B. Hayes, as the result of an assault of highwayman on Christmas eve when he was seriously injured and robbed. He was a leading citizen of Athens and Limestone County. Had he lived to the 27th of this month he and his wife would have celebrated their golden wedding anniversary.

Mr. Phillip Bruce, nearly 100 years old, who was perhaps the oldest man in the county, died at his home near Haw Ridge last week. (From Ozark, Ala. paper).

Mr. John W. Branch, who lived near Echo (Dale Co., Ala.) died suddenly at his home Tuesday. He was the father of Mrs. Major Carroll, of this place.

Mrs. S. D. Clark died at the home of her husband in this place. (Dale Co., Ala.).

Mr. J. T. Bruce, of Eufaula, died near West Point Sunday. He had been canvassing in interest of a publishing house. He had been a resident of Eufaula about five years. He leaves a wife and three children. Burial at LaGrange, Ga. (Note: This article has Mr. and also Dr. Bruce).

Atlanta, Ga., Jan. 22.-J. H. Porter, age 69, banker, died at his home here of heart disease.

Thurs. Feb. 4, 1897

Mr. George P. Swift, age 82, of Columbus, (Ga.) died recently. For many years he was a manufacturer here.

Mr. Caleb Golden, who lived near Clopton in Dale County, died of pneumonia at his home on Monday.

Mrs. E. V. Teague died at the home of her son, Mr. Angus Teague, near Shorterville (Henry Co., Ala.) on the 20th inst.- Abbeville (Ala.) Times.

Eufaula Times & News
1897

Mrs. Carmichael, wife of Judge J. M. Carmichael, died at her home in Ozark (Ala.) on Tuesday.

Mrs. E. A. Saunders, of Abbeville, died recently.

Plant City, Fla., Jan. 28.-At Turkey Creek, a station about four miles from here, W. E. Moody shot and killed in self defense his brother-in-law, John Odom.

Thurs. Feb. 11, 1897

Mr. W. H. Graham, of Morris Station, died of consumption on Wednesday, after a long illness. He lived in his store and was cared for by his faithful clerk and friend, Mr. Joseph E. Johnson.

Mrs. Martha Redding, age about 85, died at the home of Mr. F. M. Gay in Eufaula on yesterday.

Mr. George H. Thomas, Esqr., of Ozark, died Monday. He had been a sufferer of Bright's disease. Burial in Ozark with Masonic honors.

Mr. B. T. Joyner, of Dothan, died at his home last week of typhoid pneumonia. He was the father of triplets born only a few days ago, named Shadrach, Meshach and Abednego. The last named baby died a few hours before his father. Survivors are his widow and nine children.

Thurs. Feb. 18, 1897

Alva Malone, age about 14, the step son of Mr. W. T. Watford, died Sunday at his home two miles west of the city. Burial at Judson Church in Henry County.

Mr. Zack Bird, age about 43, died at his home in Eufaula on yesterday from consumption. He leaves a wife and several children.

Mr. J. C. Fuller died yesterday. He had been suffering from rheumatism, but only a few weeks since he was forced to take his bed. Survivors are his wife and three children.

Thurs. Feb. 25, 1897

Mrs. Eliza Stephens died at the home of her son-in-law, Mr. James Hatfield, on last Thursday from apoplexy. She was born 75 years ago in Fayetteville, N. C. Her parents removed to this county when she was quite young and she has lived here ever since. Burial at Bascom Church four miles west of the city.

Thurs. Mar. 4, 1897

Mrs. William E. Price died at her home near Eufaula Thursday. Survivors are her husband and several children. Burial in Eufaula.

Thurs. Mar. 11, 1897

Arthur Skipper, age 78, of Henry Co. (Ala.) died recently.

Mr. William (Buck) Cox, age 89, died at the home of his son in Linwood, Bullock County, on Wednesday. He once resided near Enon for many years.

Mrs. J. E. Pitts, age 70, of Union Springs (Ala.) died on Saturday. Burial at Sardis. She was the only living sister of Dr. L. Sessions, of Union Springs, and mother to Messrs. Whit-

Eufaula Times & News
1897

field, W. M., J. L., and T. F. Pitts and Mrs. J. A. Paulk.

Mr. M. B. Patterson, an aged citizen of Elamville (Barbour Co.) died at that place recently.

Mrs. Kittie McRae, of Clio, died there Saturday. She was the mother of Messrs. Frank and Phil McRae and Misses Jane and Mary McRae.

Thurs. Mar. 18, 1897
Mr. Fletcher Kennedy, age about 22, died at Hill House in Clayton yesterday. He took morphine to end his life. He was the son of ex-postmaster Kennedy, of Clayton.

Mr. E. H. Hobdy, age 52, of Ocala, Fla. died last week. His brother, Capt. R. L. Hobdy, lives in Union Springs. Burial at Louisville in Barbour County.

Thurs. Apr. 1, 1897
Mr. Ollen Searcy, age 74, died near County Line (Barbour and Henry Counties) yesterday.

Thurs. Apr. 15, 1897
Mr. J. L. Moultrie, age 80, and for half a century has lived on his farm near Union Springs, died recently.

Mr. Herman Hirsh, of Columbus, Ga., died recently.

Mrs. Cade received a telegram announcing the death from congestion of her brother, Mr. Louis Christian, at Gilmer, Texas, on last Sunday. He leaves a wife and one child.

Thurs. Apr. 29, 1897
Capt. W. F. Joseph, of Montgomery, died recently.

Mr. John Tindall, age 75, died at his home in Eufaula on Thursday. He had lived here for 30 years. He leaves a wife and five children. He was a war veteran.

Mrs. Sarah Morgan died at her home in Eufaula Tuesday. Survivors are her mother, with whom she lived, four children and two brothers, Mr. John and Mr. Lawrence Sauls, and two sisters, Mrs. Alonzo Durham and Mrs. Ann Curbow.

Mrs. J. A. Nobles, of Quitman Co., died last night after a long and painful illness.

Thurs. May 6, 1897
Mr. Benjamin T. Blassingame, age 87, died at his son's home in Eufaula this morning. He was born in Monroe Co., Ga. He moved to Russell Co., (Ala.) in 1840 and to Eufaula a few years ago. Burial at Glennville.

Thurs. May 13, 1897
Lexington, Ky., May 10.-Capt. William Strong, aged 72, was shot and killed recently near his home in Breathitt County by unknown persons.

Mr. R. F. Smith, age 31, died in Eufaula this morning. He was reared at Ramer, Montgomery Co., Ala., where his parents still reside.

Mrs. Lucinda Riley, wife of Rev. Daniel Riley, died at her

Eufaula Times & News
1897

home in Echo (Dale Co., Ala.) on last Thursday.-Ozark (Ala.) Star.

Mr. Barney B. Watford, many years a citizen of Dale Co., Ala., but recently moved to Sanders Post Office in Geneva Co., dropped dead 10th inst., while plowing his field.

Thurs. June 24, 1897

Mr. Junie Reeves, age about 30, shot himself at his home near White Oak on Saturday. He was the only surviving child of Mr. Daniel Reeves. His wife was the dau. of Mr. Milledge Smith. Survivors are his wife and two children.

Dr. John W. Drewry died Monday at his home in Eufaula. He practiced medicine for 50 years. He leaves five children, Messrs. John W. Drewry, of Cuthbert, James Drewry and Mrs. J. G. Guice, Mrs. J. P. Foy and Mrs. A. C. Mitchell, all of Eufaula. His wife died only a few years ago. He was born in Jones Co., Ga., Sept. 5, 1827. He moved to Spring Hill in Barbour Co., in 1850 and married Miss E. A. Etheridge, of Clinton, Ga., Dec. 1st, 1851. He moved to Eufaula in 1866.

Mrs. Carrie Butler died this morning of consumption at the home of Mr. J. E. Black. She was Miss Carrie Black, dau. of Mr. John Black. Mrs. Butler was the widow of Mr. A. C. Butler, who died several years ago. One child survives, Mr. Will A. Butler. Mrs. Butler was born 7th Aug. 1848 and married Mr. Butler in Nov. 1867.

Thurs. July 1, 1897

Dr. Absalom Ogletree died at his home this morning. He was born in Wilkes Co., Ga., 1823. He practised dentistry about ten years and moved to Quitman County from Wilks and began farming. He was married twice. He leaves two daughters, two sons and a grand-daughter.

Mrs. W. B. McLendon died at her home in Georgetown yesterday. She was the mother of Mrs. Dr. Dozier, of Quitman County and of the late Dr. J. W. Mercer.

Mr. Dick L. Blair died at his home in Clayton on Friday.

Mrs. William Link, age 79, died at her home in Eufaula this morning. Mr. Link, her second husband, died some years ago. She leaves only one child, Mrs. George A. Ferrell, who has been living with her. She was a sister to Mrs. Jacob Ramser, of Eufaula. Mrs. Link came to Eufaula nearly 50 years ago. She was born at Stuttgrat, Kingdom of Wurtemberg in 1821. She came to Lumpkin, Ga. in 1841.

Thurs. July 8, 1897

Mr. Jason Walker of Geneva County (Ala.) died recently. He leaves a family.

Thurs. July 22, 1897

Atlanta, July 16.- Emanuel Rich, age 49, a member of the firm of M. Rich & Bros., committed suicide at his home in this city by cutting his throat. He was a native of Hungary. He leaves a wife and two children.

Eufaula Times & News
1897

Mr. A. J. S. Glenn, formerly of Eufaula, but for eighteen years of Knoxville, Texas, died there in April. He was a member of the noted Glenn family of this section. He leaves his wife, Mary Russell, and two children. Mrs. Glenn is from a well known family in this section. She was the grand-daughter of Capt. A. G. Smith who lived in Eufaula.

James, the second son of Mr. Thomas Evans and his wife nee Miss Dillie Waddell, of Columbus, Ga., died at the home of his uncle, Mr. A. A. Evans, in Eufaula on 11th July.

Talbotton, Ga., July 20.-Dr. W. L. Ryder, who shot down his sweet heart in Talbotton, was the victim of a mob who took the law into their hands and he was lynched near Waverly Hall, Ga., near Mr. John W. Willis' home.

Thurs. Aug. 12, 1897

Columbia, S. C. Aug. 4.-Wicher Smith, an old citizen of Newberry County, died recently. He had two sons, Walter and Howard Smith.

Anson, the four year old son of Mr. and Mrs. W. W. Sawyer, died at his home in Eufaula yesterday.

The remains of Mr. Cal Taylor who died yesterday from the effects of a blow from a base ball bat in the hands of Charles Faulkner, were buried at Fairview (Eufaula) today.

Thurs. Aug. 19, 1897

Mrs. W. E. McKinney, living in Eufaula, died suddenly of heart trouble at her home today.

Miss Bessie Koonce, a young lady of Columbia, Ala., died suddenly at her home last night from the effects of poison which she took to be a dentifrice by mistake. Upon examination the supposed tooth powder was strychnine.

Florence, Ala., Aug. 14.- Mr. V. B. Green, age 70, of Whitehead, Ala., was shot and fatally wounded by his daughter's suitor, Eli Barney, who had been forbidden to visit the Green's home.

Thurs. Sept. 2, 1897

Mr. Adam Warr, living near Texasville (Barbour Co.) died on Saturday of typhoid pneumonia. Survivors are his wife and four children. Burial at Prospect Church.

Miss Eula McCurdy, age 21, died today at the home of her sister, Mrs. A. J. Chamblis, in Eufaula. She had typhoid fever.

Thurs. Sept. 9, 1897

Atlanta, Sept. 6.-Mr. Isaac Liebman, age 54, wealthy and prominent business man of this city, died here recently.

Mrs. A. H. Drakeford, of Tuskegee, Ala., died in Ashville, N. C. recently.

Mr. Jack Sanders, age 63, died at the home of his brother-in-law, Mr. Samuel Ogletree, in Georgetown Saturday night. He was a brother of Mr. J. R. Sanders, of Cochran station (Barbour Co.) Burial at Georgetown.

Eufaula Times & News
1897

Birmingham, Sept. 8.-George S. O'Neal, store keeper of the Sloss Iron & Steel Co., died yesterday. He leaves a wife.

Mrs. Sara Van Pelt died at Fort Deposit, Ala., recently.

Mr. Peter Mulligan died at Huntsville, Ala., recently. He was a prominent merchant.

Thurs. Oct. 7, 1897
Mrs. F. A. Pomeroy and her daughter, Miss Maggie, died from burns they received at their home in Columbus, Ga., last Saturday.

Mrs. Albert Stephens, of Columbia (Ala.), died at her home a few days ago.

Thurs. Oct. 14, 1897
Atlanta, Oct. 11.- Dr. J. T. Monroe, of Union, S. C. committed suicide at Hotel Alvin by cutting his jugular vein with a knife.

Miss Mary Peak, of Glennville, died yesterday of consumption. She was a sister of Mr. Alonza Peak, of Hawkinsville (Barbour Co.).

Mrs. Jennie Howerton, age 81, mother of our townsman, Mr. T. J. Howerton, died at her home near Wesley, on Thursday. She had been a resident of Henry County about 70 years, coming to this county from Georgia with her parents when a small child.

Thurs. Nov. 25, 1897
Alston, Ala., Nov. 19.-Mrs. Lena Walker died at her home near here on the 11th inst. Burial at Clopton. She leaves a husband and mother.

Thurs. Dec. 2, 1897
Dr. J. S. Coffin, age 65, of near Florence, (Ga.) died at his home Saturday. He leaves a family.

Thurs. Dec. 9, 1897
Mr. James Tansey, age 69, died yesterday. He had lived in Eufaula forty years. His wife died two years ago and he had no children. Burial in Eufaula.

Thurs. Dec. 16, 1897
Mr. Z. F. Nance, age 82, died at his home at Leesburg, Ala., yesterday. He leaves a wife and four children, Mr. B. E. Nance, of Leesburg, Mr. R. F. Nance, Mrs. S. F. Moreland and J. A. Nance of Eufaula. Mr. Nance lived here for many years. Burial in Eufaula.

Mrs. James W. Grant, of Louisville, died last night.

Thurs. Dec. 30, 1897
Capt. E. L. Jenkins died at his home at Louisville, Ala., yesterday from consumption. Burial in Midway. He leaves a wife and brothers.

The Clayton Record
1897

Sat. Jan. 23, 1897

The Clayton Record
1897-1898

Mr. George Grant, age 32, died suddenly Monday. Survivors are his wife and two children.

Miss Annie G. Sutlive, age 27, professional nurse, died recently at Savannah. Survivors are her mother, Mrs. E. J. Sutlive, a brother, Mr. W. G. Sutlive, city editor of the press.- Savannah Morning News.

Sat. Jan. 30, 1897
Mrs. Nancy Thomas, age 65 last Dec., died at her home here. She moved here from Henry County thirteen years ago. She leaves four children and several grand children.

Sat. Apr. 3, 1897
Mr. James Henderson, age 84, died at the home of his son near Mt. Andrew Tuesday. Survivors are several children.

Sat. May 15, 1897
Alsey, the nine year old son of Mr. John Clarke, of Beat Six (Barbour Co.), was taken suddenly sick Sunday with something like choleramorbus, and died on Monday.

Sat. Aug. 7, 1897
Huntsville, Aug. 2.- The remains of J. V. (Victor) Petty were buried yesterday in the City Cemetery by the Knights of Pythias. He is survived by his wife and one little girl. He was the only surviving brother of Mr. Will Petty, of Barbour County.

Mr. Donald Sessions died at Ashville, N. C. last Friday and was interred at Union Springs (Ala.), his old home. He was a son of Dr. Louis Sessions and a son-in-law of Maj. Culver.

Sat. Aug. 14, 1897
Little Rena, infant dau. of Mr. T. H. Ventress, died here on Monday. Her mother preceded her to the grave but a few months.

Sat. Aug. 21, 1897
Senator J. M. George died at his home in Miss. on Saturday. He had resided in that place since his eighth year. He was born in Monroe Co., Ga., on 26th Oct. 1826.

Sat. Sept. 11, 1897
Mrs. Amanda Holmes, mother of Messrs. H. S. and John Holmes, died at Mr. H. S. Holmes' house near Clayton on Wednesday last. Burial at Nebo.

Fri. Feb. 23, 1898
Mr. Ellison Baker, age about 80, died at his home near Louisville on Feb. 15th. He leaves a large family of children.

Fri. May 6, 1898
Mr. W. J. White, formerly of Clayton, Tax Collector of this county, died at his home in Eufaula on Tuesday. Survivors are his wife and three grown children, a mother, a brother and several sisters.

Fri. July 1, 1898
Mr. Daniel Norton died at his home four miles southwest of

The Clayton Record
1898

Clayton on Monday. He leaves a large family. Burial at the Floyd Cemetery.

Fri. Aug. 12, 1898
Mrs. W. J. Hendley died at her home near Abbeville (Ala.), on the 9th and was buried at Mt. Zion. Her husband is the brother of our townsman, Mr. R. M. Hendley.

Fri. Aug. 19, 1898
Mrs. Mary Foy died at the home of her dau., Mrs. J. L. Pitts, on Monday last. Survivors are several sons and one daughter.

Mrs. John Miller died at her home in Mt. Andrew on last Thursday. Survivors are her husband and several children.

Mr. G. T. Long (Dick) died suddenly in Birmingham Sunday.

Fri. Sept. 2, 1898
W. J. Rhodes, mayor of Talladega, (Ala.), died Saturday.

Mr. Norman Norton, living near Louisville, (Ala.) died on Wednesday.

Fri. Sept. 9, 1898
Mr. Cullus Fenn died at his home near Louisville, (Ala.) on Sunday. Burial at old Mt. Zion. Survivors are his wife and twelve children.

Mr. Charles Tarver died at his home near here on Wednesday and was buried in the Masonic Cemetery. Survivors are his wife, three sons and five daughters.

Fri. Sept. 16, 1898
Hon. Willis G. Clark, of Mobile, died at a Virginia resort on Saturday. He was identified with the State University.

Mrs. Brown, nee Miss Belle Hortman, died at her home in Texas last Sunday. She was the daughter of Mr. John G. Hortman.

Fri. Sept. 23, 1898
Capt. N. H. Wood, former chief of police at Bessemer, (Ala.) died in that place Friday.

Mrs. R. B. Arnold, wife of Rev. Arnold, died at her home near Clopton (Ala.), on Friday. She was buried at Pen Isle Church. She was the mother of Mr. W. A. Arnold and the mother-in-law of our townsman, Mr. M. M. Strickland.

Fri. Oct. 28, 1898
Mr. R. H. Baker, age 70, merchant of Selma (Ala.), died last week.

Duncan S. McLaughlin, age 80, died last week at Powderly, Ala. He was born in Jefferson County, Ala.

Eufaula Times & News
1898

Thurs. Jan. 6, 1898
Mr. C. G. McLeroy, an old citizen of Howe (Barbour Co.), died recently.

Eufaula Times & News
1898

Mrs. Elizabeth Wilson, age about 80, mother of Mr. J. M. Thweatt, died yesterday from burns she received when her clothing caught fire at the home of her son in Eufaula.

Thurs. Jan. 13, 1898
Mrs. A. S. Green died at Ft. Gaines on Thursday while visiting her children, Mrs. Sharp and W. J. Green. Other survivors are Mrs. Brown, of Bluffton and Mrs. Sutlive, of Savannah. She was also the mother of Mrs. Farquhar McKay.

Thurs. Jan. 27, 1898
Capt. W. F. Robinson, age 55, died yesterday. He leaves three sons, Roby, of Atlanta; Hugh, of Americus; and Fred Robinson, of Eufaula. He leaves a brother, Mr. Charles C. Robinson of Eufaula, and several sisters, Mrs. Goodwin, of Savannah, Mrs. Peacock and Miss Cornelia Robinson, of Eufaula, and Mrs. J. B. Alford, of Columbia.

Thurs. Feb. 3, 1898
Col. A. A. Thompson, age about 60, died at his home at Columbia last Saturday. Survivors are his wife and two sons, A. B., and Coy, and two daus., Miss Annie and Mrs. John McTyer, of Eufaula. Mr. I. K. Thompson, a brother, lives in Columbia.

Mr. Seaborn Ogletree, age about 50, of Georgetown (Ga.), died yesterday at the home of his brother, Mr. Sam Ogletree. He was not married.

Thurs. Mar. 3, 1898
Ada Ross, the 4½ year old child of Mr. J. L. Ross, died yesterday.

Mrs. H. M. Kaigler died at her home at Georgetown (Ga.), yesterday. She was a sister of Mrs. A. Ogletree of this city and of Mrs. R. G. Reynolds, of Henry County, (Ala.).

Mrs. C. C. Brunson, age 72, died at her home in Eufaula last night. She was the wife of Maj. W. A. Brunson. She leaves five children, Mrs. C. A. Martin, Miss Mary Brunson and Mr. Harry Brunson, of Eufaula, and Messrs. M. A. and L. E. Brunson, of Fla.

Mr. Clarence Dickinson, a young man who had just finished his education in medicine, died Friday.-Ozark (Ala.) Star.

Thurs. Mar. 10, 1898
Spartanburg, S. C., Mar. 2.-The death of T. J. Timmier occurred here recently. He leaves a family.

Pickensville, Ala., Mar. 7,-J. D. Burgy, a prominent citizen, was shot from ambush and killed.

Mr. Thomas Mooney, age over 70, father of Mr. John A. Mooney, of Eufaula, died at his home at Nashville. Survivors are his wife and children. He was a native of County Mayo, Ireland and came to this country quite young.

Mrs. Catherine Comer, age about 75, died at her home in Savannah yesterday. She leaves six sons, Messrs. H. M. and J. W. Comer, of Savannah, B. B. Comer, of Birmingham, G. L. Comer of

Eufaula Times & News
1898

Eufaula, J. F. Comer of James (Ala.), and Ed Comer of Texas. Burial at Spring Hill in Barbour County.

Mrs. J. T. Morris died at her home in Eufaula this morning. She had been living here only a few months, having moved here from Montgomery where her husband accepted a position on the train between Eufaula and Montgomery.

Mrs. Sarah Carroll, living near Ozark (Ala.), died last Friday. -Ozark Star.

Thurs. Mar. 24, 1898
Postmaster E. L. Brown left Eufaula for Sumter, S. C., due to the death of his father, age 90. He left four living children.

Mrs. S. J. Holmes, age 59, of Ozark, died Saturday. She leaves two children, Mr. James Holmes of Eufaula and Mrs. Munn of Ozark.

Silas Shirah, Esqr., age 78, died at his home in Beat 12 on last Saturday.-Barbour Journal.

Thurs. Mar. 31, 1898
Dr. Augustus W. (William) Barnett, age 74, died at his home in Eufaula on Monday. He was born in Washington, Ga., Aug. 24th, 1825, and married Dec. 18, 1849 to Miss Celeste Treutlen, who died and his second marriage was to Miss Adele Connor, of Cokesburg, S. C., Mar. 30, 1875. He lived at Glennville (now in Russell Co., Ala.) many years and moved to Eufaula in 1865. His wife survives him and nine children, Mr. Sam T. Barnett, Mr. Paul and Mr. Reese Barnett, of Atlanta; Rev. Frank Barnett of Forsyth and Mr. John T. Barnett of Eufaula, Mrs. E. T. Tullis of Montgomery, Miss Carrie Barnett, Miss Annie Dell Barnett and little Una Barnett.

Mr. W. H. Edmonds, of Baltimore, died in that city this morning. His widow, nee Anna Sylvester, was reared in Eufaula. Survivors are his wife and three children. (Note: From Sylvester Family History - the children were Richard, Asbury and Helena).

Mr. E. B. Wilson, formerly of Union Springs, died recently in Atlanta. He was well known in Eufaula.

Thurs. Apr. 7, 1898
Mrs. Margaret O'Brien Davis, of Birmingham, died recently. Only a year or less ago she married Dr. Davis.

Mrs. Celia Scott, age 95, died at the home of her son, Mr. Manning Scott in Henry County, Ala. She bore twelve sons, four of whom survive her.

Dr. John E. Price, of Headland, Ala., died suddenly of heart trouble on Saturday.-Dothan (Ala.) Siftings.

Thurs. Apr. 28, 1898
John T. McAllister, brother to W. A., J. T., and R. C. McAllister of Ft Gaines, (Ga.) was shot and killed at a lumber town of Polloek, La., recently.-Columbia (Ala.) Breeze.

Mrs. Jane Davie, age about 70, died at Spring Hill (Barbour County) Sunday. She was the mother of Dr. Mercer Davie, Judson

Eufaula Times & News
1898

Davie, Meigs Davie, Bunyan Davie and Misses Stella and Luna Davie. Burial at Midway.

The remains of Mrs. Marietta Shorter reached Eufaula yesterday and burial in Eufaula from the Baptist Church.

Thurs. May 19, 1898

Judge Elijah Teague, age 78, of Shorterville, Henry Co., (Ala.), died recently. He was Tax Commissioner of the county.

Rev. Mark S. Andrews, D. D., age 72, of Mobile died Sunday. He was born Feb. 23, 1826, at Oglethorpe, Ga. When he was eight years old his parents removed to Chambers Co., Ala. He entered the ministry after reading law. His first church appointment was Eufaula in 1852. He married in 1854 to Miss Sarah Glenn, of Auburn, Ala. She, with six children survives. The children are Mark S. Andrews, Jr., San Antonio, Texas; Dr. Glenn Andrews, Montgomery; William T. Andrews, Henietta, Texas; Mrs. Alfred G. Ward, Mobile, Miss Sallie Andrews, Mobile. Burial in Montgomery.

Mr. Paul B. Scaife, age 21, formerly of Eufaula, and Miss Annie McDonnell Moore were drowned while boating. Burial for Mr. Scaife in Eufaula.

Mrs. Jason Jones died at her home near Columbia yesterday. She was the daughter of the late Dr. H. M. Kaigler, who was buried yesterday.

Mr. Marion Craddock suicided at his home near Lawrenceville, (Henry Co., Ala.) by shooting himself this morning. He leaves a wife and about six children.

Mr. Daniel McLain, an aged citizen, died at his home at Clio on Saturday. Burial at Pea River Church.

Thurs. May. 26, 1898

Mr. F. B. Lignoski died suddenly last night. He was a representative for the Jesse French Piano Co. Burial in Troy.- Troy (Ala.) Messenger.

Mrs. G. H. Wilde, age 25, died Tuesday at her home in Eufaula. She was Miss Callie Stevens and had been married about two years. She leaves a husband and an infant a few days old.

Thurs. June 9, 1898

Mrs. Sam H. Solomon died at Shellman, Georgia on Friday.

Mrs. D. M. Seals, relict of Col. Morgan Seals, died at Headland, (Ala.) last Wednesday while on a visit to her dau. Burial at Headland. For many years she lived here in Eufaula where she raised a large family.

Mrs. Eliza Jones Price, age 70, died today in Dalton, Ga. She was a sister of Dr. Thomas S. Mitchell, of Eufaula. Burial at West Point. She was born and reared in Lafayette, Ala. Her survivors are two children, one in Texas and one in Dalton, Ga., also two brothers and one sister, Rev. R. P. Mitchell, of Miss., and Mrs. Mary A. McArthur, of Paris, Texas.

Thurs. June 16, 1898

Eufaula Times & News
1898

Mrs. Maggie (Margaret) Ludwig, age 75, died at her home in Eufaula today. She will be buried from the Catholic Church. She came here several years ago. She was the mother of Mrs. Phil Schmaeling, of Eufaula. She leaves three children, perhaps others, and a husband.

Mrs. Anthony Stow, of Atlanta, died yesterday - at a good old age. She lived in Eufaula many years ago. Survivors are two children, Mr. Ed Stow, of Albany, Ga., and Miss Kate Stow who lived with her mother. Burial in Eufaula.

Miss Bettie Goldsmith died in Atlanta yesterday. She was a sister of Mrs. A. D. Johnson, of Eufaula. Burial in Greenville.

Thurs. June 23, 1898
Mr. James Milton, a citizen of Eufaula since 1857, died Sunday. He was born in Bristol, England in 1830, removed to London and lived there until he was 21, when he came to America. He married here Nov. 1861 to Miss Louise Dunn, who died Apr. 1877. Survivors are Messrs. Victor M., James, John and Walter Milton and Misses Lula and May Milton.

Thurs. June 30, 1898
Dr. Claude Brannon, age 32, of St. Petersburg, Fla., died this morning. He was the son of the late Capt. W. B. Brannon, of Eufaula, who died in 1873. Burial in Eufaula.

Miss Gerta Watson, age 13, daughter of Mr. and Mrs. E. C. Watson of Gaino (Barbour Co.), died today of rheumatic fever.

Mr. Marcellus E. Milligan, of Geneva (Ala.), died at his mother's home in Ozark Saturday. He was a young lawyer. Survivors are his wife and several small children.

Thurs. July 14, 1898
Mr. F. C. Bush, of Iowa City, Ia., died at Bridgeport, Ala. on Wednesday enroute to Eufaula. Mrs. Bush was with him.

Miss Mary Powell died at the home of her father, Mr. John Powell, in Eufaula on Tuesday.

Thurs. Aug. 4, 1898
Mr. Simon Lewy died Sunday. He leaves a widow and three boys and three girls.

The remains of Mr. Robert Alston arrived yesterday bound for Spring Hill (Barbour Co.). They were accompanied from Miami by Orderly Sergeant W. T. Sheehan, who will stay here the utmost limit of his eight days furlough.

Thurs. Sept. 1, 1898
Mrs. R. M. Tillman, of Elamville in Barbour County, died on Aug. 14th, 1898. Survivors are her husband and eight children.

Prof. Charles R. McCall, of Troy (Ala.), died Wednesday. He was an ardent supporter of the State Normal College at Troy and a professor of ancient language.

Judge Daniel Carmichael, one of the oldest citizens of Dale

Eufaula Times & News
1898

Co., Ala., died Tuesday at Chipley, Fla., at the home of his brother. He died from hydrophabia.

Mrs. Mary L. Borders died at the home of her dau., Mrs. Mary Foster, on the 24th of Aug. She was married to Rev. A. H. Borders in 1833 and lived with him fifty-four years until the time of his death. Survivors are one son and one dau., several grand-children and great-great-grand- children.-Clayton Record.

Thurs. Sept. 8, 1898
Birmingham, Ala., Sept. 5.-Frank J. Queen, age 91 died here of paralysis at the home of his dau., Mrs. N. F. Thompson. He was Kentucky's pioneer citizens and until ten years ago he was a merchant of Bardstown, Ky. When his wife died he came to Birmingham to live with his dau. Mr. Queen married a dau. of Daniel Boone. Burial in Bardstown.

Knoxville, Sept. 5.-Col. J. C. Flanders, who has for 35 years been a leading hotel man in the city died recently. He was a native of Montpelier, Vt.

Thurs. Sept. 22, 1898
Mrs. Drucilla McRae, age 65, died this morning at the home of her nephew, Mr. C. D. Bush, at Rocky Mount. She leaves one son, Mr. Colon McRae of Star Hill, (Barbour Co.). Burial at New Hope.

Rev. D. W. Barnes, age about 40, of the Methodist Conference, died at his home at Barnes Cross Roads (Dale Co., Ala.) last night.

Thurs. Sept. 29, 1898
Sheffield, (Ala.) Sept. 26.- Mr. R. A. Solomon, age about 60, of Sheffield, took his life by taking morphine. He was formerly of Eufaula. He leaves a wife and several grown daus. and a son.

Capt. John L. McRae, of Louisville, died there Tuesday night.

Mrs. J. C. Borders died at her home in Louisville on Sunday last. She was the wife of Dr. Borders, who survives her and six small children.

Mrs. Jesse B. Searcy took her life by drowning in the river. She married Mr. Searcy about three years ago. Mrs. Searcy was Mrs. Perkins and a sister to Mr. Searcy's first wife. She had one son, Henry Perkins, about fifteen years of age and Mr. Searcy had a dau. about the same age. Burial in Fairview in Eufaula.

Thurs. Oct. 6, 1898
Montgomery Advertiser of 27.-Rev. W. F. Loveless, of Goldsboro, N. C., died last Sunday. He was a son of Rev. E. L. Loveless of the M. E. Conference. He was not married. Survivors are his parents.

Thurs. Oct. 13, 1898
Mrs. J. F. Hawkins, age 24, of Batesville, wife of the section boss on the R. R., died last night of typhoid fever.

Thurs. Oct. 20, 1898
The death of Mrs. Page Beard Nevins is announced by the Birmingham papers. She was the dau. of Rev. Dr. Thos. J. Beard and was born in this city in 1865 when her father was rector of St. James Church in Eufaula. She married William R. Nevins. She leaves three infants.

Eufaula Times & News
1898

The remains of Mr. P. H. Morris, of Atlanta, formerly of Eufaula, reached here for burial yesterday. They were accompanied by Mrs. Morris, Mr. Seymour and little Pat Morris.

Thurs. Oct. 27, 1898
Atlanta, Oct. 21.-Judge Marshall J. Clarke died yesterday from a stroke of paralysis. He was born at Lumpkin, Stewart Co., Ga., June 27, 1839. In 1855 he entered Mercer University and after graduating he was admitted to the bar. In 1885 he was appointed Judge of the City Court of Atlanta.

Mr. W. L. Bass, age about 50, died at his home at Sedalia, Mo., last Saturday. He lived in Eufaula about 20 years ago. He married Miss Lizzie Doughtie, sister to our townsman, Mr. T. C. Doughtie. He leaves a widow and two children. Burial in Eufaula with Masonic honors.

Mrs. M. L. Albritton died at her home in Ashford, Ala., last Wednesday of fever. Survivors are her husband, Judge Albritton. Burial at Cuthbert, Georgia.

Thurs. Nov. 3, 1898
Mr. James Baker, age about 55, died at his home in Eufaula on Tuesday. Survivors are his wife and one child.

Mrs. Nathan Whitaker, age about 50, of Quitman Co., (Ga.) died at her home Friday. Survivors are her husband and two children.

Thurs. Nov. 10, 1898
Mrs. Douglass, age about 78, mother of Mrs. R. A. Ballowe, of Eufaula, died in Smithville (Ga.) yesterday. She was a resident and had charge of a school at Glennville (Ala.) before the war. Burial at Thomasville.

Mrs. Ann E. Bryan, age 65, died at her home in Quitman Co., Ga., yesterday. Survivors are her husband and five children.

Mrs. John Proctor died in Albany (Ga.) on last Sunday and was interred at Dawson, (Ga.). She was Miss Annie Lewis and grew up in Eufaula and lived here several years after her marriage.

Mrs. J. D. Parker died at her home in Longstreet, La., last week. She was Miss Jessie Veal, of Louisville prior to her marriage about eighteen months ago. Burial at Louisville, Ala.

Thurs. Nov. 24, 1898
Rev. Geo. R. Pournelle, of the South Georgia Conference, died at Dover, of consumption. He was born and reared in Eufaula.-Dawson (Ga.) News.

Mr. J. H. Pruden, age about 81, died at his home in Midway, Bullock Co., this morning. He was the father of Mr. Theo. Pruden, of Eufaula. Survivors are his wife and two children and numerous grand-children. Burial in Eufaula.

Mrs. Thomas H. Carr, of Montgomery, died Friday. Mrs. Carr, nee Miss Ann Colby was reared in Eufaula.

Thurs. Dec. 1, 1898

<u>Eufaula Times & News</u>
1898-1899

Maj. Henry Russell Shorter died at his home in Eufaula on Sunday. He was born in Monticello, Jasper Co., Ga., Feb. 28th, 1833. He was the son of Dr. and Mrs. Reuben C. Shorter. He came to Eufaula with his parents in 1836. He married in 1854 to Miss Anna C. Keitt. Survivors are his wife, two daus., Mrs. W. D. Jelks and Mrs. C. C. Hanson, and a son, Henry R. Shorter, Jr.

Mr. Emmett Vigal died at the home of his mother near Lakeview (B'ham.) on Tuesday. He lived in Eufaula for a number of years. He was a younger brother of Mr. Will H. Vigal, of Eufaula. Burial in Birmingham.

Thurs. Dec. 8, 1898
Dr. Allen S. Andrews, pastor of the Methodist Church at Union Springs, (Ala.) died yesterday from apoplexy.

Mrs. Martha M. Brown, (Mrs. James H.), age about 53, died at her home in Columbus Sunday. She was born in Randolph County, but has been a resident of Columbus for 25 years. Survivors are her husband, two children, three sisters and four brothers. Her children are Mr. Watt Brown, Columbus; and Mrs. L. M. Burrus, of Augustus. Her brothers are Messrs. W. A. Doughtie, of Montgomery: Punch Doughtie, of this city; James N. Doughtie, of Tex., and T. C. Doughtie, of Eufaula; and Eugene Doughtie, of Americus. Her sisters are Mrs. W. L. Bass, of Sedalia, Mo.; Mrs. F. J. Dehonie, of Kansas City, Mo.; and Mrs. J. W. Chastine, of Montgomery, Ala.

Rev. P. M. Callaway, age 87, died at his home yesterday in Newton, Dale Co., Ala. He was a Baptist minister, but the earlier years of his life were given to law. Survivors are his wife and six children.

Thurs. Dec. 15, 1898
Mr. Thomas H. Beauchamp, age about 63, died at his home in Montgomery on Friday with a paralytic stroke. He was formerly of Eufaula. Survivors are his wife and five children, Miss Susie and Mr. Tom Beauchamp, of Montgomery; Mrs. Drake, of Atlanta; Mrs. Mabry, of Dothan; and Mrs. Wood, of Pronto. Burial at Troy.

Thurs. Dec. 22, 1897
Col. Hilliard J. Irby, age 83, died at his home in Eufaula last Thursday of pneumonia. He was born in Meckenberg County, N. C. on Mar. 31, 1816. In 1844 he married Miss M. F. Williams and in 1852 he moved to Ala. His wife died in the early 80's, and on Feb. 3rd, 1884 he married Miss Virginia P. Crawford, of this city. Survivors are his wife, two sons, Messrs. L. E. and C. C. Irby and three daughters.

Thurs. Jan. 5, 1899
Carrie, little dau. of Dr. & Mrs. C. L. Boyd, died at the home of her parents in Dallas, Texas this morning.

Richmond, Jan. 6.- Dr. Moses D. Hoge, the well known eminent Presbyterian divine, died recently.

Mr. Burt Cooper died at his home in Quitman Co., Ga., last

Eufaula Times & News
1899

Tuesday. He was one of the oldest citizens in the county.

Mr. C. C. (Charles Calhoun) Frazer, age about 40, of Union Springs, nephew of Judge Frazer, Col. N. H. Frazer and Mr. F. J. Frazer, died last night. He leaves a wife and six children.

Mrs. Argent Harrington, age 83, who lived near Georgetown, (Ga.) died Sunday. Burial at Bland Cemetery.

Mr. William R. Adams, a young of Ozark, (Ala.) died of consumption on Monday at the home of his mother. He was a brother of Mr. Joe Adams of the Ozark Star.

Maj. Willis B. Butts, age about 60, died at his home in Eufaula on Wednesday. He was born in Columbus, Ga. He lived in that city until the war. He leaves a wife and several brothers and sisters.

Thurs. Jan. 19, 1899
Miss Sue, 12 year old dau. of Hon. John B. Knox, of Troy, (Ala.) died Saturday.

Mrs. John Bass Shelton was buried at Oakwood Cemetery on yesterday. She died at the home of her sister, Mrs. B. W. Walker, in Montgomery. She was a dau. of the late Mrs. T. J. Alsop. Her husband, Rev. J. B. Shelton and Mrs. Shelton lived at Louisville, Ky., for Rev. Shelton to attend the Baptist Seminary. Survivors are her husband, one child, and two sisters, Mrs. B. W. Walker and Mrs. G. W. Townsend.-Montgomery Journal.

Thurs. Jan. 26, 1899
Mr. Henry Roberts, of Ozark, died Sunday, and was buried at Clopton. He was a long time a citizen of Henry County.

Thurs. Feb. 2, 1899
Capt. T. J. Brannon, of Montgomery, formerly of Eufaula, died at Montgomery recently. He was a brother of the late Capt. W. J. Brannon, and brother-in-law of Dr. W. P. Copeland, of Eufaula. Burial at Americus, Ga.

Mr. Lee Johnson, age about 29, died at Wickburg, Ariz. Tuesday. He had gone there for his health. Burial in Eufaula.

Mr. Eb Priest died suddenly Tuesday at his home in Eufaula. He was born at Thomasville, Mar. 10th, 1839, but moved to Eufaula when a small boy. Survivors are his wife and six children.

Thurs. Feb. 16, 1899
Leavenworth, Kan., Feb. 7.-Col. Thos. Moonlight, age 67, died here today. He was a colonel of an artillery regiment during the Civil War.

Kansas City, Feb. 7.-Col. H. I. Bledsoe of the Missouri Battery C.S.A. died recently. He was one of the last prominent Confederates in this section.

Dr. Groves Caldwell, of Bullock Co., (Ala.) died at his home in Midway Wednesday. Survivors are several grown children. Burial in Midway.

Eufaula Times & News
1899

Meta, the ten year old dau. of Mr. and Mrs. J. E. Sapp died last night.

Mr. Dozier Cade, of Batesville, died recently from pneumonia. Survivors are several grown children.

Mr. Lorenzo Jordan, age about 30, of Georgetown, Ga., died at the home of his mother Friday. Survivors are his wife and child.

Mrs. Donie Wilkinson, wife of Bunyan Wilkinson, died at Louisville on Sunday.

Mrs. John Teu (Tew?), of Louisville, who was the dau. of Nathan Walker, died recently. Survivors are her husband and several children.

Mountainboro, Ala., Feb. 11.- Mrs. Henry Ware, living near here, died from burns she received when her clothing caught fire. Survivors are her husband and son.

Thurs. Feb. 23, 1899

Mr. John Fussell, living near Ozark, died Sunday. He was very old and had lived in Dale County for many years.

Maj. Daniel D. McLeod, lawyer of Anniston, died Monday of appendicitis. He was reared at White Oak in Barbour County.

Mr. Garlington Lucas, age 88, died at his home at Bush, (Barbour Co.) yesterday. Burial at Bush Chapel. He was one of the earliest settlers of Barbour Co., coming here in the days of the Indians. He leaves seven grown children.

Mr. Columbus Benton, formerly of Eufaula, died in Birmingham Tuesday. He had been living there a short time.

Thurs. Mar. 9, 1899

Mrs. Benjamin B. Davis, age 65, died at the home of her dau. Mrs. Mary Fitzgerald in Atlanta. Burial in Eufaula. Survivors are Mr. George B. Davis of Eufaula, Mr. W. A. Davis, of Anniston, and Mrs. Fitzgerald, of Atlanta.

Mr. L. D. McLean died Friday at his home in Eufaula. He was born and reared here. His death came just beyond the meridian of his life. Survivors are his wife and child. Burial at Fairview.

Mrs. B. F. Allday, formerly of Eufaula, died at her home in Montgomery yesterday.

Thurs. Mar. 23, 1899

Mr. Henry Dawson, formerly of Glennville (Russell Co., Ala.), died recently in Denton, Texas.

Prof. Harrison Hart, age about 60, and dancing master by profession, died at Chattanooga last night. His family were at Cartersville (Ga.) when last heard from. Prof. Hart was reared in Eufaula, and was a member of that one time large family, the oldest of which was the late H. C. Hart, of Eufaula. He leaves one brother, Mr. C. B. Hart, and one sister, Mrs. L. W. McLaughlin, both of Eufaula. Burial in Chattanooga.

Eufaula Times & News
1899

Thurs. Mar. 30, 1899

Mrs. George Vaughan died at her home in Eufaula Monday. Survivors are her husband and several children. Burial in Eufaula.

Mrs. William Petry died Monday at her home in Eufaula after a long illness. Survivors are her husband, two daus. and four sons. Burial in Eufaula.

Dr. F. H. Bloodworth, formerly of Eufaula, died Monday in Savannah. In 1897 he married Miss Clara Ross, of Eufaula.

Mr. John M. Alston died Tuesday at his home near Cowikee (Barbour Co.). He was a brother of W. A. Alston, of Hawkinsville and a relative of Judge A. H. Alston of Clayton. Survivors are a large family of children. Burial at Cowikee.

Miss Jane Parker died Friday at the home of her brother, D. H. Parker, below town. She was an aunt of Messrs. H. H. and E. A. Parker. She moved here several years ago with her brother's family from Texas.

Thurs. Apr. 6, 1899

Mr. Fred Norman, age 36, died at a hospital in Atlanta on Sunday. He was born in Union Springs, Ala. He had been living in Columbus for the last five years. Burial in Columbus.

Mr. Ap Shirley, living in Henry Co., died at his home near Spivey on Friday. Survivors are his wife and several children. Burial at Mt. Zion Church.

Thurs. Apr. 13, 1899

Mr. Joe C. Clark, son of Mr. Whit (Whitfield) Clark, died at Anniston recently and was buried in Clayton yesterday.

Mr. D. C. Parkerson, an old citizen of Cuthbert, (Ga.) died yesterday. For over twenty-five years he was agent of the Southern Express Company.

Mr. George Campbell, age about 21, son of Mr. W. D. Campbell, of Otho (Henry Co.), died last Sunday.

Thurs. Apr. 20, 1899

Mrs. W. W. Lockhart, widow of the late Mr. Lockhart who died at Headland a few years ago, died at the home of her father, Mr. W. J. Davis, near Headland on Tuesday. Burial at Headland.

Ross McCormick, age about 26, was drowned in Cowikee Creek (Barbour Co.) last Thurs.

Thurs. Apr. 27, 1899

Mr. Andrew West died at his home near White Pond (Barbour Co.) on Saturday. Burial at Pond Bethel. Survivors are his wife and five small children. He leaves three brothers, Messrs. William West, Amos West and Rev. Anson West of the North Ala. Conference of the M. E. Church.

Thurs. May 4, 1899

Mr. John R. Engram died at his home near Enterprise in Coffee Co., (Ala.) last Wednesday of pneumonia.

Eufaula Times & News
1899

Mr. Jesse B. Bowden, an elderly citizen of Clayton, died Tuesday. Burial with Masonic honors in the grave yard at Union. Survivors are several sons and daus.- Clayton Record.

Mrs. Jinnie (Jennie?) Southland died at her home in Ashford (Houston Co., Ala.) last Sunday. She was the youngest dau. of Mr. W. H. Bodiford. Burial at Union Church. Survivors are her husband and three children.-Abbeville Times.

Mrs. Charles W. Sheally was buried at Fairview Cemetery (in Eufaula) yesterday. She died in Montgomery last Saturday. She was Miss Bessie Merriwether, of Fitzpatrick, Bullock Co. Several years ago she married Mr. Chas.W. Sheally, son of Mr. John W. Sheally. Survivors are her three small boys and two girls.

Col. Robert Hardaway died of apoplexy in Columbus at the home of his sister, Mrs. C. E. Johnston. Survivors are two sons, Messrs. Early H. and B. H. Hardaway and three sisters, Mrs. A. H. Flewellen, of Eufaula; Mrs. C. E. Johnston, of Columbus; and Mrs. John W. Wright, of Marian, Ark.

Miss Eliza McDonald, age about 75, died at the home of her niece, Mrs. Durham, on last Wednesday.

Thurs. May 11, 1899

Mr. E. R. King, age 73, died at his home near Georgetown, Ga., yesterday. He leaves a large family.

Thurs. May 25, 1899

Mrs. B. F. Faust died near Ozark on Saturday. Survivors are her husband and a babe only a week old.-Ozark Star.

Mr. Marcus L. Solomon, of Lumpkin (Ga.), died Saturday. He was a brother of Mrs. T. W. Zuber, of Eufaula.-Cuthbert Liberal.

Mr. O. S. Wells, age 64, died Tuesday at his home in Eufaula. Survivors are his wife and five children. Burial in Eufaula.

Mr. Heywood Graddy, age 75, died at his home in Georgetown (Ga.), last night. Survivors are five grown children.

Thurs. June 1, 1899

Mrs. John H. Clisby, of Montgomery, was killed last Tuesday when her horse ran away with her carriage.

Mr. Chas. W. Bray, age 36, died last night at his home. Survivors are his mother, Mrs. John E. Bray, and two brothers, Messrs. John W. Bray, of Eufaula, and Frank Bray, now living in Florida.

Thurs. June 8, 1899

Mrs. Pess (Julian W.) Sanders, nee Miss Laila Engram, died Sunday at her home near Eufaula. Burial at Hawkinsville in Barbour Co. She was a sister of Miss Carltie and Harry Engram, survivors are her husband and three children.

Dr. S. K. Jackson, age 83, died at "Roseland" near Eufaula this morning. He was the father of Bishop H. M. Jackson. He was a native of Virginia.

Eufaula Times & News
1899

Mr. H. J. Williamson, age 63, died at his home in Spring Hill, Barbour Co., on Wednesday. Survivors are his wife and four children.

Mrs. Mary Bledsoe, relict of Rev. John Bledsoe, died at the home of her son-in-law, Mr. W. M. Dozier, in Quitman Co., Ga., on yesterday. Burial at Antioch Church, near LaFayette, Ala.

Thurs. June 15, 1899
Miss Nellie Stephens, age 15, daughter of Mr. R. H. Stephens, of Pratts, below Clayton, died at Arlington (Ga.), where she was attending school. Burial at Pratts.

Mrs. A. H. Flewellen, age 96, died last night at her home in Eufaula. She was a sister of the late Col. Robert Hardaway. She was born in Elbert Co., Ga., Oct. 23, 1839. She married Capt. Flewellen in Columbus, Ga., Oct. 9th, 1850, when she was Miss Sallie Hardaway. Survivors are her husband and four children, Messrs. W. W., James T., of Bullock Co., G. H. Flewellen of Birmingham, and Mrs. E. Q. Smith, of Seattle, Wash. Surviving sisters are Mrs. C. G. Johnson, Columbus, and Mrs. J. W. Wright, of Bullock County.

Mrs. Rebecca Peak, age 76, died at Glennville Monday. She made her home with her son, Mr. R. D. Peak, at Glennville. She was the mother of Mr. O. T. Peak, of Hawkinsville (Barbour Co.), and Mr. J. B. Peak, of Bullock Co., Ala.

Mrs. Nicie McDaniel died at her home beyond Georgetown (Ga.), yesterday. Survivors are her husband and two small children.

Thurs. June 29, 1899
Judge Webb Foster, of Abbeville, died in a Montgomery hospital from appendicitis. Burial at Abbeville (Ala.). He was a brother of A. B. Foster, of Troy. His father was Chancellor John A. Foster. He came to Clayton from Miss. when he was a boy. Survivors are his wife and three children.

Thurs. July 6, 1899
Mr. T. J. Reeves died at his home near town on Friday. Survivors are two sons and two daughters. Burial at White Oak (Barbour County).

Thurs. July 27, 1899
Mr. James Grisman died in Eufaula yesterday. He was born many years ago in England, but early in life went to Canada where he lived until three years ago. He was a brother-in-law of Mr. James Tansey, and when his wife died her remains were brought to Eufaula and buried at Fairview. The dec'd will be buried by the Knights of Pythias.

Mr. Jehu Phillips died at his home near Springvale Sunday. Burial at Oak Grove. He had passed the three score years. Survivors are seven children. One of these, Mr. Munval Phillips lives at Morris Station. The dec'd had lived in Georgia fifty years.

Thurs. Aug. 3, 1899
Birmingham, Ala., July 31.-Col. Horace Harding, age 72, died

Eufaula Times & News
1899

in Grand Rapids, Mich. He was a citizen of Birmingham and a civil engineer.

Gainesville, Ga.- Mrs. Julius C. Cato, wife of Dr. Cato, of Eufaula, died last Saturday while visiting her family at Gainesville. She was the daughter of Mrs. J. T. Kendall. Burial in Gainesville. Survivors are her husband and children.

Rev. James Z. Henley, of Abbeville, conducted the funeral services of Capt. D. H. Zorn at Pond Bethel on Sunday.

Rev. J. W. Glenn died yesterday at his home in Midway. He was the brother-in-law Messrs. John M. and R. Q. Edmonson, of Eufaula. His son, Rev. J. M. Glenn, has been filling his father's pulpit recently. Burial at Midway.

Thurs. Aug. 24, 1899

Mrs. W. W. Hawkins died yesterday at her home at Hawkinsville, (Barbour Co.). She was a bride of a year. She was Miss Alsaza Shanks, of Glass, near Opelika, Ala. Burial at Fairview, Eufaula.

John Courtenay, the five months old son of Mr. and Mrs. J. E. O'Brien, died last night.

Mr. George M. Jordan died at his home in Eufaula on Friday. He had lived here many years. Survivors are his wife and three children, an aged father and a brother, Mr. H. L. Jordan. Burial at Fairview in Eufaula.

Thurs. Aug. 31, 1899

Mrs. J. A. Prince died Tuesday at her home in Ozark, (Ala.).

Thurs. Sept. 7, 1899

Dr. W. A. Florence, formerly of Barbour Co., died recently in Boonville, Ark. He was related to Mr. H. B. Florence and Mr. Pete Florence of the upper part of Barbour County.

Thurs. Sept. 14, 1899

Mrs. S. F. Jenkins died at her home in Louisville Wednesday.

Two prominent citizens of Randolph Co., Ga., died last week, they were Capt. T. J. Phillips, of Benevolence, and Mr. Allen Dantzler, of Shellman.

Mrs. Nancy Glass, age 95, died yesterday at her home ten miles below town. She was the widow of the late L. D. Glass. Two of her five children survive her. Burial in the family burying ground.

Mr. Sigmund Landauer, formerly of Eufaula during the latter "seventies", now a business man of Atlanta, committed suicide by taking morphine and died in the canebrake near Atlanta.

Thurs. Sept. 21, 1899

Opelika, Ala., Sept. 16.-Prof. John M. Philips, age 84, for many years a noted educator, died yesterday of general debility.

Mr. M. N. Killebrew, one of the oldest citizens in Dale Co., (Ala.) died at his home in Newton last week.

Eufaula Times & News
1899

Wednesday the remains of Mrs. John Morris, of Newton, (Dale Co.) reached Louisville for burial. Mrs. Morris, nee Miss Deila Lampley, and her husband, Dr. Morris moved to Newton several years ago. Survivors are her husband and seven children, one a baby only eight days old.

Mr. R. T. Hudspeth, age over 90, died at his home in Headland in Henry Co., recently. He leaves a family of grown children.

Thurs. Oct. 5, 1899
The funeral of Mr. J. G. Rogers, who died suddenly Thursday at his home in Howe, took place yesterday.

Thurs. Oct. 12, 1899
The funeral of Mr. W. W. Flewellen took place yesterday. Burial in Fairview Cemetery in Eufaula.

Mr. T. C. Green died at the home of Mr. Warren Baker near Louisville. He leaves several children.

Mr. John D. Rollins, an aged citizen of Pike Co., (Ala.) died Saturday.

Thurs. Oct. 19, 1899
Mr. Richard Barnett, age 83, died at his home at Headland recently. He had been married four times and had 23 children.

Mr. James Brown, another citizen of Headland, died suddenly at his home last Saturday.

Curtis Carter, age 21, the youngest son of Mr. and Mrs. J. J. Carter, formerly of Eufaula, died at his father's home in Evergreen, (Ala.).

Mr. J. G. Moor, age 42, died at his home near Violet Station, Lakeview. Survivors are his wife and 2 children. He was a native of Jefferson Co., (Ala.). He married about 15 years ago to Miss Sallie Billings, of Columbus, Ga. He was a half brother to Mr. J. W. Anderson of the firm of Moor and Anderson. Mrs. Moor was born and reared in Eufaula.

Mrs. J. C. West, age 31, nee Lillie Mitchell, died at her home in Eufaula last Thursday. Burial in Columbus, Ga., in the family burying ground of her uncle, Dr. T. S. Mitchell. Her husband survives her.

Mr. W. J. Martin, aged four score and ten, a citizen of Afton neighborhood (Barbour Co.) died at his home Friday.

Thurs. Oct. 26, 1899
Mrs. Z. T. Middlebrooks of the Elamville community (Barbour Co.) died last Monday. Her husband survives her.

Mr. R. M. Pitts, of Pittsboro, died yesterday at his home in Russell County. He leaves several grown children.

Rev. T. H. Stout died last Saturday at Molena, Ga., which was his home. He lived in Eufaula many years. His wife sometime ago preceeded him to the grave.

Thurs. Nov. 2, 1899
Oateston, Oct. 30, 1899.- Mr. Thomas S. Locke, an elderly

Eufaula Times & News
1899

citizen died at his home near White Pond (Barbour Co.) last Thursday from cancer. Burial at Rocky Mount. Survivors are his wife and several children.

Mr. Walter Petty, of Clayton, died in Georgia where he had gone some months ago with Mr. Fred Pitts to contract building a R. R. near Savannah. Burial in Clayton. His sister, Mrs. Porter King, lives in Troy.

The remains of Col. Milton A. Smith were laid to rest yesterday at White Oak Church in Barbour County.

Mrs. J. M. Buford died at her home in Portland, Oregon on Oct. 23. She was the dau. of Dr. J. S. Cowan, of Eufaula, and sister of J. G. Cowan, of Abbeville, and niece of Senator James L. Pugh. Fifteen years ago, with Maj. Buford, she moved to Portland.

Thurs. Nov. 16, 1899
Rev. Levi Moore died at his home at Bowling Green, Ohio, on Saturday. He was the father of Mr. R. B. Moore, of Eufaula. The dec'd. was born in Fairfield County, Ohio in 1824, and married Dec. 1, 1844 to Margaret Line. Five children were born to them.

Lodi, Ala. (Barbour Co.) Nov. 6th, 1899.- On the 5th, Mrs. A. J. Woodham, Sr., age about 80, died at her home. Survivors are her aged husband, three sons, Messrs. Rabe (or Pabe?), Bill and Jim Woodham and her daus. are Mrs. Julia Fillengin and Mrs. Mollie Gray. Burial at Mt. Enon.

Mrs. John N. Franklin age 30, died Tuesday of typhoid fever at her home near Georgetown, (Ga.). Survivors are her husband and five children. Before her marriage she was Miss Hendrix.

Thurs. Nov. 23, 1899
Mr. William F. Clark, age 66, died at his home in Henry Co., several days ago from cancer. He was a brother of Warren J. Clark, L. G. Clark, J. W. Clark, Mrs. Elizabeth James and Mrs. Mary Bedsole, of Barbour County. Burial at White Oak.

Mr. James Nettles, age 27, of Montgomery, died several days ago. He was the son of Mrs. Kate Nettles and grand-son of Capt. J. C. McNab.

Thurs. Nov. 30, 1899
Mr. William Thompson, age 67, farmer of Henry Co., died at home yesterday. Survivors are his wife and two daughters.

Thurs. Dec. 7, 1899
The funeral services of Mrs. Cynthia Davis was held at the home of Dr. S. G. Robertson recently, and was conducted by Rev. W. D. Hubbard. Burial at Fairview in Eufaula, Ala.

Thurs. Dec. 14, 1899
Mrs. George W. Thompson, age 65, living near town died Dec. 10th. Survivors are her husband, two daus., Mrs. Sallie E. Thompson

Eufaula Times & News
1899

and Georgia Ella Thompson and two sons, Messrs. Robert and Charles N. Thompson.

Mr. Reuben Rogers, an aged citizen of Eufaula, died last night from the effects of the severe cold.

Thurs. Dec. 21, 1899
Died in Birmingham on Dec. 14th, Mrs. T. M. Allen, wife of Dr. Allen. She was formerly Miss Hance. Survivors are her husband and four children. Burial in Oak Hill Cemetery, Birmingham, Ala.

Mrs. William Danford, age 67, died last evening at the home of her daughter, Mrs. Andrew James, on Dale Road in Eufaula. Burial at White Oak.

Thurs, Dec, 28, 1899
Mr. W. A. James, a young man living near Eufaula, died Friday from typhoid fever. He was the son of Mr. J. Berry James. Survivors are his wife and two small children. Burial at Christian Grove Church.

The Clayton Record
1899

Fri. Jan. 6, 1899
Dr. J. O. Keener, President of the Southern University at Greensboro, Ala., died Saturday with paralysis.

Mr. Frank Blue, a young man of Mt. Andrew, died on Wednesday of last week.

Fri. Feb. 10, 1899
Rev. J. F. Smith died at his home in Talladega, Ala., on Saturday. He was one of the best known ministers in Alabama and was for a number of years rector of St. Peter's Episcopal Church.

Fri. Mar. 31, 1899
Mrs. Y. E. Smith, nee Miss Babbitt, died at her home near Solomon's Mill (Barbour Co.) on last Friday. Burial at Zion Cemetery east of town.

Mrs. Victoria Gillis, wife of Malcolm Gillis, died at her home seven miles west of Clayton on Saturday. Survivors are her husband and several children. She was the daughter of Timothy Lee and sister of Mrs. Daniel J. Walker. (Note: The above was taken from the Eufaula and the Clayton papers).

Fri. May 5, 1899
Mrs. Gussie Smart, widow of Press Smart, died suddenly last Thursday while attending the wedding of her niece, Miss Charlotte Reynolds to Mr. A. D. Card. She leaves a six year old son.

Mr. David K. Thomas died at his home here Friday. Survivors are his wife and one son.

Fri. June 9, 1899
Mrs. Annie Clarke died in Anniston Sunday and was buried in Clayton by the side of her husband. She leaves two children, Mr. Whit (Whitfield) Clarke and Mrs. Kilby.

The Clayton Record
1899

Mr. Tip (Elias) Matthison dropped dead at the public well in Clayton on Wednesday.

Fri. June 23, 1899
    Dr. Benj. F. Meek, Professor of English Language and Literature at the University of Alabama, died at his home on the campus on Friday.

Fri. July 28, 1899
    Mr. Dell Robson, of Louisville, died at his home there Saturday

Fri. Aug. 11, 1899
    Mr. James R. Cowan, aged 70, ex-tax assessor of Etowah Co., (Ala.), died at Gallant on Saturday after an illness lasting from Christmas.

Fri. Aug. 25, 1899
    Mrs. E. A. Smith, age over 80, died at the home of her dau., Mrs. H. W. B. Price, on Friday.

Fri. Sept. 29, 1899
    Mr. A. M. Redding, age 60, formerly a citizen of Barbour Co., died at Headland (Ala.) last night.

Fri. Nov. 10, 1899
    Dr. A. Turner, age four score years and more, living near White Oak, died Saturday. Burial at Palmyra. Survivors are two sons, Messrs. Jerre and Alley Turner, both of White Oak.

Eufaula Times & News
1900

Thurs. Jan. 4, 1900
    The remains of Mrs. Sarah A. Danforth arrived yesterday from Augusta, Ga., accompanied by Mr. E. C. B. Danforth and Mrs. James Campbell, her niece of Augusta. Services were held at St. James Episcopal Church. Burial at Fairview Cemetery in Eufaula.

    Mr. Phil Oliver, age 40, died from typhoid fever at his home at Morris Station, Ga., on Saturday. Burial at Cotton Hill.

    Mrs. T. A. Craven, age 54, of Union Springs (Ala.) died suddenly at her home of heart failure. She was a sister of Mr. A. A. Couric, Sr., of Eufaula.

    Mrs. Forrest D. Hatfield of Eufaula died from typhoid fever yesterday. Survivors are her husband and three small children.

    Mr. Irwing L. Miller died in Eufaula Dec. 29th. He was born in Orangeburg Dist., S. C. in 1818. He came to Ala. in 1838 and located about 20 miles from Eufaula on the Cowikee Creek. In 1845 he married Sophia Furgurson, third dau. of Gen. John Lingard Hunter, also a native of S. C. After the war he emigrated with a colony of southern families to Brazil, South America, settling near Rio De Janeiro. He returned to the U. S. in 1884 with his wife and little grand-dau., Maude, a dau of their second son, Hayne. His wife died in Eufaula in 1890, and his oldest dau. died in Brazil. Of the six children surviving, five are living in Brazil. Mrs. (or Miss ?) Teresa Miller lives in Eufaula.

Eufaula Times & News
1900

Mr. L. L. Teague, of Earpville, Gregg Co., Tex., died last Monday. He was one of Gregg County's pioneer settlers. He was born in Columbia, Henry Co., Ala. Dec. 20th 1829. He married Apr. 18th, 1852 to Miss Mary Koonce. He moved with his family to Texas in Dec. 1871.-Longview (Tex.) Times Clarion.

Thurs. Jan. 11, 1900
Mr. Ed Stow, formerly of Eufaula, died in Albany, Ga., from apoplexy yesterday. Burial in Eufaula. He leaves a family.

Thurs. Jan. 18, 1900
Died at his home in Eufaula on Monday, Mr. Swin Pilcher, age about 70. Survivors are his wife and several children. Burial in Dale County, his old home.

Mr. Ed. McLeod, age 38, living near Palmyra Church, died at his home last night with typhoid pneumonia. Burial at Palmyra. He was the son of Mr. Daniel McLeod of Bush and brother to the late D. D. McLeod of Anniston.

Mrs. M. C. Woodruff died at Dothan yesterday. She was the mother-in-law of Mr. D. T. Sheehan of Eufaula. Burial in Eufaula. Survivors are Mrs. D. T. Sheehan and Mrs. J. C. Hickey.

Capt. LeGrand Guerry, age about 60, died at his home in Eufaula on Saturday. Survivors are his wife and nine children. Burial at Fairview Cemetery in Eufaula.

Mrs. A. A. (Sallie) Couric died Tuesday at her home in Eufaula. She and her husband had recently celebrated their 28th wedding anniversary. She was formerly Miss McLeroy. Survivors are her husband and nine children. Burial at Fairview in Eufaula.

Thurs. Feb. 1, 1900
Mrs. Bettie Cook, formerly of Eufaula, nee Bettie Brown, died yesterday at her home in Columbus, Ga. She was born and reared in Eufaula, and was a sister to L. H. Brown.

Thurs. Feb. 8, 1900
Chattanooga, Feb. 5.-The funeral of the late Judge D. M. Key was held today from the family residence. Burial in Forrest Hill Cemetery.

Elamville, Ala., Feb. 3.-Mr. V. F. Commander was killed by a piece of timber at his father's saw mill last Thursday. Survivors are his wife, two children, parents, sisters and brothers

Elamville, Ala., Feb. 3.-Mr. Homer Patterson died at the home of his mother Jan. 26th of typhoid fever.

Thurs. Feb. 15, 1900
Mrs. Charles Moore, of Perry, Ga., died recently. She was the mother of Mrs. P. B. McKenzie and Miss Mary Moore of Perry (Ga.). Her husband survives her.

Thurs. Mar. 8, 1900
Atlanta, Mar. 5.-The funeral of Thomas Reed, age 67, took place today at Oakland Cemetery. He was one of the oldest citizens of Atlanta, having come here driving a tobacco wagon from North Carolina in 1847.

Eufaula Times & News
1900

Thurs. Mar. 15, 1900

    Mr. Judson Key, age about 40, son of H. E. Key, died at his home in Dale County last Wednesday.-Ozark (Ala.) Star.

Thurs. Mar. 22, 1900

    Oateston, (Barbour Co.) Ala. Mar. 19th.- Mrs. B. E. G. Parmer died at her home Sunday from dropsy. Burial at Rocky Mount.

    Mrs. T. R. McTyer, of Clayton died at her home yesterday. She was a sister-in-law to Misses Bessie and Maggie McTyer. Survivors are her husband and sons.

Thurs. Mar. 29, 1900

    White Pond (Barbour Co.), Mar. 19.- Mrs. Ann Parmer died at her home Sunday. Survivors are her husband and several children.

Thurs. May 3, 1900

    Mr. Sam M. Garrett, age 27, born in Eufaula, died last Friday. He was the son of the late Mr. James Garrett. His mother died in his infancy, leaving him to the care of his sister, Mrs. Ann Cobb. Survivors are his wife and baby and one brother and sister.

Thurs. May 10, 1900

    Mr. S. C. Benton, age about 35, formerly of Eufaula, died here of pleurisy on Wednesday. Burial at Pratt City.- B'ham. Tribune.

    Oateston (Barbour Co.), May 7.-Mr. A. A. Richardson, an old citizen of Baker Hill, died on 29th ult. He leaves a wife and two brothers, Messrs. John and Israel Richardson.

    The funeral of Mr. Wells J. Bray, formerly of Eufaula, took place in Conn. last Sunday. Survivors are one child, Mrs. B. L. Guice of Eufaula, two brothers and two sisters, Mr. Nathan Bray, of Eufaula, Mr. James P. Bray, Mrs. Lester P. Mallory and Mrs. Sarah B. Ixes, of New Haven. New Haven (Conn.) Courier.

    Bishop Henry Melville Jackson died at his home at "Roseland" near Eufaula on Monday. He was born in Leesburg, Va. on July 29th 1849.

    Mrs. Kate Stephens, age 45, wife of Mr. Calvin J. Stephens, died at her home in Eufaula this morning. Besides her husband, she leaves a dau. and two sisters and three brothers.

    Mr. J. H. Whitlock died last Thursday at his home in Eufaula. Survivors are his wife and son and a brother.

    Judge Ike Feagin, formerly of Eufaula, died at his home in Union Springs on Wednesday.

    Mr. Will Bray, formerly of Eufaula, died at Glennville last Thursday.

Thurs. May 24, 1900

    Mr. J. E. Griffin, formerly of Eufaula, died in Montgomery Friday where he had gone for treatment. Burial at his home in Midway, Ala. Survivors are his wife and two children, Misses Bennie and Ethel Griffin.

Thurs. May 31, 1900

    Dr. Albert Goodwin died in Eufaula yesterday. Survivors are

Eufaula Times & News
1900

four sisters and brother, Mrs. Griggs and Miss F. L. and Mamie Goodwin, of Atlanta; Mrs. Warren Huff, Waverly, Ga., and Rev. Sam Goodwin of New York. Dr. Goodwin was born Mar. 15, 1850 in Tolbotton, Ga.

Thurs. June 7, 1900

Louisville, Ala. June 5.- Mrs. Mary Grubbs, who has long been a resident of this place, died last Saturday at her home.

Spivey, Ala. June 4.- Mr. N. L. Hawley, age about 60, died at his home in Lawrenceville on the 3rd of June of heart dropsy. Survivors are his wife and nine children.

Thurs. June 21, 1900

Mrs. Lizzie Driggers, age 82, died at the home of A. R. Chestnut last Tuesday.- Baker Hill.

Mr. Jim Moore, of Clayton, died Tuesday while working in his farm. Survivors are his wife and five children.

Mr. J. W. Blair died at his home near Spring Hill in Barbour County this morning.

Thurs. June 28, 1900

Mr. Mose Benton, formerly of Eufaula, but now of Clayton, died in that town Sunday.

Capt. A. Flewellen, age over 70, of Eufaula, died at the home of his son, Mr. Jim Flewellen at Flora, Ala. He had made his home in Eufaula with his son, the late W. W. Flewellen. He had been a resident of Andrew Female College at Cuthbert, Ga. His only surviving son is Mr. J. T. Flewellen, of Flora, and his dau.-in-law Willie Mae Flewellen. Burial in Cuthbert, Ga.

Mrs. Mattie Jones, age 57, wife of Joseph Jones, died yesterday at her home in Eufaula. She was born near Louisville in Barbour Co., May 24, 1843. Survivors are her husband and seven childre Burial at Fairview in Eufaula.

Thurs. July 5, 1900

Mrs. J. E. Pinkston died at her home at Louisville on June 27. Survivors are her husband and two children. Burial at Midway, Ala.

Mrs. Bettie Brown, proprietor of the Josephine Hotel at Union Springs, died Saturday.

Thurs. July 12, 1900

Mrs. W. E. Guilford died at her home in Dale County on the 3rd of July and was buried at Prospect Church. She leaves a family

Mrs. Mary Powers, age about 82, died at her home near Belcher (Barbour Co.) last Saturday. She leaves a large number of relatives Burial at Antioch.

Mrs. Lucie Tennille Emory MacKenzie, wife of Mr. Geo. Norbury MacKenzie, died at Belair, Md., yesterday. She was the dau. of Ambrose Marechal Emory, of Baltimore. Survivors are a son, named for his father, and two daus., Misses Mary Mackall and Anna Vernon

<u>Eufaula Times & News</u>
1900

MacKenzie.-<u>Baltimore</u> <u>News</u>.
Mrs. MacKenzie was a grand-dau. of Gideon Emory, of Eufaula and Georgetown during the '40's and '50's.

Thurs. July 19, 1900
Mrs. Lizzie Hall, wife of Mr. William Hall, living near Terese (Barbour Co.) died at her home July 13th. Survivors are her husband and six children. Burial at Christian Grove.

Mr. G. Walker Williams, age over 81, died at his home at Afton (Barbour Co.) on the 10th. Survivors are his wife and children.

Mrs. Ann Johnson died at the home of Mr. Pilot Floyd in Clayton on Friday last. She was the dau. of the late Walker Williams.

Mrs. Julia Hales, age nearly 90, died at her home in Eufaula. Survivors are one son, who lives near Ozark.

Thurs. July 26, 1900
Mrs. G. P. Cook, of Star Hill (Barbour Co.) died July 16th. She is survived by her husband and eight children. Burial at Bathesda.

Thurs. Aug. 9. 1900
Mr. J. G. McIntosh, over age 76. died at Cowikee and was buried at Spring Hill (Barbour County).

The funeral of Mr. James Sherry took place today from the Catholic Church.

Mrs. Z. Dancer, age four score and one year, died at the home of her niece, Mrs. Van Robinson in Eufaula yesterday. She was born in Edgefield, S. C. and came to Columbus where she lived for some years. She had been living in Eufaula the last 20 years.

Thurs. Aug. 16, 1900
Rev. J. D. Stallings, age 32, pastor of M. E. Church at Alston, (Barbour Co.) died Thursday. Survivors are his wife and four children.

Mr. George W. Hendrix died yesterday at his home in Eufaula of typhoid fever. Survivors are his wife and four children.

Dr. H. E. Brooks, nearing four score years, died at his home in Eufaula yesterday. Survivors are his wife and two daus., Mrs. O. Worthy, of Troy, and Mrs Fannie Raleigh, of Eufaula.

Prof. John D. Yerby, Supt. of Mobile Schools, died in Mobile on the 9th. He was born in Greensboro, Ala. forty years ago. He married Miss Gabrielle Bullock of Mobile, who with a dau. survives him. He also leaves a father, two brothers and four sisters, the majority of whom reside at Greensboro. <u>Mobile</u> <u>Register</u>.

Thurs. Aug. 23, 1900
Mrs. E. J. Clarke, age 72, died at her home Sunday of bronchial pneumonia in Eufaula She had lived here since 1864. Survivors are three daus., Mrs. Kirkpatrick , Mrs. A. J. Smith of Montgomery and Mrs. C. J. Smith of Eufaula.

Eufaula Times & News
1900

Thurs. Aug. 30, 1900
Dr. Dan Goldsmith, of Atlanta, died in Bonhomie, Miss., yesterday. He was born in Greenville (Ala.) and was a brother to Mrs. J. B. Johnson, of Eufaula.

Thurs. Sept. 6, 1900
Mrs. George Jordan, age 48, died at her home in Eufaula Tuesday from Cancer. She leaves three orphan children, Emma, Earnest and Carrie Lou, the youngest is about eight years old. Relatives will take care of the children.

Thurs. Sept. 13, 1900
Mrs. W. J. Miller died at her home in Eufaula Tuesday from heart trouble. Survivors are her husband and five children. Burial at Mt. Aereal Church.

Thurs. Sept. 20, 1900
Mr. Robert Moulthrop, Sr., age about 63, died in New Haven, Conn., while on a visit to his sister, Mrs. Frank Parmer. He was born there in 1827 and came to Eufaula about 1867. Survivors are his wife and two children, Robert, Jr., and Albert Moulthrop. Burial at Fairview Cemetery in Eufaula.

Thurs. Sept. 27, 1900
Mr. R. A. Passmore and Dr. Christopher McDonald, of Louisville, both died at that place yesterday. The former a victim of consumption, the other died of typhoid fever.

Thurs. Oct. 11, 1900
Mrs. Oscar Davis, nee Miss Mamie Calhoun, died at her home in Texas where she had been living only a short time.

Thurs. Nov. 8, 1900
Mrs. A. A. Dantzler, of Shellman, (Ga.) died last Thursday. She was the grandmother of Mr. Ed Dantzler, of Eufaula.

Thurs. Nov. 15, 1900
Mr. Allen Wallace died yesterday at Batesville, Ala. at the home of his dau., Mrs. R. S. Smith. Survivors are his five daus. Burial at Clio.

Thurs. Nov. 29, 1900
Mrs. Lizzie Daniel Hortman, the young wife of three years of Mr. James Hortman of Batesville, died yesterday. Burial in Dawson, her old home.

Thurs. Dec. 13, 1900
Mrs. Sarah King, age 78, wife of William King, died at her home at Bush in Barbour Co. this morning. She was the mother of Mrs. S. J. Belcher and Mrs. Ben Clark. Burial at White Oak.

Mr. D. S. Reeves, age 79, of White Oak Springs in Barbour County died on Dec. 6th. Six children survive him, three sons and three daughters. Burial at Mount Serene.

The death of Mr. Duncan McRae, age about 40, occurred yesterday at his place at Louisville. Survivors are his wife and two children.

Eufaula Times & News
1900

Thurs. Dec. 20, 1900

The funeral of Mr. John Moore took place at his home at Hatchers Station, Ga. on Friday. Burial in Fairview Cemetery in Eufaula. Survivors are his wife, four daus. and two sons.

Mrs. Clara Belle McKenzie, wife of Mr. W. R. McKenzie, died at her home in West End, near Birmingham. The deceased formerly resided in Eufaula, but removed to Birmingham about ten years ago. Burial at Tuskegee, Ala.

Mrs. Marian Spurlock, age 98, of Linwood, Ga., died last week. She was the mother of Mrs. Lizzie Vining and Mrs. Shade Thompson, of Eufaula. She resided near Eufaula many years ago. Her husband, Mr. Solomon Spurlock is buried at the old family church burying ground just north of the city. Mrs. Spurlock is stepmother of J. M. Spurlock, formerly of Eufaula, and step-grand mother of Mr. O. O. Spurlock.

The Clayton Record
1900

Fri. Jan. 5, 1900

Mrs. Maggie Ponder, wife of Mr. John Ponder, died Friday before Christmas. She was Maggie McCraney, dau. of the late Norman McCraney and was the last of the girls. She leaves a husband and six small children and several brothers.

Fri. Feb. 23, 1900

The death of Mr. William Holland occurred last Saturday. He leaves a wife and several grown children.

Mrs. James Orr died Thursday at her home here. Survivors are her husband and several sons and daughters.

Fri. Mar. 16, 1900

Col. John D. Roquemore died at his home in Montgomery last week. He was a native of Barbour County. In 1887 he moved to Montgomery to practice law.

Fri. May 25, 1900

Col. James G. Gilchrist, age 86, died at his home in Montgomery on Friday.

Fri. July 13, 1900

Capt. James Lang died at his home in Louisville Wednesday. Late in life he began to practice law. Survivors are his wife and several children.

Col. William Houston Burr, age 63, died at Talladega Friday. He was a native of Camden, S. C. and moved to Alabama when he was 13 years of age.

Fri. Sept. 14, 1900

Mr. T. R. Efurd died Friday and was buried with Masonic Honors.

Fri. Sept. 21, 1900

Mr. J. H. Hollingsworth, age about 68, of Mt. Andrew, died Tuesday. Survivors are his wife and several children.

Eufaula Times & News
1901

Thurs. Jan. 17, 1901
Died on Friday, Mrs. Dan Tiller of Newtopia in Barbour Co.

Mrs. Dan Tyler died of consumption Fri. at Elamville. Survivors are her husband and eight months old babe. Mrs. Tyler is the daughter of Mr. Harrison Lewis.

Mr. Henry Stern, age about 35, died at Vicksburg, Miss. last night. He was reared in Eufaula and went to Mississippi 15 years ago. He was the youngest child of Mrs. Mina Stern of Eufaula. He was stricken with small pox. He leaves a wife, a mother, four brothers and five sisters. Mr. Silas Stern, J. Stern, Ben Stern of San Antonia, Tex., and Mesdames M. Baer, J. Freidman, J. K. Sams and H. Bloom of Eufaula; also Mr. Seigman Stern, of Centerville, Miss.

Thurs. Jan. 24, 1901
Mr. Tom Taylor, age 85, died last week at Solomon's Mill in Barbour County.

Mrs. Frank Whitney died Saturday at her home on Southside in Eufaula.

Mrs. H. C. Thornton, age 75, grandmother of Mrs. R. A. Ballowe of Eufaula, died yesterday at the home of her dau., Mrs. C. E. Estes in Columbus. Burial at Cuthbert, Ga.

Thurs. Jan. 31, 1901
Mrs. Violetta Wyatt Hunter Hoole, wife of Mr. Bertram J. Hoole, died in Eufaula on Tuesday. She was born in S. C. nearly 80 years ago. She married Mr. Hoole Nov. 27th, 1839. Their daus., Mrs. E. L. Brown and Miss Victoria Hoole are the surviving children. Her sisters surviving are Mrs. Victoria Clayton, of Eufaula, and Mrs. James L. Pugh, of Washington, D. C.

Thurs. Feb. 7, 1901
Mr. H. J. Spivey, age 67, died at his home of pneumonia in Sanford, Ga., recently.

The remains of Mr. P. J. Tully arrived in Eufaula Thursday for burial in Fairview, which will be only temporary, later the body will be removed and buried beside his wife at the family burying ground at Lockport, N. Y.

Thurs. Feb. 21, 1901
Mr. Bertram J. Hoole died last night. He was born in Darlington, S. C. on June 1811, and came to Eufaula in 1835. In Nov. 1839 he was married to Miss Violetta Hunter, of Eufaula. Survivors are his daus., Mrs. E. L. Brown and Miss Victoria Hoole.

Mrs. E. Brooks, age 80, of Eufaula, died yesterday in Troy, Ala. at the home of her dau., Mrs. O. Worthy. She was the widow of the late E. H. Brooks, of Eufaula. Her remains were accompanied by her daus., Mrs. Fannie Raleigh and Mrs. O. Worthy. Burial at Fairview in Eufaula.

Thurs. Feb. 28, 1901
Died on 4th Feb, 1901, Mr. John R. Lewis, of Texas. He leaves

Eufaula Times & News
1901

a wife and seven children in Texas. In this county he leaves the following brothers and sisters: Messrs. Quinn, G. W., A. J., and Straton Lewis; Mrs. Martha A. Williams, Mrs. L. A. Jernigan, Mrs. Nancy Mosley and Mrs. Mollie Floyd, of Clayton.

Col. Arthur Hood, age 42, of Cuthbert, Ga., died last night at his home. Survivors are his wife and three children.

Mrs. H. Hortman died at her home in Batesville, Ala., last Thursday. She was born in Warren County, Ga., in 1828 and married Mr. Hortman 51 years ago. Most of her married life was spent in Batesville. Survivors are her husband and six daus. and two sons. Burial in Eufaula.

Thurs. Mar. 7, 1901

Mr. Richard Quinn Edmonson, Jr., age about 30, died Friday at Waxahatchee, Texas. He married Miss Tessie Meridith. Survivors are his wife and two little children, his father, mother, two brothers, Messrs. E. L. and John Edmonson and two sisters, Mrs. W. H. Flowers and Mrs. J. H. Flowers, both of Dothan, Ala.

Thurs. Apr. 4, 1901

Rev. W. H. Patterson died Wednesday at his home in Eufaula. He was born in Dooley Co., Ga., Oct. 9th, 1836, but was reared in Hancock Co., and had been a resident of Eufaula more than thirty-five years. Survivors are his wife and two sons, Messrs. F. M. Patterson of Eufaula and W. R. Patterson of Greensboro, N. C.

Mrs. R. D. Shropshire, age about 50, died Monday at her home in New York from pneumonia. The remains were accompanied by her son Mr. William Shropshire and her sister, Miss Mollie Barnett and friends of Montgomery. Burial in Eufaula.

Miss Mary Butt, age about 40 years old, died at her home in Eufaula Saturday.

Thurs. Apr. 18, 1901

Mr. John Toole, age about 40, died at his home near Poston's Mill last Sunday. Burial at Christian Grove Cemetery. His wife died only a short time ago. Several small children are left orphans.

Washington, Ga., Apr. 10.-Mr. Guy Smith died at his father's home in this county recently. Mr. Smith has relatives in this city.

Mr. F. S. Sparrow, of Birmingham, was killed Apr. 2nd near Stephens, Ark., one hundred miles from Texarkans, Texas, by an overloaded car breaking and falling on him while he was performing his duties as an employee of the R. R. He had been in Ark. about four months. He was born in Eufaula about 33 years ago and had been a resident of Birmingham twelve years. He was the son of Mr. W. J. Sparrow. He leaves a wife and four children.

Mrs. Katherine McMurry, age 83, died in Eufaula yesterday. She was born in Ireland and came to Eufaula fifty years ago. Survivors are one son, Mr. George McMurry.

Thurs. May 2, 1901

Eufaula Times & News
1901

Mr. Wyley Hartzog died at the home of his son, Henry Hartzog on Apr. 23rd. Burial at Pond Bethel. Survivors are several children.

G. H. Howell died last night near Baker Hill in Barbour Co.

Mrs. Mittie E. LaHattie, age 56, died yesterday at her home in Atlanta. She is survived by her husband, Rev. C. B. LaHattie, two sons, C. O. and Albert LaHattie and two daus., Mrs. Emmett Brogden and Miss Lucile LaHattie, of Atlanta. She was also the mother of the late Mrs. Stake Brewer of Elberton, and sister-in-law of M. T. LaHattie. She was born in Eufaula and was the dau. of Oliver Ingram of Eufaula. She lived with her father until a short time before the war, when she married Rev. LaHattie.-Atlanta Journal.

Mrs. LaHattie is the sister of J. E. Engram, of Eufaula.

Thurs. May 9, 1901

Mr. Shelley D. Dowling died at his home in Ozark on last Thursday. Burial at Claybank.

Mr. Jesse Kay, age 51, died at his home near Eufaula last night. His wife died ten years ago. Survivors are one girl and four boys. Burial at Epworth Church.

Mr. Cephas J. Knox, age 48, died Monday at his home in Auburn, Ala. He formerly lived at Troy. He married Miss Annie Jennings of this city. Survivors are his wife, one son and one daughter.

Mr. William Graddy, age 84, died at his home near Georgetown, Georgia, yesterday.

Thurs. May 23, 1901

Mrs. Harrison Rogers, of Dawson, Ga., the mother of Mrs. W. F. Locke, of Eufaula, died at her home in Dawson this morning.

Rev. J. P. Margart died at his home in Batesville, Ala., on yesterday. He was born in Charleston, S. C. in 1816, moved to Barbour Co. in 1861. He leaves a wife and two sons, Messrs. S. F. and S. T. Margart and one dau., Mrs. Otis(? print bad). Burial in Fairview in Eufaula.

Rev. John Wesley Solomon, age 79, died at his home near Seale yesterday. He was a Methodist minister. Burial at Seale, Alabama.

Miss Sue Butt, age 55, died at her home in Eufaula last evening.

Dr. J. E. Crews, age 83, died Sunday in Clayton. He leaves a wife and brother, Mr. Anderson Crews, of Clayton.

Dr. E. M. Heron, age 91, died at the home of his dau., Mrs. R. Q. Edmonson in Eufaula. He was born in Charleston, S. C. and came to Eufaula 75 years ago. He leaves one son, D. J. Heron, of Elamville, Ala., and his dau., Mrs. R. Q. Edmonson of this city. Burial at Fairview in Eufaula.

Eufaula Times & News
1901

Thurs. June 13, 1901

Mrs. Mary A. Perryman, age 81, died yesterday. She was Miss Mary Hudspeth, when just grown she married Mr. J. W. Pippin and after his death she married Mr. D. A. Perryman, who preceded her to the grave about four years ago. She leaves one son, Dallas Pippin, of Eufaula and grand-sons, Messrs. Weeks, Gordon and George Pippin and one grand-daughter, Mrs. J. T. Morris.

Mrs. L. J. Lewis, age about 60, sister of Mr. A. J. Locke and Hon. R. D. Locke, of Macon, died in Montgomery today.

Thurs. June 20, 1901

Mr. E. L. Kaigler, age 33, died Friday at his home in Macon. Survivors are his wife and children. Burial at Georgetown, Ga.

Mrs. Emily Thompson Tharp, age 66, wife of Mr. V. D. Tharp, died at her home in Eufaula recently. She was born in Philadelphia, Penn., of Quaker parents. She came with them to Columbus, Ga., and was married there in 1856 to Mr. Tharp. They moved to Eufaula 28 years ago. Survivors are her husband and a niece, Mrs. T. W. Howard, of Columbus, Ga., and one brother.

Mrs. W. A. Juhan died yesterday at the home of her son, Mr. W. J. Juhan, in Macon. Before her marriage she was Miss Elizabeth J. Brooks, of Clinton, Jones Co., Ga. Her husband died a few years ago. Survivors are her four children, Messrs. Charles, William, Louis and Mrs. Susie Guice, of Eufaula.

Thurs. June 27, 1901

Mrs. Johanna McIntyre, age 75, died at her home in Eufaula Friday. She was born in County Kerry, Ireland, and came to America in her childhood. She was married to Mr. Patrick McIntyre. Survivors are her three nephews, Messrs. Mike, John and Dan Coffee, of Macon, Ga. Burial at Fairview.

Thurs. July 4, 1901

Mrs. J. A. Bennefield died suddenly at her home near Solomon's Mill on Monday. She leaves a husband and six children. Burial at Bethlehem.

Mr. John McL. McRae died at his home in Eufaula on Friday. He was born in Marlboro Co., S. C. in 1838 and moved with his parents to Alabama when he was 15 years old. He was married in Eufaula in 1862 to Miss Amma Williams, of White Plains, Ga. Survivors are his wife and three daus., Misses Julia, Jennie and Amma; and two sons, Messrs. Louie and John McRae, two sisters, Mrs. J. T. Kendall of Eufaula and Marie Young of Anniston, and one brother, Mr. Jabez McRae of near Louisville, Ala. Burial at Fairview in Eufaula.

Thurs. July 25, 1901

Dr. W. A. Mitchell died Tuesday at his home in Eufaula. He was born in Glennville, Ala., in 1848. He moved to Eufaula in 1875. Survivors are his wife, a dau., Mrs. Robert M. Ormond of Atlanta and a brother. Burial in Atlanta.

Thurs. Aug. 4, 1901

Eufaula Times & News
1901

Mrs. Amanda Gaston, age 76, wife of Mr. J. B. Gaston, died at her home at Howe, near Eufaula recently. Survivors are her husband, three sons, Messrs. John Johnson of Howe, T. L. Johnson of Elba, Ala. - children by her first husband, Mr. Richard Johnson, Judge Zell Gaston, Butler Co., Ala., and Mrs. Abe Leham, Greenville, Ala. Burial at Howe.

Mr. William Spence, age 50, died this morning of paralysis at his home in Quitman, Ga. Burial at Union Church.

Mr. J. H. Faulk of Clio, (Ala.) died there yesterday of heart disease.

Mr. James Cameron, age 74, died yesterday at his home near Eufaula. He was a veteran of the Mexican War and the Confederate War.

Thurs. Aug. 8, 1901

Mrs. J. W. Clark died at her home this morning in Eufaula of typhoid fever. Mr. and Mrs. Clark moved here from Ozark 12 years ago. The deceased was born Mar. 22, 1852. Burial at Fairview in Eufaula.

Thurs. Aug. 22, 1901

Enterprise, (Ala.) Aug. 20, 1901.-Mr. Ruben A. Davis died at his home this morning. He moved from Barbour County about eight months ago.

Mr. I. B. Adams, age about 35, died at his home at Coffinton, Stewart Co., Ga., last Friday. He leaves a wife and two children. Burial at Coffinton.

Thurs. Aug. 29, 1901

Mr. James B. Shorter died at the home of his mother, Mrs. Carrie Lomax in Montgomery. He was born in Clinton, Ga., 12 July 1849.-Montgomery Advertiser.

Thurs. Sept. 19, 1901

Mrs. C. R. Barbaree, age 69, died while visiting Mr. and Mrs. J. W. McCrae in Louisville, Ala. recently. Burial at China Grove.

Thurs. Oct. 3, 1901

Mr. H. F. Lunsford, age 45, died at his home near Eufaula last night. He was married to Miss Henrietta Hughes, sister of Mr. John Hughes, of Eufaula; to whom eleven children were born - nine of whom are living. Burial at Mt. Airy Church.

Thurs. Oct. 17, 1901

Mrs. Hannah Ray, age four score and ten, died in the Bush neighbor-hood recently. Her husband died twenty years ago. Survivors are seven children. Burial at Mount Pleasant Cemetery.

Mrs. J. B. Stewart, age 51, died at her home in Eufaula. She came here about 15 years ago. Burial at Columbus, Ga., her old home.

Thurs. Oct. 24, 1901

Eufaula Times & News
1901

Mrs. Aaron Parmer, of near Baker Hill, died this morning. Survivors are her husband and several children.

Thurs. Nov. 7, 1901

Maj. M. F. Perry died at his home at Thompson Station, Bullock County on Friday and was buried at Fairview in Eufaula. Survivors are his wife and several children.

Mr. J. R. Saunders, age 75, of Cochran (Barbour Co.) died at his home yesterday and will be buried there. He was a brother of Mrs. Ogletree of Georgetown.

Mrs. Carrie McLeod Brady, wife of Mr. John L. Brady, died at her home at Rose Hill, Columbus, Ga. Monday of typhoid dysentery. She was Miss Carrie McLeod of Eufaula. She leaves three children, Albert, age 12; Robert, age 10; and Nellie, age 3. Mr. H. J. McLeod of Columbus, Mr. F. McLeod of Texas and Mr. W. L. McLeod of Birmingham are her brothers. Mrs. Lizzie Brown, of this city, is her sister. Burial at Columbus.

Thurs. Nov. 21, 1901

Died this morning, Mrs. S. A. Moore, age 73. She was the mother of Mrs. W. A. Cargill of Eufaula. Survivors are three children, Mrs. Cargill, Mrs. Hart of Quitman Co., Ga., and Mrs. Hendricks of Lakeland, Fla.

Mr. J. G. Hortman died accidentally by falling down the stairs at J. K. Sam's store and breaking his neck. He was born in S. C. in 1818 and lived a long time in Georgia. About 54 years ago he moved to near Batesville, Ala. Survivors are Miss Emma Hortman of Eufaula, Mrs. Lelia Daniels, Weston, Ga., Mrs. Belle Brown of Cleveland, Tex., Mrs. Lizzie Mallet of Mobile, Ala., Mrs. Lou Sandifer of La., Mrs. Edna Sandifer of Merrill, Miss., J. W. Hortman of Batesville and W. H. Hortman of Clayton.

Thurs. Nov. 28, 1901

Mrs. Lockland McLain died last night in Eufaula. Her husband died in the 1870's. Miss LeElla, her dau., was a companion and nurse to her mother. Burial in Chrystal Springs, Miss., beside her mother.

Thurs. Dec. 5, 1901

Mr. T. R. (Thomas Rembert) Sylvester died at his home at Terese in Barbour Co. this morning. He had passed four score and two years. He is survived by his wife, Allethia Turner Beckham Sylvester, one dau., Mrs. Mary Emma Fields and sons William Oscar, Taylor, Thomas R. and Edgar Forest Sylvester. Burial at Terese.

Mr. W. H. Birdsong, age 70, of near Clayton, died last night. His two sisters, Miss Joe Birdsong and Mrs. F. E. McLeod live here. Burial at Fairview in Eufaula.

Thurs. Dec. 26, 1901

Mrs. C. R. DeJarnette of Autaugaville died Friday. Her dau., Mrs. J. L. Godwin of Eufaula, was called to her bedside and had only been there a short time before she died.

Eufaula Times & News
1901

Dr. Richard Lemeul Butt of Midway, Ala., died Wednesday at his home. The remains were carried to Montgomery and interred in the Vandiver lot. He was born in Columbia Co., Ga., Nov. 1st, 1824. He begun practicing at Columbus, Ga. On July 29, 18?? he married Miss Eliza C. Leonard, of Morgan Co., Ga. She died in Memphis, Tenn,. 15 Nov. 1861. The second marriage of Dr. Butt was with Mrs. Martha J. Gamsnell. She died 12 Aug. 1870. His third wife whom he married 22 Nov. 1876 was Mrs. Mary E. Henderson, dau. of William Moss, a native of New York.

Dr. Butt first located in Midway in 1853. He left there and returned in 1875. He is survived by his wife, one brother, Rev. M. E. Butt, of Childersburg,, Ala; a son, Mr. R. L. Butt of Montgomery, Ala., and one dau., Mrs. Mary Virginia Wood of Las Negas, N. M., two grand-children, Eldridge Johnson and G. B. Johnson of Montgomery, and four step-children, R. M. Henderson and W. F. Vandiver of Montgomery, Mrs. Mattie L. Thompson and Mrs. T. R. McCarty of Demopolis, (Ala.).

The Clayton Record
1901

Thurs. Jan. 17, 1901

Mr. J. E. Borders, age 79, and Mrs. Borders, age 75, who for some time made their home in Fla. and were the aunt and uncle of A. S. Borders and Mrs. Mary Foster of Clayton, died of la grippe, Mr. Borders died Monday and Mrs. Borders died Sunday. Burial in the Masonic Cemetery.

Thurs. Feb. 7, 1901

Mrs. J. L. Morrell died at her home in Cartersville, Ga., on Jan. 24th last. She leaves a husband.

Thurs. Feb. 14, 1901

Mrs. H. E. Brooks, age 80, died at Troy Tuesday. She formerly lived in Eufaula, but after the death of her husband last year she moved to Troy to live with her dau., Mrs. O. Worthy. Burial in Eufaula.

Mr. S. G. Pruett died in Montgomery Monday. He was a brother of Judge W. H. Pruett, of Clayton.

Mr. Miles Heath, an old citizen of Alston in Barbour Co., died Thursday from la grippe.

Thurs. Mar. 7, 1901

B. D. Givens age about 55, a Tuscaloosa County farmer, died suddenly of heart failure Thursday.

Hon. Francis L. Peters, of Dallas County, (Ala.) died in Montgomery at the home of a friend on Wednesday. He was Speaker of the House in the state legistature.

Thurs. Mar. 14, 1901

The funeral of Mr. J. S. Espy took place yesterday at County Line Church.-Eufaula Times.

Thurs. Mar. 28, 1901

The Clayton Record
1901

Mr. J. J. Bradley returned Friday last from Pensacola where he went to attend the funeral of his brother, Mr. Hobbs Bradley.

Thurs. May 2, 1901

Mr. George Wiley Hartzog, age 84, of Lindsey, died on March 22nd from cancer. Burial at Pond Bethel Church in Barbour County.

Thurs. May 9, 1901

Mrs. Jane McLeod, age 76, nee Jane Cunningham, wife of the late Mr. John McLeod, died May 2nd at the home of her son-in-law, Mr. Charles Stewart, Sr., near White Oak Springs. Burial at Palmyra. She leaves Mrs. Stewart, her only child.

Thurs. May 16, 1901

Mr. C. P. (Calab) Reese, father of Mr. J. W. Reese, died at the home of the latter on 27 Apr. 1901. He was born 22 Feb. 1819. He married 1 Mar. 1840 to Miss N. E. Kates in S. C., where both were born. He moved from Ga. to Ala., settling first in Cherokee Co., thence to Barbour County. He came with his companion to spend the remainder of his life with his son at Enterprise, (Ala.). Weekly (Ala.) Enterprise.

From Clayton Record: Mr. Reese has two sons in Texas, one in Geneva Co., and one in Coffee Co., two daus., Mrs. W. H. Craigg and Mrs. Berry Johnston.

Thurs. May 23, 1901

Mr. W. O. Monroe, age about 60, editor of the Eutaw Whig & Observer, died at his home in Eutaw recently.

Rev. J. W. Solomon died at his home in Seale, (Ala.) last week.

Thurs. June 6, 1901

Mr. John E. Crews, age 82, died Sunday. He was born in Georgia, in Jones County, 1st Jan. 1819. He married 25 Mar. 1851 to Miss Margaret E. Dubose, who survives him, also a brother, Mr. Anderson A. Crews and a half brother and sister.

Thurs. Aug. 1, 1901

Mrs. Sarah Williams, age 74, died 8 July at the home of her son, Mr. J. W. Williams. She was the dau. of Mr. William Searcy and was born in North Carolina in 1827. Survivors are her son and dau., Mrs. Westbrook.

Thurs. Aug. 15, 1901

Mr. L. F. Rich, of Bullock County, died at his home last Saturday. Survivors are his wife and one son, G. A. Rich.

Mr. Frank Robson, formerly of Clayton, died suddenly last Friday in Bullock County.

Thurs. Aug. 22, 1901

Mrs. Martha Jane Williams, wife of Mr. Nathan Williams, died at her home in Barbour Co. on 15th Aug. She was a dau. of Mr. John Lewis- and with her family moved here from North Carolina when a girl. Survivors are her husband, three sons, Messrs. John, Nathan and George Williams, and one dau., Miss Savannah Williams. Burial at Pond Bethel.

The Clayton Record
1901

Thurs. Aug. 29, 1901
Mrs. W. T. Shehane, wife of Will Shehane, of the *Montgomery Journal*, died in Eufaula at the home of her parents, Mr. and Mrs. Virgil Crawford on Saturday of typhoid fever.

Thurs. Sept. 27, 1901
Judge P. Wood, Probate Judge of Dallas County, died recently in London where he was attending the Encemental Conference of the Methodist Church as one of Alabama's delegates.

Eufaula Times & News
1902

Thurs. Jan. 2, 1902
Mrs. Betsey Clark, age 98, died at the home of her son-in-law, Mr. J. A. James, eleven miles south of the city yesterday. Burial at Rocky Mount.

Thurs. Jan. 23, 1902
Mrs. Mary Rhody, wife of Mr. Barney Rhody, age 49, died yesterday at her home in Eufaula. She was Mary McFadden, born in Dougald, Ireland and came to Eufaula about twenty years ago. Survivors are her husband and eight children, Mrs. P. T. Brannon, Mrs. John Cherry, Emma, Annie, Maude, James, Maggie and Theressa Rhody. Burial in Eufaula.

Mr. Thomas S. Bryant died at his home in Quitman Co., Ga., yesterday. He was born in Virginia on 2nd Sept. 1815 and moved to Georgia about fifty years ago. He has five children to survive him and four that preceded him to the grave. His wife died on 8th Nov. 1868.

Thurs. Jan. 30, 1902
Mrs. Catherine Chambers, age 82, died at her home near Clayton Saturday. She was Miss Catherine McSwain. She first married Mr. Berry Crews and after his death she married Rev. W. H. Chambers. Survivors are her husband and two daus., Miss Nannie Crews and Mrs. Dr. J. J. Winn, of Clayton. Burial at New Hope.

Mrs. Cyntha Lanier, age 58, died at her home in Eufaula on Friday. She had been a resident of Eufaula fourteen years, coming here from Georgia. At the age of 20 she was married to Mr. Nowland, of Georgia, whose death left her with five small children They are Mrs. Girard Brown of Dawson, Ga., Mrs. R. S. Folsom, Messrs. John and Robert Nowland of Eufaula and Mr. Butler Nowland of the U. S. Army, Fort McPherson, Ga. Sixteen months ago she married Mr. J. M. Lanier, who with her children survive her.

Thurs. Feb. 13, 1902
Mrs. Wilber C. Baker of Little Rock, Ark., died in Eufaula on Saturday while on a visit to her parents, Mr. and Mrs. Seth Mabry. She gave birth to twins on Friday, one of which died. Burial in Clayton.

Thurs. Mar. 6, 1902
Dr. L. P. Dozier, age 71, died yesterday at his home at

<u>Eufaula Times & News</u>
1902

Hatchers Station in Quitman Co., Ga. Survivors are his wife and four sons, J. E. Dozier, E. M. Dozier of Shellman, Ga., W. M. Dozier of Hatchers Station and L. H. Dozier of Tallahassee, Fla., and two daus., Mrs. James J. Hill of Bronwood and Mrs. T. J. Ramser of Eufaula.

Mrs. J. B. Clark, age about 26, died of consumption at her home in Eufaula yesterday. Survivors are her husband and three little children.

Col. Abb Borders of Ozark died yesterday. Burial in Clayton.

Mr. Louis Dowling, age about 40, died at his home in Ozark last night.

Mrs. Anna Beall Dent died yesterday. She was the eldest dau. of Edward B. Young and Anne Fendell Beall. She was born in Eufaula in June 1840. She married Capt. S. H. Dent June 5, 1860. Survivors are her husband and six children, Mr. Edward Y. Dent, Mrs. Nannie Dent Long, S. H. Dent, Jr., Lieut. Henry A. Dent, Mrs. Louise Hurt and Miss Caroline Dent.

Thurs. Mar. 13, 1902
Mr. Will Martin died at the home of his mother-in-law, Mrs. Christian Martin, near Oatston in Barbour County last Thursday. Survivors are his wife and several small children. Burial at Bethel.

Mrs. J. J. James, formerly of this place, but moved to Ozark about 12 years ago, died there yesterday. Mr. W. H. Clifton of Eufaula is a brother-in-law. The deceased leaves a family.

Thurs. Mar. 20, 1902
Mr. Allen West of Crocket, Texas, died at his home a few days ago of pneumonia. He was born and reared in Barbour County. He has three brothers living, Rev. Anson West, William and Amos West. He has two sisters living in Texas. Survivors are his wife and children in Texas, and one dau. in this county.

Mrs. Mattie Adams, wife of Asa Adams of Lodi (Barbour Co.), died on the 11th and was buried at Adams Chapel.

Mr. John G. Singer, age 87, a pioneer of Lumpkin, (Ga.) died here today. Survivors are his aged wife and several children. He was a brother to Mrs. Mary Ramser of Eufaula.

Thurs. Apr. 3, 1902
Mr. John R. Espy, age 46, of Gordan Ala. died Friday. He was the son of the late J. S. Espy, who died about a year ago, and a brother to Mrs. Dr. W. G. Lewis. He was formerly a resident of this city. Survivors are his wife and seven children and several brothers and sisters. Burial at Gordan.

Thurs. Apr. 17, 1902
Mr. Alexander McKay, age 53, died at his home in Eufaula Tuesday from a stroke of paralysis. He was born in Louisville, Ala., Jan, 4th, 1849. He and his family came to Eufaula in 1887. Survivors are his wife and children. Burial at Fairview in Eufaula.

<u>Eufaula Times & News</u>
1902

Thurs. May 1, 1902
A Memorial to Susie A. Deshazo, who died 9th Oct. 1901. She was born near Eufaula and married Rev. J. B. Deshazo on 1st Dec. 1881. Survivors are her husband and eight children.

Thurs. May 29, 1902
Mrs. William Foy died this morning. She was Nellie Beall Foy. Survivors are her husband and two small sons, Levy and Fred, her father, mother, sisters and brothers.

Mrs. Mary Roberts, age 73, died at her home at Hatchers Station, Ga. on Friday. Burial at Palaula Cemetery.

Thurs. June 12, 1902
Mrs. L. E. Willford, age 75, died suddenly at the home of Mr. J. W. Simmons in Eufaula on Tuesday of congestion.

Mr. G. W. Carter, of Albany (Ga.), died at his home recently. He was formerly a citizen of Eufaula.

Thurs. June 19, 1902
Mr. T. J. Methvin, an aged citizen of Quitman Co., Ga., died at his home at Kipling suddenly from heart disease yesterday. Burial at Pataula Cemetery. Survivors are his aged wife, five sons, Bob, Daniel, Jack, William and Ralph Methvin and three daus. Mrs. Ray, Misses Clifford and Anna Methvin.

Thurs. July 3, 1902
Mr. A. C. Mitchell, age 52, of Eufaula, died this morning. He was born and reared at Glennville and married Miss Lillie Drewry who survives him and one son, Mac, their only child. Burial in Eufaula.

Mr. Phil Pierce of Eufaula received news this morning of the death of his father, Mr. Phil Pierce, Sr., age 62, of Springvale.

Mrs. Lizzie McNab Reeves, age 46, wife of Mr. J. H. Reeves of Eufaula, died in a Montgomery hospital yesterday where she had gone for treatment. Survivors are her husband and five children. Mrs. Reeves was the dau. of Mr. John McNab, of Eufaula.

Mr. Farquhar McKay of Louisville (Ala.), died yesterday. He was a brother of Mr. Alex McKay of Eufaula who died a few months ago. Survivors are his wife and five children.

Thurs. July 10, 1902
Mr. Marion Boyd, age 86, died at his home at Zeigler in Barbour Co., last Monday.

Dr. Henry Urquhart died at Tate Springs, Tenn. on the 6th inst. He was at one time Presiding Elder of this district, and was editor of the <u>Alabama Christian Advocate</u>. Burial in Eufaula.

Thurs. July 17, 1902
Mr. W. M. Wilhem, an aged citizen of Eufaula, died at his home last Friday. Burial at Fairview in Eufaula.

Thurs. July 24, 1902
Mrs. William F. Tibbetts (or Tebbitts), wife of Capt.

Eufaula Times & News
1902

Tibbetts of Mobile, died at the home of her mother, Mrs. John M. McKleroy and brother, Capt. W. H. McKleroy in Anniston. Survivors are her husband, an infant son, her mother and brother.

Capt. Samuel M. Stanford, age about 60, died at his home at Bush, near Eufaula, last night of cancer. Survivors are his wife and five grown children.

Thurs. Aug. 7, 1902
Lafayette, Ala., Aug. 4.- Rev. Eugene H. Hawkins, age 31, Presiding Elder of the Lafayette District of the Southern M. E. Church, died here Saturday of typhoid fever. He was the son of Dr. V. O. Hawkins of Dadeville, (Ala.), Survivors are his wife and three children.

Thurs. Aug. 14, 1902
Sylvania, Ga., Aug. 9.-Col. T. W. Oliver died at his home this morning. He was the oldest and most prominent lawyer here. Survivors are his wife and two children. He was the brother of Mrs. J. C. West of Eufaula.-Augusta (Ga.) Herald.

Thurs. Sept. 4, 1902
Mrs. Frank W. Stevens of Selma died suddenly this morning. She had been married only a little over a year. She was the mother of a week old babe. Mr. Stevens is a brother to Mr. Charles A. Stevens of Eufaula.

Mr. John C. Williams, age 68, an old citizen, died at his home in Clayton Sunday. He held the office of Justice of the Peace in Beat 7 for many years.

Thurs. Sept. 11, 1902
Mrs. Sarah Hudson, age about 75, died at her home in Monttezuma, Ga. at few days ago. She was the mother of Mr. E. A. Hudson, of Eufaula.

Thurs. Sept. 18, 1902
Mrs. Betsey Beasley, age over 97, died at the home of her son, George W. Beasley five miles south of Clayton on the 6th inst.

Prof. T. A. Craven died at Union Springs this morning from the effects of a stroke of paralysis.

Mr. Thomas Stovall, age 93, died last night at the home of his dau. Mrs. J. M. McGee in Eufaula. He was born and reared in Franklin County, Ga. He came to Eufaula about 35 years ago. Survivors are six children, Mrs. J. M. McGee of Eufaula, Mrs. L. A. Hudgens of Abbeville, Mrs. Susie Scoot, Abbeville, Dr. J. H. Stovall of Columbia, Mrs. Fannie Ray and Mr. George Stovall of Texas.

Thurs. Sept. 25, 1902
Mrs. Mary E. King, age 67, died at her home in Montgomery where she moved from Eufaula about 25 years ago. She died yesterday. Survivors are her husband and five sons. She was the mother of Mr. W. G. Hamilton. Burial at Fairview in Eufaula.

Mrs. W. S. English died at her home in Hawkinsville in

Eufaula Times & News
1902

Barbour County this morning. She was a sister of Messrs. R. S. and Joseph Jones. Survivors are her husband, a grown son and three grown daughters.

Thurs. Nov. 20, 1902

Mrs. Margaret Sutton, age 54, died at her home in Barbour County on the 31st Oct. She was the wife of B. H. Sutton and the mother of twelve children, all of whom survive her save two daus.

Thurs. Nov. 27, 1902

Died last Monday at her home at Gaino (Barbour Co.), Mrs. L. G. Clark of typhoid fever. Burial at Rocky Mount.

Thurs. Dec. 11, 1902

Mrs. Christian A. Searcy, age 78, died at her home in Skipperville in Dale Co. (Ala.), this morning, She was the mother of Messrs. J. B. and Ed Searcy of Eufaula.

Mr. J. R. Pierce died at his home in Springvale, Ga., yesterday of typhoid pneumonia.

Thurs. Dec. 18, 1902

Mr. Thomas Ramser died at his home in Eufaula this morning. He was born 7 Dec. 1858 and was educated at Greencastle and Jefferson, Ind. On July 12th 1893 he married Miss Annie Dozier, dau. of Dr. L. P. Dozier of Hatchers Station, Ga. Survivors are his wife and three small children, Julian, Dozier and Mary, an aged mother and six sisters, Mrs. E. P. Blair, Mrs. B. Crawford of Eufaula; Mrs. Daniel McNeal of Ozark, Mrs. C. H. Tripp of Waelder, Texas, Mrs. T. W. Bowers of Waelder, Tex., and Mrs. L. C. Bell of Nashville, Tenn.

Thurs. Dec. 25, 1902

Mrs. S. S. Barr, age 95, died this morning at the home of her grand-son, Capt. J. R. Barr. She was the mother of Dr. J. R. Barr of Eufaula. Burial in Richmond, Va., beside her husband.

Mr. Edward P. Blair, age 41, died at his home in Eufaula last Saturday. He was born at Cuthbert, Ga. In 1884 he married Miss Laura V. Ramser. Survivors are his wife and four children, Marie, Osie, Edna and Charles. His mother, Mrs. D. M. Scarborough, lives in La. He has three sisters, Mrs. C. D. Diggers of Mansfield, La., Mrs. J. D. Danzier of Eufaula and Mrs. J. F. Stapleton of El Paso, Texas, and one brother, Mr. C. W. Blair of Mansfield, La.

Mr. Jesse Allen died at his home in Eufaula this morning with lung trouble.

The funeral of Mrs. J. M. Magee was held at her late home in Eufaula yesterday.

The Clayton Record
1902

Fri. Jan. 3, 1902

Mrs. Rebecca Parish, age 81, died at the home of her dau.,

The Clayton Record
1902

Mrs. Simonton, in Enterprise Hotel last Saturday. She was born at Wilmington, N. C. and when she was eight years old moved to Alabama with her father who settled near Brundidge in Pike Co., Ala. Her husband died a few years ago.

Fri. Jan. 24, 1902

Mr. Martin Brabham, age 40, died Monday at his home near Clayton. About five years ago he married Miss Willie Smith, who survives him, and two children, a boy and a girl.

Mr. Pete (P. E.) Florence, age 45, was accidently killed at Cowikee (Barbour Co.) when his shot gun discharged while he was mounting a horse. Survivors are his wife, four daus. and one son. Burial at Spring Hill in Barbour County.

Fri. Feb. 7, 1902

Mrs. J. A. Green died at her home near Clayton last Tuesday. She is survived by her husband and several children.

Fri. Feb. 14, 1902

Mrs. Eliza Nix died at her home near Clayton last Thursday. She had lived to a ripe old age. Burial at Pleasant Plains.

Fri. Feb. 28, 1902

Mr. A. T. Borders died in Ozark. He was the son of Mr. A. S. Borders. The deceased was born in Clayton in 1868. He married Miss Pauline Carmicheal, who with one son survives him.

Mr. O. J. Anglin, age 81, died at his home in Union Springs on Friday.

Mrs. Narcissa Petty, the mother of Messrs. Ed and Dick Petty, who were once citizens of Clayton, died at her home near Arkadelphia, Ark., last Saturday.

Fri. Mar. 7, 1902

Mr. Gideon Nix died at his home north of town Sunday of consumption. His wife and several children survive him.

Mrs. S. H. Dent of Eufaula died in an infirmary at Montgomery on Thursday. She was the dau. of the late Dr. Young. Her husband and children survive her.

Mrs. Jane McCraney, age 85, died at the home of Mr. William McEachern on Feb. 24th, 1902. She was born Mar. 12, 1816 in South Carolina.

Fri. Mar. 14, 1902

Mrs. Asa Adams died at her home near Texasville in Barbour County on Tuesday.

Fri. Apr. 11, 1902

The death of N. W. (Wes) Vinson occurred on Monday. He came here when quite a youth. He was a Confederate War veteran. He leaves his wife and two children.

Mr. J. B. Reynolds died at his home in Clio on Wednesday from heart failure. He leaves a family

The Clayton Record
1902

Fri. Apr. 18, 1902
    Mr. John Martin, an elderly citizen, died at his home near Clayton on Saturday. Burial at Pleasant View.

Fri. May 2, 1902
    Mr. S. F. Singleton died at his home last Wednesday. He was a Confederate Veteran. Burial at Pleasant Grove Baptist Church.

Fri. May 9, 1902
    Mr. T. C. Norton, an elderly citizen, died at his home near Clayton on Sunday. He is survived by an aged sister and two children. Burial at Miller's church.

    Mr. T. C. Helms, an elderly citizen, died at his home at Louisville, Ala., last Friday.

Fri. May 30, 1902
    Mr. T. L. Smart, formerly of Barbour County, died at his home in Terrill, Texas recently. He was the father of Mrs. J. T. Grubbs at Louisville, Ala., and an uncle of Dr. W. A. Smart of Clayton.

    Mrs. R. N. Pitts, the only dau. of Maj. W. W. Screws, of Montgomery, and niece of Mrs. J. N. Williams, died at her home in Montgomery last Monday. Survivors are her husband and three little children, two boys and a girl.

Fri. June 13, 1902
    Mr. William Wood, age 94, died at his home in Beat 10 on Monday. He was one of the first settlers of the county.

Fri. June 20, 1902
    Mr. John Taylor died at Midway on last Thursday.

Fri. June 27, 1902
    Mr. F. McKay died suddenly at his home in Louisville, Ala., on Wednesday. Survivors are his wife and several children. Burial at Pea River Cemetery.

Fri. July 4, 1902
    Mrs. H. C. Glenn died June 18th at her home in Clayton. She was Miss Lucy Curtis Cotton, dau. of Rev. James L. Cotton, D. D. of The M. E. Church, South. Her mother was Lucy Ann Curtis. Mrs. Glenn was born at Cahaba, Ala. 18 Nov. 1858. Her only surviving sister is Mrs. Martha Cotton Banks of Opelika, Ala. On Apr. 18, 1878 she married Mr. Henry Clarence Glenn at Hurtsboro, Ala. She was the mother of seven children, six of whom and her husband survive her.

Fri. July 18, 1902
    Mr. W. Z. Graves, age 33, died at his home in Girard, (Ala.) yesterday. Survivors are his wife and three children, Lottie, age 11 years, Lucy, 8 years old and Parish, a boy, age 6; besides one sister in Clayton.-Columbus (Ga.) Enquirer-Sun.

    The subject of the above sketch lived for a number of years in Clayton.

The Clayton Record
1902

Mrs. Jasper Adkinson died at Clio on Tuesday. Burial at Louisville, Ala.

Fri. Sept. 5, 1902
Mr. John C. Williams died last Sunday. When a mere lad he entered the Confederacy and served the entire four years.

Fri. Sept. 19, 1902
Mrs. Elizabeth Clarke Cowan died Sept. 9th. She was the dau. of James Clarke and was born in Columbus, Ga. on Sept. 19, 1833. Her father moved to Clayton when she was 3 years old and she has lived here since that time. She married in 1854 to William R. Cowan who died long ago. She is survived by her dau., Mrs. W. A. Bishop, one sister and several grand children.

Fri. Oct. 3, 1902
Earnest Laseter died at his home near Clayton yesterday of typhoid fever. He leaves a family.

Fri. Nov. 7, 1902
Mrs. B. H. Sutton, an aged citizen, died at her home near Elamville, (Ala.) on Friday.

Fri. Dec. 5, 1902
Mr. David Edward Nix, age 81, died last Saturday. He was born in Cobb County, Ga., and moved to Ala. in 1855. Burial in Clayton.

Mr. N. K. Stephens, age 62, died at his home at Louisville, Ala. Burial at Louisville.

Eufaula Times & News
1903

Thurs. Jan. 8, 1903
Mr. Joe Seaborn, formerly of Barbour County, died at his home at Webb Station in Henry Co., Ala., on the 28th of Dec. Survivors are his wife (Note: Clayton paper states she is the dau. of Mr. Allen Adams of Lodi in Barbour Co.) and four children. Mr. Seaborn was the son of the late William Seaborn.

Mr. Eugene Gibbons, age about 35, formerly of Eufaula, died at his home in Slocum, Geneva Co., Ala., of consumption this week. Survivors are his wife and five children, his mother and one brother.

Thurs. Jan. 22, 1903
Mr. Merrill A. Sheehan, age 58 died at his home in Atlanta this morning of heart failure. Survivors are his wife and two sons in Alabama and a dau., Mrs. Ada Langston of Atlanta. He has three brothers in Eufaula, Mr. D. T. Sheehan, Mr. E. S. Sheehan and R. E. Sheehan.

Thurs. Jan. 29, 1903
Capt. W. L. (William Littleberry) Burnett, age 62, died at his home in Eufaula yesterday. He had a short time ago moved here from his plantation in Quitman Co., Ga. He was born in Clay Co.,

Eufaula Times & News
1903

Georgia on 6 Oct. 1841, and was the son of Dr. Swan Pritchard Burnett and Mrs. Martha Harden Burnett. He married Miss Augusta Gorden of St. Catherine's Canada, on Dec. 15, 1880.

Mr. William C. Tanton died yesterday at his home in Eufaula. He had been a resident here only five months. He was born at Wartha, Ga., where he lived the greater part of his life. Survivors are his wife and five children. Burial in Eufaula.

Mrs. J. N. Lewis, formerly of Eufaula, died Jan. 15th in her 70th year of age, at Ensley, Ala. Survivors are her dau., Mrs. Will Johnson and one brother, Mr. John Veal of Athens, Ga., one sister, Mrs. Lizzie Federick of Jacksonville, Fla.

Thurs. Feb. 5, 1903

Mrs. Leonard Barron, living near Ozark, died suddenly Saturday. Mr. and Mrs. Barron moved from Clayton about two years ago.

Dr. C. C. Robinson received a telegram Friday announcing the death of his brother-in-law, Dr. S. A. Goodwin who died in New York. He is a brother to the late Dr. A. Goodwin and brother-in-law of Mrs. O. H. Peacock of Eufaula. He was born and reared in Harris Co., Ga., and moved to New York to practice medicine.

Mr. William M. Petry, age 62, died at his home in Eufaula Friday of heart failure. He was born in Bavaria in 1840 and came to Eufaula from Apalachicola, Fla. about 1866. His wife preceded him in death some years ago, was Miss Mollie Hyatt. Survivors are their children, Messrs. Louis Petry of White Plains, N. Y., Clifford A. Petry of Andalusia, (Ala.), William M. Petry and Frank Petry of Eufaula, and Mrs. Hamp Stewart, Miss Lottie Petry of Eufaula, and a sister, Miss Mina Petry.

Tuscaloosa, Ala., Feb. 5.-Mrs. Louise Ware of Tuscaloosa died at her home here. She was born Mar. 1819 near Northport, (Ala.). She is survived by a dau., Miss Lou Ware, two sisters who are living in Texas and two brothers, Col. I. J. Lee of Ensley (Ala.) and Frank Lee. Burial at Northport Cemetery.

Mrs. J. W. Rollins, second wife of Prof. Rollins, died suddenly at Kincey in Henry Co., last Tuesday. She was a dau. of Mr. Giles Richards. Burial at County Line.

Thurs. Feb. 26, 1903

Mrs. Susan Samantha Elizabeth Reeder died at her home near Reeder's Mill Dec. 28th, 1902, and was buried at Old Bethel Church near Blue Springs in Barbour Co. She was the dau. of Mr. and Mrs. John F. McGlaun, and was born Oct. 10, 1852 near Clopton in Dale Co. She married Mar. 2, 1871 to Mr. W. N. Reeder of Barbour Co. and has lived at Reeder's Mill since that time. Survivors are her husband and nine children, seven boys and two girls.

Mr. L. P. Mallory died at his home in New Haven, Conn., on Saturday of a stroke of paralysis. His wife is a sister of Mr. N. M. Bray of Eufaula.

Eufaula Times & News
1903

Thurs. Mar. 5, 1903
   Hon. H. B. Tompkins died at his home in Atlanta yesterday. He was born and reared at Clayton, Ala. (Note: From the Clayton Record - Mar. 6, 1903 - He was married twice. By his first wife there were three daus., and by the second wife there were two sons, Henry and Lawrence Tompkins. His sister, Mrs. Walter S. White of Sheffield, survives him.).

Thurs. Mar. 12, 1903
   Died near Hagler's Mill in Barbour Co. on Friday, Mrs. Adam Tyler, age about 24. Survivors are her husband and three children.

Thurs. Mar. 19, 1903
   Mr. Eli Stevens, formerly of Eufaula, but now Montgomery County, died Friday. Survivors are his wife and children. Burial near Eufaula at the family burying grounds.

   The death of Mr. Andrew Dowling, living in the White Oak neighborhood, occurred today. Burial at White Oak Chapel.

   Col. E. Troupe Randall died suddenly at his home in Union Springs Saturday of heart failure.

   Mrs. Tom Allday, formerly of Eufaula, died at her home in Dothan on Monday. Survivors are two children. She was a sister of Mrs. Dan Sheehan. Burial in Eufaula.

Thurs. Mar. 26, 1903
   Mr. John Tillman, age about 90, died on the 15th inst., and was buried at New Prospect. He had been a citizen of Henry County for 50 years.

   Mrs. Irene Carter, age 28, of Terrell, Texas, died recently. She was formerly Miss Irene Harwell of Barbour County and was a sister to Mrs. O. S. Wells. Survivors are her husband and one child six years of age.

Thurs. Apr. 2, 1903
   Mr. Jeff Koonce of Columbia, Ala., committed suicide yesterday by shooting himself.

   Died at Baker Hill in Barbour Co. on Wednesday, Mr. Carlton Thomas. Survivors are his wife and two children. Burial at Clayton Cemetery.

Thurs. May 7, 1903
   Mr. John C. McEachern, age 66, died at his home in Eufaula on Friday. Survivors are his wife and two children, Mr. M. McEachern and Mrs. Dr. Davie of Dothan. Burial in Eufaula.

   Mrs. R. L. Hobdy died this morning at her home in Union Springs. She was formerly Miss Mary Bufford and spent her early life in Eufaula. She was the dau. of Judge Jefferson Bufford. She was married near Tuskegee to Mr. Hobdy in 1868 (? print bad). Survivors are her husband and five children, Messrs. Robert and Bufford Hobdy and Misses Anne, Marie and Jenny Hobdy. She is a relative of Mr. R. Q. Edmonson's family and the late

Eufaula Times & News
1903

Mr. William Petry's family of Eufaula. Burial in Eufaula.

The funeral of Rev. Azor Van Hoose took place yesterday in Eufaula. His remains were followed to its last resting place by relatives and friends.

Mr. W. B. Lee, living on the Farrior farm near Clayton, was killed Friday when the mule he was driving was frightened at a bicycle. He leaves a wife and six young children.

Thurs. May 14, 1903
Tuscaloosa, Ala., May 7.-Mrs. Mary Thornton Bostick died Mar. 25th in Chefoo, China. She was formerly Miss Mary Thornton and graduated at the Alabama Central Female College of this city. She was a foreign missionary to China in 1890 and in 1891 she married Rev. George P. Bostick, also a missionary. She is survived by her husband and four children and one step-child.

Thurs. May 21, 1903
Mr. W. B. McLendon, age 90, of Georgetown, Ga., died last night.

Mr. John W. Simmons, living near Blue Springs in Barbour County, died at his home Saturday.

Thurs. June 4, 1903
Mr. James H. Evans died at his home in Eufaula yesterday of Bright's disease. He was born in Orangeburg Dist., S. C., on Feb. 8, 1835, married in Eufaula Feb. 7, 1859 to Miss Angeline Patterson, dau. of T. D. Patterson. The dec'd lost an arm in the Civil War. Survivors are his wife and five daus., Mrs. J. W. Stacey of Dallas, Tex., Mrs. Sallie McLendon of Fort Gaines, Ga., Mrs. Charles Cory of Dallas, Tex., Mrs. J. W. Talley of Clarksville, Tenn., and Mrs. A. B. Belcher of Bainbridge, Ga. Burial at Fairview Cemetery in Eufaula.

Thurs. June 11, 1903
Judge J. E. Cobb, of Tuskegee, (Ala.) died last Tuesday at East Las Vegas, N. M., where he had gone for his health. Burial at Tuskegee.

Mr. Robert B. Lee died at his home between Lodi and Baker Hill in Barbour County on Sunday. He was born in South Carolina on Dec. 11, 1822. He married Miss Mary Parmer Dec. 15, 1842. There were four children of this union, Mrs. Jim Creel of Blufton, Ga., Mrs. Joe Searcy of White Pond in Barbour County, Mrs. George Zorn of Lodi and Mr. Needham Lee of White Pond. He married second to Miss Ida Griffin on Sept. 27, 1887 and from this union there were two daus. and a son, Jeffie, Edna and Robert Lee. Burial with Masonic honors at Pond Bethel in Barbour County.

Thurs. June 25, 1903
White Oak, (Barbour Co.) Ala., June 22.- Mr. H. F. Tiller died at his home on Feb. 19, 1903.

Mrs. J. Seaborn Espy died at the home of her son, Mr. G. B. Espy near Bush in Barbour County last Sunday. Burial at County Line Church.

Eufaula Times & News
1903

Mrs. J. B. Farrior died at her home in Clayton on Thursday. Burial in Clayton.

Mrs. David Nix, relict of the late Mr. Nix who died at his home in Clayton several months ago, died at her home recently.

Mrs. Martha F. Henry died at Columbus, Ga. this morning. She was the dau. of the late John Q. Evans of Villula, Ala., and married Mr. Beverly M. Henry. She was one time a resident of Russell County. She leaves seven children and three brothers, one of whom is Judge A. A. Evans of Clayton.

Thurs. July 2, 1903

Atlanta, June 22.-Dr. S. A. Taylor took his life by shooting himself at his home near East Point on Saturday. Survivors are his wife and six children.

Thurs. July 9, 1903

Mrs. Floyd, age about 80, wife of Mr. Page Floyd, died at her home ten miles southeast of Clayton on Thursday. Survivors are her husband and several grown children.

Judge H. M. Beach died at his home in Columbia, Ala., on Wednesday.

Postmaster A. J. Locke received notice of the death of his sister, Mrs. Mary Montgomery, age 84, who died at her home in in Lorma, Texas, recently.

Mrs. Willie S. Mitchell, wife of Dr. Thomas S. Mitchell, died at her home yesterday in Pensacola, Fla. She was born in Muscogee Co., Ga., Apr. 1838 and was married Mar. 4, 1856. She was the mother of Dr. James W. Mitchell of Atlanta, Mrs. W. A. Hill of Georgetown, Ga., Mrs. Stella Matthews, Mrs. Chris Thiesen and Drs. E. S. and C. Ray Mitchell of this city. Burial at Columbus, Ga., in Lynwood Cemetery beside her two sons, Dr. T. Rudledge Mitchell and William Cooper Mitchell, and her niece, Mrs. Lizzie West.-Pensacola Journal.

Mr. W. T. Heigler who moved from near Blue Springs in Barbour Co., to Slocomb in Geneva Co., died Sunday. Ozark Star.

Mr. Jason G. Guice died at his home in Eufaula last night. He was born in Talbot Co., Ga. on Nov. 19, 1840 and was reared to boyhood in Columbus, Ga., was educated in Barbour Co. where his parents moved when he was ten years old. He lost an arm as the result of the Civil War. He married July 1, 1873 to Miss Stella Drewry, dau. of Dr. J. W. Drewry. His mother is Mrs. L. C. Guice, his brothers and sisters are Mrs. T. L. Crew of Mt. Andrew, Ala., Mrs. W. H. Jenkins of Louisville, Ala., Mrs. W. A. L. Haynie of Marion, Ala., Mrs. H. L. Brannon and Miss Cordie Guice, Messers. John G. and T. J. Guice of Evergreen, Ala., B. L. Guice of Birmingham and E. Tandy and Ike F. Guice of this city.

Thurs. July 23, 1903

Newman, Ga., July 18.-Rev. James H. Hall, D. D., pastor of

Eufaula Times & News
1903

the Central Baptist Church of this city, died this morning. Survivors are his wife and several children, among whom is Hon. Hewlett A. Hall.

Mrs. T. H. Ferrell, age 84, died at the home of her dau., Mrs. W. T. Moore, seven miles from Georgetown, Ga., this morning. Burial at Pataula Cemetery in Quitman County, Georgia.

Mrs. Annie E. Caffee, wife of Judge Caffee of Alabama, died in Ashville, N. C. yesterday. She had been visiting many health places for lung trouble, but could get no relief.

S. L. Bradley, a respected and prominent citizen of Mt. Andrew, (Barbour Co.) died Wednesday.-<u>Clayton</u> <u>Record</u>.

Mr. William Colbert, age 65, died at his home yesterday. He was an old soldier and had lived in Eufaula nearly all his life. Survivors are two sons, Charles and Avery Colbert.

Thurs. July 30
The sad intelligence was received from Montgomery last night that Mrs. Lucy Hart, wife of the late B. Frank Hart had died. Mrs. Hart is the dau. of Maj. H. W. B. Price, now of Atlanta, Ga., and mother of Mr. Beall Hart and Charles Hart and sister of Mrs. C. C. Skillman, of Eufaula. Besides her sons, she leaves a dau., Mrs. E. T. Naftel of Montgomery and a son, B. Frank Hart of Lumpkin, Ga. Burial from the Episcopal Church to Fairview Cemetery in Eufau

Thurs. Aug. 6, 1903
The remains of W. N. Reeves, Jr., age about 25, arrived from Birmingham where he had been living for about a year. Survivors are his wife and two children, Florine and Lillian Reeves.

Thurs. Aug. 13, 1903
Mrs. H. C. Alexander, age 84, died in Mobile yesterday. She was the mother of Rev. I. O. Adams of Eufaula.

The remains of Mrs. Van Hoose arrived here from Gainesville, Ga. for burial. Her remains were accompanied by Dr. Battle of Macon and her son, Rev. Asa Van Hoose and her daughter.

Thurs. Aug. 27, 1903
Mrs. Nancy Stephens, age 89, relict of the late D. D. Stephens died at her home in Louisville, Ala., on Tuesday. She had been a resident of Barbour County over 70 years.

Mrs. Elizabeth Folsom, age about 90, was buried in Fairview in Eufaula this morning. She was the mother of Mrs. Amanda Carroll and Mrs. Martha Sawyer and Messrs. James and Wash Folsom, all of Eufaula.

Thurs. Sept. 3, 1903
Mrs. B. B. James, age 41, died at her home in Eufaula Friday with typhoid fever. She was a dau. of Mr. Richard Turner of Barr's Mill in Pike Co., Ala. Survivors are her husband and five children Burial at Barr's Mill.

Thurs. Sept. 10, 1903

Eufaula Times & News
1903

The remains of Mrs. Elizabeth Taylor, wife of James Taylor, who died at her home near Zeigler (Barbour Co.) on Friday were buried at Mt. Zion. Survivors are her husband and children.

Mrs. N. A. Oppert, age 59, died last Tuesday at her home near Smyrna Church, four miles from Dothan. She was born and reared in Barbour County at Blue Springs.

Thurs. Sept 17, 1903
Mr. John T. Britt, age about 55, a merchant of Clayton, died at his home suddenly yesterday of an acute indigestion. He leaves a mother, Mrs. Weaver, and a brother, M. W. Britt of Midway, also a wife and four children, Mrs. Robert Milligan at Geneva, Miss Mabelle and Masters Wade and John Britt.

Mr. W. S. English, an old resident of Hawkinsville in Barbour Co., died at his home Sunday. He was found dead by his son.

Mrs. John F. Lunsford, living about nine miles south of Eufaula, died Friday of heart dropsy. Burial at White Oak.

Mrs. Luna Rau, formerly of Eufaula, died suddenly at her home in Macon, Ga., last night. She was the wife of Ed J. Rau, who was an engineer on the Central R. R.

Mr. John W. Beasley, age about 65, died at his home near Pratt's Station (Barbour Co.) on Saturday. He was the son of the old pioneer citizen, Mr. William Beasley, deceased.

Thurs. Sept. 24, 1903
Mrs. John Cooper died at her home on Dale Road in Eufaula Sunday. Survivors are her husband and five children. Burial at Rocky Mount in Barbour County.

J. W. Barnes died yesterday at his home on Dale Road in Eufaula. Survivors are his wife and four children. Burial at White Oak Cemetery.

Thurs. Oct. 22, 1903
Mrs. W. J. Miles died yesterday at her home near Zeigler in Barbour County. She leaves a family . Burial at Mt. Zion.

Ex-Governor H. L. Mitchell died at his home in Tampa, Fla., on Saturday. He was a native of Jefferson County, Ala., and many years ago located in Florida. He served as governor of the state and a member of the supreme court.

Mr. Noah S. Laney of Fort Worth, Texas died recently. He was an old acquaintance of Mr. L. E. Irby of Eufaula and was a visitor here this summer.

Thurs. Oct. 29, 1903
Yesterday at the Jewish Temple the funeral services of Mrs. Minna Stern were conducted by Rabbi Messing from Montgomery. Burial in Fairview Cemetery in Eufaula. She was born in Hamburg, Germany, Jan. 23rd, 1825, came to New York when she was 18 years of age, where at twenty she married Mr. David Gabriel Stern who died in Eufaula Jan. 1881. They settled in Pike County,

Eufaula Times & News
1903

Georgia, before the war and came to Eufaula 35 years ago. She reared ten children to be grown, eight of whom survive her. They are Madames M. Bear, J. Friedman, J. Stern, J. K. Sams and H. Bloom, Mr. Silas Stern, York and Leigman Stern of Woodville, Miss.

Dr. J. T. Battle, formerly of Hawkinsville in Barbour Co., died with heart failure at his home in Montgomery. Survivors are his wife and daughter. Burial in Montgomery.

Thurs. Nov. 5, 1903

Mr. James Hinson, age 36, of Clayton, died at his home Saturday with a stroke of paralysis. Survivors are his wife and four children. Burial in the Masonic Cemetery at Clayton.

Mrs. Louis Crane, formerly a resident of Springhill in Barbour Co., died at her home in Ensley, Ala., a few days ago. Burial at Springhill.

Mrs. N. W. Roberts of Eufaula received a telegram yesterday from New Jersey announcing the death of her sister-in-law, Mrs. J. W. Young. She was also sister-in-law of Col. E. B. Young and Mrs. George Dent of this place.

Thurs. Nov. 26, 1903

Mr. Hughey McLean, an aged citizen of Barbour County, died Friday from the effects of a fall. Burial at White Pond.

Mrs. S. E. Reeves, of Johnston, Pa., died yesterday. She was the mother of Messrs. J. W. and W. E. Reeves of the Gas and Electric Company in Eufaula.

Mr. E. Lingo, age about 70, died yesterday at his home at Texasville in Barbour Co., with paralysis. He had lived in Henry and Barbour Counties all his life. Burial at Clopton.

Mr. Charles A. Stevens, age 54, died last Sunday at his home in Eufaula with a stroke of paralysis. He was born in Conn. and was an architect and has built many houses in Eufaula. Survivors are four children, Mrs. Annie Lou Dick, Bob, Edward and Charlie Stevens and two sisters, Mrs. Hattie Brady of Columbus and Miss Nellie Stevens of Eufaula, and one brother, Mr. Frank Stevens of Selma. His wife preceded him to the grave about ten years ago. Burial in Eufaula.

Thurs. Dec. 3, 1903

Dr. John A. Hickman, age 76, died at his home in Cynthia, Ky., Friday. His wife was reared in Eufaula and is a sister of Miss Cornelia Robinson, Mrs. O. H. Peacock and Mr. C. C. Robinson. His second wife was Miss Emma Sanford, of Alabama.

Mr. William T. Simpson died at the home of his son, Mr. W. T. Simpson, Jr., at Florence. The dec'd. was born in Macon, Ga., Dec. 24, 1825. At an early age he moved to Eufaula where he spent most of his life. He was married to Miss Mary Daniels, who survives him, and five children, Mrs. L. Y. Dean of Eufaula, Mrs. Ed Cargill of Columbus, Ga., Mrs. William Keesee of Clarks-

Eufaula Times & News
1903

dale, Tenn., Dr. Lee Simpson of Omaha and W. T. Simpson, Jr., of Florence. Burial in Eufaula.

Thurs. Dec. 10, 1903
    Col. R. D. Locke died in Macon, Ga. this morning. He was a brother of Mr. A. J. Locke of Eufaula. Burial at Union Springs.

    Mr. E. H. Roberts of Eufaula died last night at Brewton while visiting. He was married three years ago to Miss Mary Lou McKenzie of Eufaula. Survivors are his wife and one child and five brothers. Burial in Eufaula.

Thurs. Dec. 17, 1903
    Mrs. S. D. White, who at one time lived in Eufaula, died at her home in LaGrange, Ga., Saturday.

Thurs. Dec. 31, 1903
    Mr. Nathan Marks Bray, age 74, died at his home in Eufaula last night. He was born in Fairhaven, Conn., Aug. 9th, 1829. He came to Macon, Ga. in 1853 and to Eufaula in 1857. He married June 2, 1859 to Miss Kate E. Mills. Survivors are his wife and two daughters in the city and a son in St. Louis. Burial in Eufaula.

The Clayton Record
1903

Fri. Jan. 2, 1903
    Mr. E. P. Smith died at his home near Clayton last Monday from a stroke of paralysis.

Fri. Mar. 20, 1903
    Mrs. Andrew Dowling died last Tuesday from gun wounds received when an intruder invaded the home and shot her. She leaves a husband and children.

Fri. Mar. 27, 1903
    Mrs. J. J. Bradley died at her home at Mt. Andrew last Thursday of paralysis.

    Mr. J. C. Thomas, Jr., died at his home at Baker Hill in Barbour County last Thursday of pneumonia. He was the son of Mr. and Mrs. Carter Thomas. He is survivied by his wife and two small children. Burial at Clayton.

Fri. Apr. 24, 1903
    Mr. Gilbert McCall, age 82, died Apr. 8, 1903. He was born near Fogetteville (?) in Cumberland County, N. C., and when quite young came to Alabama.

Fri. June 19, 1903
    Mrs. David Nix died at the home of her son, Mr. Frank Snead, on Saturday. Burial in the family cemetery.

Fri. Nov. 6, 1903
    Mrs. Polly Broxton, wife of Mr. I. B. Broxton of near Louisville, died a few days ago. Burial at Bethlehem Church.

Fri. Nov. 27, 1903

The Clayton Record
1903

Mr. Hugh McLean, age 73, died at his home Thursday in Beat Ten in Barbour County. He was a pioneer citizen of Barbour County. Burial at Pond Bethel Cemetery. He was born in Scotland, emigrated early in life to the U. S. and spent more than 40 years in Barbour Co. Survivors are his wife and eight children.

Fri. Dec. 11, 1903
Mrs. Charlotte Isabelle Hooper of Opelika, Ala., widow of George W. Hooper, died yesterday at the home of her sister, Mrs. N. L. Laney. She was the dau. of Col. Haynes and Mary Fleming Waddell of Hillsboro, N. C. She was a sister of the late James F. Waddell of Russell Co., Ala., and Rev. deB. Waddell of Meridian, Miss., and Mrs. N. L. Laney of this city. She is survived by three children, Mrs. Belle H. Collier of Birmingham, Mrs. Rinaldo Williams of Atlanta, Mr. George B. Hooper of Birmingham and an adopted child, Mrs. A. A. Evans of Clayton, Ala.-Columbus (Ga.) Enquirer Sun.

Eufaula Times & News
1904

Thurs. Jan. 14, 1904
Rev. Angus Dowling, age 70, son of Noel and Sarah D. (nee McDonald) Dowling, died at his home in Daleville, (Ala.). He was the father of Mr. H. B. Dowling of Eufaula. Burial near Ozark.

Thurs. Jan. 21, 1904
Mrs. Lizzie West, age about 40, wife of W. M. West, died on the 13th inst. of typhoid pneumonia. She was before her marriage Miss Lizzie Hawkins, dau. of T. A. J. Hawkins of Texasville and sister of Prof. A. N. Hawkins of Ozark, Mrs. Jessie Adams of Spio, (Barbour Co.) Mrs. John Middlebrooks of Elamville in Barbour Co. She leaves several children, two of whom are grown, a son, Prof. Cornelius West of Alto, Texas and a dau. Miss Almar West. Burial at Pond Bethel.

Thurs. Jan. 28, 1904
W. H. Thomas, age 61, died at his home in Clayton on Friday. Burial at Clayton.

Thurs. Feb. 4, 1904
Mrs. R. G. Smith died at her home in Montgomery last night. She lived in Eufaula when Mr. Smith was employed by the R. R. Burial at Old Presbyterian Church four miles below Louisville in Barbour County.

Thurs. Feb. 18, 1904
Mrs. James Horn age about 25, died at her home at Louisville on Friday. She was Miss Ila Hobdy, the dau. of Mr. John Hobdy, who moved to Texas years ago and died there, leaving a large family of children. She had been married less than two years. Mrs. M. H. Parish of Clayton and Mrs. Dr. Ellis of Dothan are her sisters.

Mrs. J. F. McGilvary, who recently moved from near Mount

Eufaula Times & News
1904

Pleasant Church to Enterprise, Ala., died after a short illness and was buried in Enterprise on the 5th Jan. 1904. Survivors are her husband and two children, her mother, sister and brothers.

Thurs. Feb. 25, 1904

Washington, D. C., Feb. 22.-Mrs. B. H. Hill, Sr., of Atlanta, died at the home of her dau., Mrs. Thompson. Her sons, C. D. and B. H. Hill, Jr., were with her. Burial in Atlanta.

Mrs. W. L. Richardson, age 65, died at her home in Eufaula yesterday. Survivors are her husband and five children. Burial in Eufaula.

Thurs. Mar. 3, 1904

Mrs. Louise M. Dickerson, age four score, died at the home of her son, Alfred Dickerson in Eufaula this morning.

Thurs. Mar. 17, 1904

Mr. W. E. Gay, age 66, died at his home in Quitman Co., Ga., yesterday.

Thurs. Apr. 7, 1904

Rev. T. F. Mangum died this morning. He had been a minister for fifty years. Survivors are his wife, five sons and one dau. His sons are T. F. Mangum, Jr., of Cuba, Tom Mangum of Tallahassee, Ala., Robert Mangum of Selma, W. W. Mangum of Eufaula and Miss Helen Mangum. Burial at Selma.

Mr. Hugo Schloss left today for Cincinnati, Ohio to attend the funeral of Mrs. Schloss' father, Mr. Nathan Menderson.

Thurs. Apr. 14, 1904

Mr. Arthur Peach, age 38, died of consumption at the home of his brother, Mr. George W. Peach, Esqr., last Thursday in Clayton. He was a son of John H. Peach, living at Perote in Bullock County, Ala. His wife, the former Miss Lila Andrews died about a year ago leaving a baby boy, who is now living with his sister, Mrs. Robert Petty. Burial at Union Springs.

Thurs. Apr. 21, 1904

Mrs. Hannah Dasinger, age 84, died at her home at Cox's Mill in Barbour County last Tuesday. She was the mother of Thomas and George Dasinger and Mrs. Daniel Grissitt, who moved to Texas a few years ago.

Thurs. Apr. 28, 1904

Mrs. Mary Scott, wife of Windfield Scott of Lawrenceville, Ala., died Mar. 30th. She was born 9 Mar. 1850 and was married Dec. 1875. Survivors are her husband, two sons, Crawford and George Scott and two daus., Mrs. Dora Hudspeth of Clopton, Ala., and Miss Lucy Scott.

Mr. J. W. Sparrow received a message that his only son, William Abbey Sparrow had died at his home in Birmingham. He was about 40 years old.

Thurs. May 5, 1904

Mrs. M. F. Smith died at her home in East Burnsteadt, Ky.,

Eufaula Times & News
1904

on April 26th. Survivors are her aged father, her husband, three children. Her father is Mr. W. J. C. Harrell, one brother, Judge J. M. Harrell and two sisters, Mrs. G. B. Gay and Mrs. S. H. Nesbitt of Hatchers Station, Ga. Burial at Hatchers Station at the old family burying ground.

Thurs. May 12, 1904
Mr. V. D. Tharp, age 80, died last night at the home of Dr. S. G. Robertson in Eufaula. He had lived in Eufaula for 33 years, coming here from Columbus. His wife survives him.

Mrs. Margaret Belcher, wife of J. T. Belcher, living near Floyd City (Barbour Co.) died last Sunday.

Thurs. June 9, 1904
Mrs. Ed M. Johnson, wife of the editor of the Geneva (Ala.) Reaper, formerly of Eufaula, died in Geneva recently.

Mrs. Robert (R. E. L.) Martin, age about 45, died at the home of Mr. John Kendall in Eufaula last Saturday of consumption. She had been living in Memphis until a few months ago. Survivors are her husband and three children. Burial in Eufaula.

Thurs. June 16, 1904
George Warr, age about 50, died with cancer of the eye at his home near Lindsey last Friday. Survivors are his wife, a son and four daughters. Burial at Prospect Cemetery.

R. Y. Caniell died at Hill's Infirmary at Montgomery and his remains were shipped to his home at Geneva (Ala.). Mrs. Britt and Mrs. Simonton, his sisters-in-law left Wednesday to attend the burial services.

Mrs. Elizabeth Warr, age 70, widow of the late Mr. Ezekiel Warr and mother of Aaron and Sam Price and step--mother of G. W. Warr who died recently of cancer, was found dead in her bed Wednesday. Burial at Prospect Church near where she lived.

Thurs. June 30, 1904
Mrs. John W. Clark, widow of the late Capt. Clark, died at Lake City, Fla., recently. The remains will be brought to Eufaula today for burial. Mr. C. Locke received the telegram announcing the death of his mother.

Thurs. July 7, 1904
Dallas Holmes died Monday and was buried at County Line. He leaves a wife and several small children.

Thurs. July 15, 1904
James M. Buford died on the 10th of May in Los Angeles, Calf. He formerly lived in Eufaula. His death was the result of a fall from a street car.

Thurs. Aug. 4, 1904
Mrs. Richmond Fuquay, of near Prospect Church, died suddenly on Thursday. Survivors are her husband and two children. Burial at Antioch.

Eufaula Times & News
1904

Thurs. Aug. 11, 1904

Mr. M. H. Edwards died at his home near Batesville last night. He moved to Barbour County from Atlanta six or eight years ago. Burial in Atlanta beside his wife and other members of his family.

Mrs. J. R. Sanders, age 70, died at the home of her dau., Mrs. L. Peak in Eufaula of heart disease yesterday. Survivors are her two children, Mr. Pres. Sanders who is on the police force at Montgomery, and Mrs. Peak in Eufaula. Burial at the old Shorter Cemetery ten miles north of town.

On Tuesday morning the sad intelligence was received in the city that Mrs. Nancy Bishop, age 86, mother of Mrs. M. S. Passmore, had died Monday at Spring Hill (Barbour Co.). She was the mother of four sons and three daughters.

Thurs. Aug. 18, 1904

Mrs. Eliza Gilchrist died yesterday at her home at White Oak. She leaves a number of children, all grown and several grand-children.

Hon. Harry J. Gillam died suddenly at Alexander City, Ala., on Friday at the home of his dau., Mrs. J. O. Thomas. Mr. Gillam resided at Wetumpka, Ala., and the funeral took place there.

Thurs. Aug. 25, 1904

Mr. A. J. Locke, age 70, died at his home in Eufaula yesterday.

Mrs. W. W. Mangum, age 36, died at the home of Capt. B. B. McKenzie in Eufaula on Friday. Survivors are her husband, Dr. W. W. Mangum and two children, Annie Will and Elizabeth, a father, mother and several sisters and brothers. Mr. B. B. McKenzie is the father of Mrs. Mangum.

Mrs. Elizabeth Vining, age 72, died yesterday in Eufaula. She leaves ten grand-children, seven daus. and three sons, all were at her bedside except one son, Bob Vining, who was in Fla.

Sept. 1, 1904

Mrs. Rebecca Winslett, age 79, died at the home of her son, Joe Winslett near Hatchers Station, (Ga.) yesterday from injuries she received by a fall several days age. She had lived in Quitman County, (Ga.) for 50 years and was an Ely before her marriage. Burial at Mt. Zion near Hatchers.

Thurs. Sept. 29, 1904

Mr. Patrick O'Byrne, age four score and five years, died at his home in Eufaula this morning. Survivors are his wife and small son. Burial at Fairview from the Catholic Church.

Mrs. J. W. Beauchamp, wife of John W. Beauchamp, died at her home two miles south of Hatchers Station last night.

Thurs. Oct. 10, 1904

C. S. J. Buchanan died in his pasture near his home at Springvale on Wednesday. He was one of the oldest citizens of the vicinity and had been justice of the peace at Springvale, (Ga.) for 38 years.

Eufaula Times & News
1904

Thurs. Oct. 27, 1904

Mr. Ed B. McCrary, an old citizen of Eufaula, died at the home of E. Z. Martin in Birmingham recently. Survivors are his wife and three children, Miss Nell McCrary, Mrs. Edgar Z. Martin and Mr. E. D. McCrary.

Mr. F. J. Allday, age 72, died at the home of his son-in-law, C. B. Fisher on the Dale Road in Eufaula. Survivors are one son and three daughters. Due to the family lot at Fairview being full, burial will take place at the Georgetown, (Ga.) Cemetery.

Mrs. Brazzell, the aged mother of Robert Brazzell, died Friday at her home in Eufaula. Burial at Christian Grove Church.

Thurs. Nov. 3, 1904

Mrs. John H. Poston, age 54, died in her sleep last night at her home in Eufaula. She was born in Barbour County and married in 1867. About fourteen years ago the family moved to the city from their old home ten miles below town at Poston's Mill. Survivors are her husband and six daughters and two sons, Mrs. C. C. Lidden of Marianna, Fla., Mrs. R. C. Curry of Miss., Mrs. E. H. Ross, Misses Stella, Johnnie and Russie Poston of Eufaula and James Poston of Eufaula, Bates Poston of Montgomery. Burial in Fairview in Eufaula.

Mrs. Thomas Roney died Saturday at her home about eight miles from the city. Burial at Corinth Church.

Thurs. Nov. 10, 1904

Mr. Taylor Lott died Oct. 18th, 1904. He lived in Barbour County all his life. He married Miss M. J. Lee in Feb. 1874.

Dr. P. H. Brown, father of Dr. A. P. Brown of Eufaula, died yesterday in Troy. He was originally from Georgia. He was married twice; first to Miss Calista Mildred Tarver and to them several children were born. After her death on Dec. 18, 1877, he married Miss Louise T. Perry, who survives him and four sons, Charles Brown, M. P. Brown, Dr. P. U. Brown and Dr. A. P. Brown.

Mr. John M. Moore died Friday at his home in Atlanta. He was a son-in-law of Dr. M. B. Wharton of the first Baptist Church of Eufaula.

The Clayton Record
1904

Fri. Mar. 4, 1904

Mrs. T. Emmett Thrower died at her home in Bainbridge, Ga., last Sunday. She was Lucile Bowdon and lived in Clayton. Survivors are her husband and a baby girl about a week old.

Fri. Apr. 1, 1904

Mr. J. H. Muller, book-keeper in the East Alabama National Bank, died in Eufaula last Saturday from blood poisoning. Burial in Charleston, S. C., his former home.

Fri. Apr. 8, 1904

The Clayton Record
1904

Fri. Apr. 8, 1904
Mr. John W. Efurd, formerly of Clayton, died at his home in Louisville on Tuesday of last week.

Fri. Apr. 15, 1904
Arthur M. Peach died last Thursday at the home of his brother, Mr. George W. Peach. The deceased was born Mar. 21, 1866 at Perote in Bullock County, Alabama. On Aug. 23, 1898 he married Miss Lila Andrews, who died on Dec. 28, 1901. Survivors are one child, a little boy who is in the care of his aunt, Mrs. R. L. Petty. Burial in Union Springs besides his wife.

Fri. May 6, 1904
The remains of Colon Norton, the son of Mr. and Mrs. L. Norton, who died in Meridian, Miss., reached Clayton Monday. Burial at Pleasant Plains Church.

Fri. May 13, 1904
Mr. James Warr, age 61, citizen of Barbour County, died at home near Louisville last Tuesday. Burial at Bethlehem. Survivors are his wife and two daughters.

Fri. May 20, 1904
Mr. John McRae, an aged citizen of Clio, dropped dead while plowing on last Tuesday. Burial at Pea River Presbyterian Church.

June 3, 1904
Mr. George Roberson, age 45, died at his home six miles south of Clayton last Saturday. He leaves a wife and children.

Mr. W. G. Hunt, an aged citizen, died at his home in Clio, Ala. last week.

D. M. Day, merchant of Newton, Ala., died last Friday from an accident while charging his soda water fount. Burial at Union Springs.-Ozark (Ala.) Tribune.

Fri. July 29, 1904
Mrs. J. J. Hagood (Anna Bartlett Hagood) died at the home of her mother-in-law near Evergreen, Ala., last week.

Fri. Aug. 5, 1904
Mr. William Greene, formerly of Clayton, died at his home at Fort Gaines, Ga., recently.

Fri. Sept. 16, 1904
Mrs. Peter Sanders, age 76, died at her home near Clayton on Monday. Survivors are her husband and two children, Mr. H. V. Sanders and Mrs. Reid.

Fri. Sept. 23, 1904
Mr. J. T. Cameron, age 79, died Sunday at the home of his daughter, Mrs. G. Y. Nix, near Clayton. Survivors are several sons and daughters, among them are Mrs. G. Y. Nix, Mrs. J. E. Bush and Mr. J. T. Cameron, Jr.

Fri. Oct. 28, 1904
L. B. (Brown) Bush died in Montgomery Monday. He was born and

The Clayton Record
1904

reared in Barbour County. He has lived to see most of his family grown young men and women.

Fri. Dec. 9, 1904
Mr. Joel Helms, age 74, died on Nov. 27th at his home below Fresco.-*Troy Messenger*.

Fri. Dec. 16, 1904
Mrs. Aaron Green died at her home southwest of Clayton on Wednesday. She was a sister of Messrs. Mark and Frank Snead.

Fri. Dec. 30, 1904
Mrs. Mary Godwin, age 56, died at her home in Eufaula this morning. She was the eldest daughter of Capt. and Mrs. John McNab and wife of Mr. John D. Godwin. She was born in Clayton, where she married 35 years ago and came to Eufaula where they have since resided except a few years spent at Selma, Ala., and Lexington, Ky. Survivors are her aged father and mother, her husband, one son, Mr. J. S. Godwin and six sisters, Mesdames Kate Nettles of Montgomery; Laura McGint of Tallahassee, Fla.; J. B. Gibson of Autaugaville, Ala.; S, M. Collins, Pike Road, Ala.; J. B. Bland of Texas; and W. B. McComb of New York.-*Eufaula Times*.

Eufaula Times & News
1905

Thurs. Jan. 12, 1905
Mr. J. G. Smith, age 71, died Jan. 1st at his home 14 miles north of Eufaula. Survivors are his wife and one daughter. Burial at Midway, Ala.

Thurs. Jan. 19, 1905
Mr. J. T. Brown, age 62, died at his home near Eufaula yesterday. Burial at Epworth Church.

Thurs. Jan. 26, 1905
Mrs. Francis E. Wood, age 84, died at her home near Eufaula yesterday. Seven children survive her. They are J. C., W. M., S. P. and Benjamin Wood and Mrs. P. A. Murphey of Lorina, Texas, and Mrs. A. L. Richards of Ray in Barbour County. Burial at Mount Pleasant Church.

Thurs. Feb. 2, 1905
Mr. W. M. Jimmerson, age about 43, died at his home at Baker Hill yesterday. Burial at Bethel.

Mrs. E. B. Barton, age 77, died last evening at the home of son, W. J. Barton at Kipling in Quitman Co., Ga. She was a sister of W. J. C. Parrell. Survivors are her husband and one son, W. J. Barton.

Mrs. Eva Bullock of Eufaula received a telegram this morning announcing the death of her sister, Mrs. P. P. Watson (Addie Martin Watson, wife of Penn P. Watson) at Martinsville, Va. She was reared in Eufaula and was the eldest daughter of Mr. and Mrs. Queen John O. Martin and sister of Mrs. Eva Martin Bullock. She married in Eufaula 23 years ago.

Eufaula Times & News
1905

Mr. M. H. Parish of Clayton died Tuesday. He was in a sanitarium for his health. His daughter, Miss Eddie, and his brother, J. E. Parish were with him.-Clayton Record.

Thurs. Feb. 16, 1905
Mr. Harrell Flowers, age 79, living at White Oak in Barbour County, died today. He leaves a family. Burial at White Oak.

Col. J. R. Hogue, age 77, died yesterday at his home in Eufaula. Survivors are his wife and one son, Mr. Fred Hogue.

Thurs. Feb. 23, 1905
Mrs. W. N. Reeves, age about 58, died Sunday. Survivors are her husband, Rev. W. N. Reeves, and three sons, Dr. John Reeves, Charlie Reeves and David Reeves and one daughter, Mrs. Harmon H. Lampley. Mrs. Reeves was the daughter of the late banker, Mr. John McNab.

Died Tuesday night at the home of her son, William T. Simpson, in Florence, Ala., Mrs. Mollie Daniel Simpson, wife of the late W. T. Simpson. She was born in Tuskegee, Ala. 70 years ago. She lived in Eufaula nearly 50 years. Her children are Mesdames L. Y. Dean of Eufaula, J. W. Keesee of Clarksville, Tenn., E. H. Cargill of Columbus, Ga., Dr. Lee J. Simpson of Omaha, Ga., and Mr. William T. Simpson of Florence Ala. Burial in Eufaula.

Thurs. Mar. 2, 1905
Mrs. Joe Patterson of Enterprise died in Montgomery recently. Burial at Pinckard, Alabama.

Mr. Eason Bush, age 73, died Monday at Belcher in Barbour County. Today his wife, age 75, died at her home.

Capt. Benjamin H. Screws, brother of Maj. W. W. Screws of the Montgomery Advertiser died in Montgomery yesterday. He was a native of Barbour County and his aged mother lives at Clayton.

Mr. Isaac Wells died last night. His wife survives. Burial at Epworth Church.

Mrs. Flora McNab Reeves, wife of Dr. William N. Reeves, died Sunday at her home in Eufaula. Survivors are her husband and children.

Thurs, Mar. 9, 1905
Mr. J. P. Perkins, age about 60, died at his home last night near Oak Grove in Georgia. Survivors are his wife and several children.

Mrs. W. A. Andrews, age three score and six years, died at her home at Spring Hill in Barbour County last night. Burial at the family burying ground near Spring Hill. She was the mother of Mrs. Joe Grant and Mr. Fred Andrews and step mother to Mr. W. D. Andrews, of Clayton.

Mrs. Elizabeth McGilvary, formerly of Barbour Co., died at the home of her son, J. F. McGilvary in Enterprise, Ala. on last Friday.

Eufaula Times & News
1905

Thurs. Mar. 23, 1905

Rev. W. N. Reeves died at his home in Eufaula this morning.

Thurs. March 30, 1905

Mrs. Emma Debose, wife of Shelly Debose, died at her home near Blue Springs in Barbour County last Saturday. Burial at Bethel.

Mr. Jim Scroggins, age 76, a citizen of Solomon's Mill, died on March 22. Burial at the family cemetery near his home. He was married three times, first to Miss Liza Harrell, second to Miss Emma Tomberlin and third to Miss Callie Debose. He leaves thirteen children.

Mrs. Elizabeth Rollins, age 78, wife of the late G. W. Rollins, who was killed by a R. R. train near Ozark ten years ago, died at Dothan on Mar. 15th of lagrippe. She was the mother of sixteen children, twelve boys and four girls. Burial at Rocky Mount in Barbour County.

Mrs. Sarah Moore, age 53, wife of J. B. Moore, died in Macon at her home yesterday. Survivors are her husband and six children, Miss Ola Roberts, C. F. Roberts, J. R. Roberts and C. L. Roberts, Mrs. W. F. Herman and Mrs. W. T. Bloodworth. Burial at her old home at Haddock's Station on the Georgia road at Salem Cemetery.-Macon (Ga.) Telegraph.

Rev. W. H. Reeves, D. D., age 74, died March 20th at his home in Eufaula. He was born in Dallas County, Ala., in 1831, the son of Rev. Jeremiah Reeves. His wife died only a month ago.

Thurs. Apr. 6, 1905

Mr. John J. Flowers, of Montgomery, died while on a visit to his son, W. H. Flowers at Jakin, Georgia.

Thurs. Apr. 27, 1905

Ben J. Daniel, editor of the Columbus (Ga.) Ledger, died yesterday at his home in Columbus. He was a native of Alabama.

Mrs. Egletine Boylston Thomas, age 30, wife of Mr. John C. Thomas, died at Uniontown, Ala., yesterday. She was born near Clayton, but had lived since childhood at Apalachola, Fla. Burial at Eufaula. Survivors are two brothers, Messrs. Boylston and one sister, Mrs. M. Brash, all of Apalachola, and her mother-in-law, Mrs. M. V. Thomas, of Eufaula.

Thurs. June 1, 1905

Mrs. Virginia Irby of Eufaula died suddenly while visiting in Columbus, Ga. Her brother, Mr. Virgil Crawford, went to Columbus to accompany the remains to Eufaula. Burial at Fairview.

Mrs. Alice Cook, age 65, died at her home eleven miles west of Eufaula yesterday. She was the mother of Mrs. R. G. Braswell of Eufaula. Burial at Prospect Church in Henry County, Ala.

Thurs. June 8, 1905

Mrs. C. E. Anderson died May 28th at the home of her dau., Mrs. G. A. Searcy of Lawrenceville, Ala. She was born in S. C. Aug. 1st, 1827. From there she moved to Fla., later to Columbus,

<u>Eufaula Times & News</u>
1905

Georgia and thence to Eufaula. In 1844 she married M. W. Anderson and had been a citizen of Barbour County for 50 years. Two years ago she went to live with her daughter. She was the mother of six sons and one daughter, five children survive her. There are T. S. Anderson of Bush, Ala,, P. H. Anderson of Malvern, Ala., W. C. Anderson and Mrs. G. A. Searcy of Lawrenceville, Ala., and M. W. Anderson of Blocton, Ala. Her husband died in 1877. Burial in the family grave yard.

Dr. P. R. Holt, formerly a druggist of Eufaula, died at his home in Newman, Ga., yesterday. He was a brother of Dr. S. A. Holt, formerly of Eufaula.

Mr. E. T. Randall of Eufaula died in a Montgomery hospital yesterday. Burial in Union Springs, Ala.

Thurs. June 15, 1905
Mrs. John Beard, formerly of Eufaula, died yesterday at her home four miles from Georgetown in Quitman Co., Ga. Survivors are her husband and three children, two of which are married.

Thurs. June 29, 1905
Mrs. M. G. Sutlive of Fort Gaines, Ga., died at her home there recently. She was a sister of E. A. Graham and was well known in Eufaula.

Mrs. Elizabeth Rhodes, wife of the late Mr. Chauncey Rhodes, died at her home in Eufaula Sunday. She was Miss Elizabeth Daniel of Tuskegee. She was married in Tuskegee Apr. 28, 1854, and her twin sister, Miss Mollie Daniel was married at the same time to Mr. William T. Simpson. They came to Eufaula to live. Survivors are her son, Mr. Jamie D. Rhodes and daughters, Mrs. E. T. Long and Mrs. W. Y. Dent.

Thurs. July 6, 1905
The remains of Mr. Paul Holder, age 30, who died Tuesday in Americus, Ga., were brought to County Line Church in Stewart Co., Ga. for burial. He was a brother of G. G. Holder of our city.

Thurs. July 13, 1905
G. C. Brabham, age 78, of Zeigler in Barbour Co., died July 3rd. Survivors are his wife, six sons and five daughters.

Mrs. Charley Thomas died July 2nd. Burial at Judson Cemetery. Survivors are her husband, two daughters, Misses Hassie and Estell Thomas, two brothers and a sister.

Mrs. J. C. Wood died at her home at Dewitt in Henry County on Sunday. Survivors are her husband and several children. Burial at Mr. Pleasant Church.

Mr. Nathan Williams, age 75, died at his home at Baker Hill in Barbour County on Friday. He was the father of Nat and J. D. Williams and other children.

James Allen Drewry died Thursday in N. C. where he had gone for his health. He was born at Spring Hill in Barbour County 40 years ago, the son of the late Dr. John W. Drewry. In Nov. 1892 he married Miss Mamie Harrison, who survives him with their three

Eufaula Times & News
1905

children, John, Hattie and Stella Drewry, a brother, Mr. J. W. Drewry of Cuthbert and sisters, Mesdames Stella D. Guice, John P. Foy and Lillie D. Mitchell.

Thurs. Aug. 17, 1905
   Mr. Edward Aiken Crawford, of Tallahassee, Fla., brother of Mr. J. B. Crawford of this city, died yesterday.

Thurs. Aug. 24, 1905
   Mrs. Sarah A. Jordan, age three score and ten, died last night at the home of Mrs. Flewellen in Eufaula. She moved here two years ago from Edgefield, S. C. Survivors are two children, Robert A. Ballowe of this city and Mrs. Trofford of Nashville.

Thurs. Sept. 14, 1905
   Dr. S. G. Robertson, age about 75, died at his home in Eufaula yesterday from a stroke of paralysis. Burial at Fairview in Eufaula.

   Mrs. John Drewry died suddenly today at her home at Cuthbert, Georgia.

   Mrs. H. A. Davis died at her home in Midway, Ala., yesterday. She spent the greater part of her life about four miles north of Eufaula.

Thurs. Sept. 28, 1905
   Mrs. Frances Griggs Davis died at her home in Midway, Ala., on Sept. 8th, 1905. She was born in Eaton, Ga., July 17th, 1846, and was reared at Glennville, Ala. She graduated at LaGrange, Ga., and on Nov. 16th, 1865 she married Mr. Hiram A. Davis, who with six daughters and two sons survive her.

   Mr. J. (John) H. Peach died at his home at Perote (Bullock Co.) yesterday. He was the father of Messrs. G. W., John and Dr. N. E. Peach and Mrs. Robert Petty of Clayton.

   Mrs. W. M. Brazzell, age about 35, died last night at her home near Cotton Hill in Barbour Co. Survivors are her husband and several children, the youngest being about four months old.

Thurs. Oct. 5, 1905
   Mr. Nathan Whitaker, age 75, died Saturday at the home of his son-in-law, E. N. King at Kipling (Quitman Co., Ga.) and was buried in the Georgetown Cemetery.

   Mayor Thomas H. Carr, age 61, died at his home in Montgomery yesterday.

Thurs. Oct. 26, 1905
   Mrs. James Rogers, age three score and ten, died at her home in Eufaula Saturday.

Thurs. Nov. 9, 1905
   Prof. C. (Clarence) A. Castellow died at his home in Leesburg Tuesday with hemorhagic fever. He was a brother of J. J. Castellow of Quitman Co. Survivors are his wife and two small children, a boy and a girl.

Thurs. Nov. 30, 1905

Eufaula Times & News
1905

E. B. Beasley received a telegram yesterday announcing the death of his sister, Mrs. Ellen Langford, age 54, of Ozark, Ala. Survivors are three sons and two daughters.

Thurs. Dec. 21, 1905
Mr. D. W. Flowers of White Oak (Barbour Co.), died 10th inst. of pneumonia. Survivors are his wife, four children, three brothers and five sisters.

Mr. John Flowers died at his home in Beat Six on Monday. Survivors are his wife and several children.

The remains of Mr. G. W. Hancock, who was killed Saturday in Birmingham, arrived in Eufaula yesterday. They were carried to his daughter's home, Mrs. W. C. Dunnaway from where the funeral took place.

Thurs. Dec. 28, 1905
Mrs. M. C. Roquemore, an aged citizen of Georgetown, died Saturday. She made her home with her relative, Mrs. Sallie Lee.

Mr. Charlie Colbert, age 45, died last night at his home in Eufaula from gastritis. He was a painter by trade.

The Clayton Record
1905

Fri. Jan. 13, 1905
Mr. R. P. Adams of Bullock County died suddenly at his home near Midway last Friday.

Fri. Jan. 27, 1905
Mr. Martin H. Parish, age 53, of Clayton, died at a sanatorium at a distance the last few days. Miss Eddie, his daughter, and his brother, J. E. Parish were summoned Tuesday. He was born in Macon County on June 1851. He was the son of the late Mr. and Mrs. Joseph Parish. He married Miss Addie Hobdy over 20 years ago and she with five of the seven children born of this union, survive him.

Fri. Feb. 3, 1905
Mr. Winston Andrews of Midland City (Ala.), died last week at his home. He was born Mar. 19th, 1839. In Mar. 1856 he married Miss Florida Adams and became the father of twelve children, ten of whom are living.-Ozark (Ala.) Tribune.

Fri. Feb. 10, 1905
Mrs. Sanford Kennedy died at her home in Beat Eight in Barbour County last Wednesday. Survivors are her husband and several children.

Fri. Feb. 17, 1905
Mrs. John S. Nix, age nearly 61, died at her home in Clayton on 26th Jan. She was the daughter of James B. and Margaret C. Norton. She leaves a husband and four children.

Fri. Mar. 10, 1905
Rev. M. McGilvary died at his home in Childersburg, Ala., last Friday from pneumonia. He once served the Presbyterian Church in Clayton.

The Clayton Record
1905

Fri. Mar. 17, 1905

Mrs. Susan A. White died at her home in Clayton on Mar. 9th. She was Miss Susan A. Lewis, born Jan. 6, 1844. On Jan. 17, 1861, she married John C. White, who with seven children who were born to this union survive her.

Mrs. C. C. Skillman received a telegram announcing the death of Maj. H. W. B. Price, age 88, the father of Mrs. Skillman. He died at his home in Kirkland, near Atlanta. The burial will be in Decatur. He was formerly a citizen of Eufaula.

Mr. J. (Julius) E. Meadows died in Clayton on Wednesday of Brights disease. He was born at Carrelton, Ga., Apr. 1st, 1863, and had been a resident of Clayton for about 20 years. (Following item: Mrs. Leila Meadows and Mr. A. S. Borders and family request that we express their thanks to their friends for the many kindnesses extended during their recent bereavment.).

Fri. Apr. 7, 1905

Mrs. W. L. Kennedy, of near Clayton, died Friday from paralysis She was born Oct. 29, 1836 in Russell Co., Ala. She married a Mr. Thomas who died leaving her with several small children, little more than 36 years ago she married Mr. Kennedy. On Apr. 1st her remains were laid to rest at Pleasant Plaines Cemetery. Survivors are her aged husband several sons and four sisters.

Fri. June 2, 1905

Mrs. F. B. Pierce, formerly Miss Willie Veal, died at her home in Louisville on Monday. Survivors are her husband and six children.

Dr. W. F. Wright, age 55 died at his home in Clayton on the 13th inst. He was a native of Habersham Co., Ga. About 20 years ago he moved here from Walhalla, S. C., and Clayton has been his home ever since. In 1876 he married Miss Mamie James of Walhalla, S. C., and she with four children survive him. They are Mr. S. J. Wright, Mrs. Allen Bradham of Manning, S. C., Miss Claud Wright and Mr. Winn Wright, and brother, Mr. J. H. Wright of Washington, D. C. and his sister Mrs. A. L. Martin.

Fri. Sept. 8, 1905

Mrs. James F. Hurst died Sept. 2nd inst. at her home near Clayton. She was the youngest daughter of Mr. Wes Norton of Clayton. She was born July 29th, 1874 and was married to Mr. Hurst about eleven years ago. Survivors are her husband and four children, also two sisters, Mrs. Ed Bell of near Clayton and Mrs. Americus Baker of Plains, Ga., and her aged father.

Fri. Sept. 29, 1905

Mr. J. B. Fryer died at his home at Clayton Thursday of paralysis. He was born at Monticello, Pike Co., in 1859. Early in life his parents moved to South Carolina, and it was in that state he grew to manhood. He came back to Alabama, settling in Perote (Bullock Co., Ala.). He moved to Clayton about 12 years ago. He married Miss Susan McGrady and she with six children survive him.

The Clayton Record
1905

Fri. Nov. 3, 1905

    Mrs. Fern M. Wood died at her home in Eufaula last Sunday from the effects of injuries she received when her horse ran away. Her late husband was once a prominent attorney of Barbour County.

Fri. Nov. 10, 1905

    Mr. Enoch Mills, age 78, died at the home of his son, Mr. Bartow Mills, last Sunday. He was the father of Mr. Sisler Mills and Mrs. A. Berlien. Burial at Louisville beside his wife.

Abell, George, 30
Adair, J. D., Dr., 48
Adams, Allen, 95
Adams, Asa, 89
Adams, Clara, Mrs., 29
Adams, Florida, 115
Adams, I. B., 84
Adams, I. O., Rev., 22, 100
Adams, J. L., 4
Adams, Jessie, Mrs., 104
Adams, Joe, 64
Adams, Lizzie, Mrs., 41
Adams, Mattie, Mrs., 89
Adams, R. P., 115
Adams, William R., 64
Adkinson, Jasper, Mrs., 95
Ainsworth, J. C., Capt., 27
Albritton, Judge, 62
Albritton, M. L., Mrs., 62
Alexander, H. C., Mrs., 100
Alexander, William, 41
Alford, J. B., Mrs., 57
Allday, B. F., Mrs., 65
Allday, F. J., 108
Allday, Tom, Mrs., 97
Allen, Dr., 72
Allen, Jesse, 92
Allen, T. M., Mrs., 72
Allison, J. F., 31
Alsop, T. J., Mrs., 64
Alston, A. H., Judge, 66
Alston, Chas. N., Dr., 4
Alston, John M., 66
Alston, John M., Mrs., 49
Alston, Robert, 60
Alston, W. A., 66
Anderson, C. E., Mrs., 112
Anderson, Charley S., 36
Anderson, J. W., 70
Anderson, Jubal, Gen., 29
Anderson, M. W., 113
Anderson, P. H., 113
Anderson, P. P., 34
Anderson, T. S., 113
Anderson, W. C., 113
Andrews, Allen S., Dr., 63
Andrews, Annie, Mrs., 17
Andrews, Fred, 111
Andrews, Glenn, 59
Andrews, J. B., 43
Andrews, J. D., Mrs., 10
Andrews, James, 30
Andrews, Lila, 105
Andrews, Mark S., Jr., 59
Andrews, Mark S., Rev., 59
Andrews, Nannie, Mrs., 30
Andrews, Roscoe C., 42
Andrews, S. A., 17
Andrews, Sallie, 59
Andrews, W. A., Mrs., 111
Andrews, W. D., 111
Andrews, W. R., 31
Andrews, Will, 22
Andrews, William T., 59
Andrews, Winston, 115
Anglin, O. J., 93
Ansley, Marion, Mrs., 4
Appling, David, 15
Appling, Otho, Mrs., 49
Armstrong, J. C., Dr., 14
Armstrong, Lucinda B., Mrs., 39
Arnold, R. B., Mrs., 56
Arnold, W. A., 56
Atchley, Walter, 31
Avery, Mollie, Mrs., 31
Babbitt, Miss, 72
Baer, M., Mrs., 80
Baer, see Bear
Bailey, Hosea, Mrs., 34
Baker, Alpheus, Gen., 11
Baker, Alpheus, Mrs., 25
Baker, Americus, Mrs., 116
Baker, Ellison, 55
Baker, James, 62
Baker, Nathan, 41
Baker, R. H., 56
Baker, Warren, 70
Baker, Warren, Mrs., 29
Baker, Wilber C., Mrs., 88
Baldree, John Q., 13
Baldwin, Dr., 5
Baldwin, Will O., 5
Ball, B. W., Mrs., 6
Ballowe, R. A., Mrs., 62, 80
Ballowe, Robert A., 114
Barbaree, C. R., Mrs., 84
Barefield, John, 19
Barlett, Arthur E., 8
Barlow, A., 27
Barnes, D. W., Rev., 61
Barnes, J. W., 101
Barnett, Addie, Mrs., 27
Barnett, Annie Dell, 58
Barnett, Augustus W., 58
Barnett, Carrie, 58
Barnett, Frank, Rev., 58
Barnett, John T., 58
Barnett, Jule C., 43
Barnett, Mary, Mrs., 43
Barnett, Mollie, 81

Barnett, Paul, 58
Barnett, Reese, 58
Barnett, Richard, 70
Barnett, Sam T., 58
Barnett, Una, 58
Barney, Eli, 53
Barr, J. M., Mrs., 26
Barr, J. R., 92
Barr, J. R., Capt., 26
Barr, J. R., Dr., 92
Barr, S. S., Mrs., 92
Barron, Leonard, Mrs., 96
Barry, William, 6
Barton, E. B., 110
Barton, W. J., 110
Bass, John H., Capt., 8
Bass, Josiah, 1
Bass, W. L., 62
Bass, W. L., Mrs., 63
Bates, Maj., 40
Bates, Andrew, 9
Bates, Sarah, Mrs., 40
Bates, W. M., Maj., 9
Battey, Robert, Dr., 37
Battle, Dr., 100
Battle, J. T., Dr., 102
Battle, Sallie B., 40
Baxley, Simon, 19
Baxter, Dan, 24
Baxter, Sol., 4
Baxter, Viccie, Mrs., 24
Baxter, W. I., 4
Beach, Amzi, 38
Beach, H. M., 99
Beal, C. W., Col., 17
Beale, C. W., 9
Beall, Anna, Mrs., 89
Beall, Samuel, 7
Bear, M., Mrs., 102
Beard, John, Mrs., 113
Beard, Thos. J., Dr., 61
Beasley, Betsey, 91
Beasley, E. B., 115
Beasley, George W., 91
Beasley, John W., 101
Beasley, William, 101
Beauchamp, J. W., 107
Beauchamp, John W., 107
Beauchamp, Thomas H., 63
Beauchamp, Tom, 63
Beauchamp, Susie, 63
Beckham, Thomas M., Rev., 32
Bedsole, Mary, Mrs., 71
Belcher, A. B., Mrs., 98

Belcher, J. T., 106
Belcher, Margaret, Mrs., 106
Belcher, S. J., Mrs., 78
Bell, Ed, Mrs., 116
Bell, John, 1
Bell, John T., Jr., 28
Bell, L. C., Mrs., 92
Bell, M. C., 47
Belton, Solomon D., Col., 38
Bennefield, J. A., Mrs., 83
Bennett, Dr., 21
Bennett, Mrs. Dr., 21
Bennett, B. F., Dr., 48
Bennett, Carrie, 48
Benton, Columbus, 65
Benton, Mose, 76
Benton, S. C., 75
Berlien, A., Mrs., 117
Bernstein, Ben, 13
Bernstein, Henrietta, 13
Bernstein, Henry, Mrs., 13
Bernstein, Melinda, 13
Bernstein, Minnie, 13
Bernstein, Phil, 13
Bernstein, Theodore, 13
Berry, Davis, 37
Berry, William, 14
Bickley, W. M., 35
Bickley, William, Mrs., 35
Billings, John D., Mrs., 39
Billings, Sallie, 70
Bird, Zack, 50
Birdsong, Joe, Miss, 85
Birdsong, W. H., 85
Bishop, Boland, 8
Bishop, C. H., 22
Bishop, D. B., 43
Bishop, Euna, 43
Bishop, Fred, 43
Bishop, Nancy, Mrs., 107
Bishop, Richard, 8
Bishop, W. A., Mrs., 95
Bishop, W. S., 43
Black, Carrie, 52
Black, E. J., 39
Black, J. E., 52
Black, John, 52
Blackwell, D. C., 16
Blair, C. W., 92
Blair, Charles, 92
Blair, D. L., Mrs., 45
Blair, Dick L., 52
Blair, E. P., Mrs., 92
Blair, Edna, 92

Blair, Edward P., 92
Blair, Henry, Dr., 1
Blair, J. W., 76
Blair, Marie, 92
Blair, Mike, 32
Blair, Mollie, 32
Blair, Ossie, 92
Blanchard, Tom, 31
Blancho, Felix, 13
Bland, J. B., Mrs., 110
Bland, John B., 30
Blassingame, Benjamin T., 51
Bledsoe, H. I., Col., 64
Bledsoe, John, Rev., 68
Bledsoe, Mary, Mrs., 68
Bloodworth, Mrs., 2
Bloodworth, F. H., Dr., 66
Bloodworth, Frank, Mrs., 26
Bloodworth, J. D., 37
Bloodworth, W. D., 37
Bloodworth, W. T., Mrs., 112
Bloom, H., Mrs., 80, 102
Blue, Frank, 72
Blue, John H., Dr., 28
Blue, O. R., Rev., 21
Bodiford, W. H., 67
Boone, Daniel, 61
Borders, Dr., 61
Borders, Mrs., 86
Borders, A. H., Rev., 61
Borders, A. S., 86, 93, 116
Borders, A. T., 93
Borders, Abb, Col., 89
Borders, J. C., Mrs., 61
Borders, J. E., 86
Borders, Janie E., 10
Borders, Mary L., Mrs., 61
Borland, Thos. M., 9
Bostick, George P., Rev., 98
Bostick, Mary T., Mrs., 98
Bowden, Jesse, Mrs., 24
Bowden, Jesse B., 67
Bowdon, Lucile, 108
Bowen, Jesse B., 27
Bowers, T. W., Mrs., 92
Boyd, C. L., Dr., 63
Boyd, C. L., Mrs., 63
Boyd, Carrie, 63
Boyd, Marion, 90
Boyd, N. W., 46
Boyer, Geo., Mrs., 4
Boykin, Frank, 11, 40
Boykin, J. W., 11
Boylston, Mr., 112
Boylston, H. McD., 45

Brabham, G. C., 113
Brabham, Martin, 93
Bradford, C. H., Mrs., 33
Bradford, Carrie, Mrs., 39
Bradham, Allen, Mrs., 116
Bradley, Mrs., 8
Bradley, Henry, 8
Bradley, Hobbs, 87
Bradley, J. J., 87
Bradley, J. J., Mrs., 103
Bradley, Robert, 1
Bradley, S. L., 100
Brady, Albert, 85
Brady, Carrie M., Mrs., 85
Brady, Hattie, Mrs., 102
Brady, John L., 85
Brady, Nellie, 85
Brady, Robert, 85
Bragan, Annie Sue, 49
Bragan, G. W., 49
Bragan, G. W., Mrs., 49
Branch, John W., 49
Brannon, A. M., Mrs., 29
Brannon, Claude, Dr., 60
Brannon, H. L., Dr., 44
Brannon, Mary A., Mrs., 44
Brannon, P. T., Mrs., 88
Brannon, R. Means, 29
Brannon, T. J., Capt., 64
Brannon, W. B., 44
Brannon, W. B., Capt., 60
Brannon, W. H., Jr., 29
Brannon, W. J., Capt., 64
Brash, M., Mrs., 112
Braswell, R. G., Mrs., 112
Braswell, Robert, Mrs., 18
Bray, Charley, 42
Bray, Chas. W., 67
Bray, Frank, 67
Bray, Fred W., 42
Bray, James P., 75
Bray, John E., 67
Bray, John W., 42, 67
Bray, N. M., 96
Bray, N. M., Mrs., 1
Bray, Nathan, 75
Bray, Nathan M., 103
Bray, W. M., Mrs., 27
Bray, Wells J., 75
Bray, Will, 75
Brazwell, Jasper, 39
Brazzell, Mrs., 108
Brazzell, Robert, 108
Brazzell, W. M., Mrs., 114
Brewer, Stake, Mrs., 82

Briggs, Rev., 49
Brinson, Mrs., 4
Brinson, S. S., Capt., 4
Britt, Mrs., 34, 106
Britt, John, 101
Britt, John T., 23, 101
Britt, Mabelle, 101
Britt, M. W., 23, 101
Britt, Wade, 101
Broadus, John A., Rev., 34
Brogden, Emmett, Mrs., 82
Brooks, E., Mrs., 80
Brooks, E. H., 80
Brooks, Elizabeth J., 83
Brooks, H. E., Dr., 77
Brooks, H. E., Mrs., 86
Brown, Mrs., 56, 57
Brown, A. P., Dr., 108
Brown, Belle, Mrs., 85
Brown, Bettie, 74
Brown, Bettie, Mrs., 76
Brown, E. L., 58
Brown, Charles, 108
Brown, E. L., Mrs., 80
Brown, Girard, Mrs., 88
Brown, J. T., 110
Brown, James, 70
Brown, James H., Mrs., 63
Brown, L. H., 74
Brown, Lizzie, 85
Brown, M. P., 108
Brown, Martha M., Mrs., 63
Brown, P. H., Dr., 108
Brown, P. U., Dr., 108
Brown, Reuben, 13
Brown, Steve, Mrs., 18
Brown, Watt, 63
Bruce, J. T., 49
Bruce, Phillip, 49
Bruns, Henry M., 38
Bruns, John Dickson, Dr., 38
Brunson, C. C., Mrs., 57
Brunson, Harry, 57
Brunson, L. E., 57
Brunson, M. A., 57
Brunson, Mary, 57
Brunson, W. A., Maj., 57
Bryan, Ann E., Mrs., 62
Bryan, George, 31
Bryan, J. C., 10
Bryan, Simpson, 31
Bryant, Archy, 45
Bryant, J. C., Maj., 32
Bryant, James, 30

Bryant, Thomas S., 88
Buchanan, C. S. J., 107
Buchanan, Franklin, 10
Bufford, Jefferson, 97
Bufford, Mary, 97
Buford, Maj., 71
Buford, Annie, 43
Buford, J. M., Mrs., 71
Buford, James M., 106
Buford, Jeff, 43
Buford, Jefferson, Maj., 43
Bullock, Eva, Mrs., 110
Bullock, Gabrielle, 77
Bullock, Seymour, Dr., 12
Burbanks, G. B., Mrs., 33
Burdeshaw, J. W., Mrs., 26
Burdette, Rosana, Mrs., 25
Burgy, J. D., 57
Burkhead, J. D., Rev., 19
Burlison, Elizabeth, Mrs., 46
Burlison, George, 46
Burnett, Martha H., Mrs., 96
Burnett, Swan P., Dr., 96
Burnett, W. L., Capt., 95
Burr, William H., Col., 79
Burrus, L. M., Mrs., 63
Bush, A., 24
Bush, A. B., 24
Bush, C. D., 61
Bush, Council, 28
Bush, Eason, 111
Bush, F. C., 60
Bush, Frank, Mrs., 35
Bush, J. E., Mrs., 109
Bush, L. B., 109
Bush, R. O., 22
Bush, Ryan, 22
Bussey, Nathan D., Dr., 4
Butler, A. C., 52
Butler, Carrie, Mrs., 52
Butler, Frank S., 3
Butler, G. W., Mrs., 12
Butler, Will A., 52
Butt, M. E., Rev., 86
Butt, Mary, 81
Butt, R. L., 86
Butt, Richard L., Dr., 86
Butt, Sallie, Mrs., 27
Butt, Sue, 82
Butts, Mittie, 22
Butts, Willie, 22, 44
Butts, Willis B., Maj., 64
Cade, Mrs., 51
Cade, Dozier, 65

Caffee, Judge, 100
Caffee, Annie E., Mrs., 100
Calder, George A., 43
Caldwell, Groves, Dr., 64
Calhoun, Mrs., 27
Calhoun, B. F., Mrs., 40
Calhoun, Mamie, 78
Callaway, P. M., Rev., 63
Caller, Mrs., 45
Caller, Pearla, 45
Cameron, J. T., 109
Cameron, J. T., Jr., 109
Cameron, James, 84
Campbell, A. D., Rev., 31
Campbell, George, 66
Campbell, James, Mrs., 73
Campbell, M. L., Mrs., 31
Caniell, R. Y., 106
Capels, Charles, Mrs., 32
Caraway, H. H., 19
Card, A. D., 72
Card, J. H., Dr., 32
Cargile, Louisa A., Mrs., 18
Cargile, Thomas, 18
Cargill, Austin C., 26
Cargill, Ed, Mrs., 102
Cargill, W. A., Mrs., 85
Cariker, M. M., Mrs., 39
Carmichael, Mrs., 50
Carmichael, Daniel, Judge, 60
Carmichael, J. M., 50
Carmichael, Pauline, 93
Carr, G. Tate, 3
Carr, Thomas H., 114
Carr, Thomas H., Mrs., 62
Carr, Tyron, 45
Carroll, Mrs., 49
Carroll, Amanda, Mrs., 100
Carroll, Sarah, Mrs., 58
Carson, R. A., Mrs., 29
Carter, Curtis, 70
Carter, G. W., 90
Carter, H. J., Mrs., 17
Carter, Irene, Mrs., 97
Carter, J. J., 70
Carter, William, Judge, 31
Cartledge, G. T., Mrs., 40
Cary, W. A., Mrs., 6
Castellow, C. A., 114
Castellow, J. J., 114
Cato, Dr., 69
Cato, Julius C., Mrs., 68
Causey, Mary A., Mrs., 40
Challis, Luther C., 31

Chambers, Catherine, Mrs., 88
Chambers, Elizabeth, 8
Chambers, I. H., 16
Chambers, J. H., 18
Chambers, J. W., Mrs., 34
Chambers, W. H., Rev., 88
Chamblis, A. J., Mrs., 53
Chastine, J. W., Mrs., 63
Chazel, J. P., Dr., 21
Cherry, John, Mrs., 88
Cherry, Robert, 14
Chestnut, A. B., 76
Chestnut, Chas., 6
Christian, John A., 39
Christian, Louis, 51
Clapp, J. J., Dr., 45
Clark, Ben, Mrs., 78
Clark, Betsey, Mrs., 88
Clark, E. J., Mrs., 77
Clark, Horry D., 22
Clark, J. B., Mrs., 89
Clark, J. W., 71
Clark, J. W., Mrs., 84
Clark, Joe C., 66
Clark, John W., Mrs., 106
Clark, L. G., 71
Clark, L. G., Mrs., 92
Clark, Lint, 26
Clark, Missouri, 26
Clark, Warren, 26
Clark, Warren J., 71
Clark, S. D., Mrs., 49
Clark, Whit, 66
Clark, William F., 71
Clark, Willis G., 56
Clarke, Alsey, 55
Clarke, Annie, Mrs., 72
Clarke, James, 95
Clarke, John, 55
Clarke, Marshall J., 62
Clarke, Whit, 72
Clayton, Victoria, Mrs., 80
Clendinen, R. J., Mrs., 38
Clifton, W. H., 89
Clisby, John H., Mrs., 67
Cobb, Mrs., 18
Cobb, Ann, Mrs., 75
Cobb, H. T., Mrs., 26
Cobb, J. E., 98
Cobb, Jesse, 18, 26
Cobb, Jesse, Jr., 18
Cody, M., Mrs., 4
Coffee, Dan, 83
Coffee, John, 83

Coffee, Mike, 83
Coffin, J. S., Dr., 54
Coker, J. T., Mrs., 7
Colbert, Avery, 100
Colbert, Charles, 100
Colbert, Charlie, 115
Colbert, William, 100
Colby, Ann, 62
Collier, Belle H., Mrs., 104
Collins, S. M., Mrs., 110
Colquitt, Alfred H., 30
Colquitt, Walter T., 30
Comer, B. B., 57
Comer, Catherine, Mrs., 57
Comer, Ed, 58
Comer, G. L., 57
Comer, H. M., 57
Comer, J. F., 58
Comer, J. W., 57
Comer, Wallace, Mrs., 26
Commander, V. F., 74
Connor, Adele, 58
Cook, Alice, Mrs., 112
Cook, Bettie, Mrs., 74
Cook, G. P., Mrs., 77
Cook, Phil, Gen., 30
Cooper, Burt, 63
Cooper, Jason, 15
Cooper, John, Mrs., 101
Copeland, Dr., 2
Copeland, W. P., Dr., 64
Copes, Robert, 32
Cory, Charles, Mrs., 98
Cotton, James L., Rev., 94
Cotton, Lucy C., 94
Cotton, Martha, Mrs., 94
Couric, A. A., Mrs., 74
Couric, A. A., Sr., 73
Cowan, A. S., Mrs., 39
Cowan, Elizabeth C., 95
Cowan, J. G., 71
Cowan, J. S., Dr., 71
Cowan, James R., 73
Cowan, William R., 95
Cowart, Miss, 47
Cox, Ann, 16
Cox, Craft., 20
Cox, Elizabeth, 16
Cox, Emanuel, Mrs., 14
Cox, W. J., Mrs., 12
Cox, William, 50
Craddock, Lem, Mrs., 41
Craddock, Marion, 59
Craig, Miss, 42

Craig, C. C., 42
Craig, John C., Mrs., 42
Craig, M. L., 42
Craigg, W. H., Mrs., 87
Crane, Louis, Mrs., 102
Craven, T. A., 91
Craven, T. A., Mrs., 73
Crawford, B., Mrs., 92
Crawford, Edward A., 114
Crawford, J. B., 114
Crawford, J. W., Mrs., 18
Crawford, Virgil, 88, 112
Crawford, Virgil, Mrs., 88
Crawford, Virginia P., 63
Creel, Jim, Mrs., 98
Crew, Hilliard, 19
Crews, A. A., Mrs., 20
Crews, Anderson, 82
Crews, Anderson A., 87
Crews, Berry, 88
Crews, J. E., Dr., 82
Crews, John E., 87
Crews, Nannie, 88
Crocket, Allen W., 89
Croff, John, 9
Croft, Willie, 9
Culver, Maj., 55
Culver, Abe, 13
Cummings, Henry, Mrs., 3
Cummings, J. B., Rev., 47
Cummings, S. J., Mrs., 44
Cummings, S. J., Rev., 44
Cummings, Seaborn J., 47
Cunningham, Charley, Mrs., 47
Cunningham, Jane, 87
Curbow, Ann, Mrs., 51
Cureton, S. O., 18
Currie, Mrs., 14
Curry, R. C., Mrs., 108
Curtis, Lucy Ann, 94
Dancer, Z., Mrs., 77
Danford, Joe, 30
Danford, William, Mrs., 72
Danforth, E. C. B., 73
Danforth, Sarah, Mrs., 73
Daniel, Ben J., 112
Daniel, Elizabeth, 36, 113
Daniel, Mollie, 113
Daniels, Lelia, Mrs., 85
Daniels, Mary, 102
Dansby, John, 43
Dantzler, A. A., Mrs., 78
Dantzler, Allen, 69
Dantzler, Ed, 78

Danzier, J. D., Mrs., 92
Dasinger, George, 105
Dasinger, Hannah, Mrs., 105
Dasinger, Thomas, 105
Davie, Mrs., 97
Davie, Bunyan, 59
Davie, J. B., Mrs., 4
Davie, Jane, Mrs., 58
Davie, Judson, 59
Davie, Luna, 59
Davie, Meigs, 59
Davie, Mercer, Dr., 58
Davie, Stella, 59
Davis, Mr., 58
Davis, Benj. B., 8
Davis, Benj. B., Mrs., 65
Davis, Cynthia, Mrs., 71
Davis, E. L., 45
Davis, Frances G., Mrs., 114
Davis, George B., 65
Davis, H. A., Mrs., 114
Davis, Hiram A., 114
Davis, Jane, 6
Davis, Jesse T., 44
Davis, John, 6
Davis, John S., 5
Davis, Macy L., 20
Davis, Margaret O'B., Mrs., 58
Davis, Martha B., 8
Davis, Oscar, 78
Davis, Ruben A., 84
Davis, W. A., 65
Davis, W. J., 66
Dawson, Annie, Mrs., 23
Dawson, George, 48
Dawson, H. F., 46
Dawson, Henry, 65
Dawson, L. G., 48
Dawson, N. H. R., Col., 33
Dawson, W. C., Col., 21
Day, D. M., 109
Dean, Abe, 36
Dean, L. Y., Mrs., 102
Debose, Callie, 112
Debose, see Dubose
Debose, Emma, Mrs., 112
Debose, Shelly, 112
Dehonie, F. J., Mrs., 63
Dehoney, F. J., 46
DeJarnette, C. R., Mrs., 85
Deloch, Ben, 30
Dent, Caroline, 89
Dent, Edward Y., 89
Dent, George, Mrs., 102
Dent, George H., 2

Dent, Henry A., 89
Dent, Nellie Beall, 7
Dent, S. H., 2, 89
Dent, S. H., Jr., 89
Dent, S. H., Mrs., 93
Dent, W. Y., Mrs., 36, 113
Dent, Warren F., 2
Deshazo, H. L., 25
Deshazo, J. B., Rev., 90
Deshazo, Susie A., 90
Deshazo, Wilson, 20
Dewitt, John M., 6
Dick, Annie Lou, Mrs., 102
Dickerson, Alfred, 105
Dickerson, Florence, Mrs., 36
Dickerson, Louise M., Mrs., 105
Dickerson, Clarence, 57
Diggers, C. D., Mrs., 92
Doriety, J. B., 35
Dorman, Mrs., 7
Dorman, A. A., 46
Dorman, Alex, 7
Doster, S. J., Col., 31
Doughtie, Mrs., 48
Doughtie, Edward C., 17
Doughtie, Eugene, 63
Doughtie, James N., 63
Doughtie, John, 48
Doughtie, Lizzie, 62
Doughtie, Punch, 63
Doughtie, T. C., 62, 63
Doughtie, Tom., 48
Doughtie, W. A., 63
Doughtie, W. A., Mrs., 23
Douglass, Mrs., 62
Dow, Buena V., Mrs., 34
Dow, C. Q., 34
Dowling, Prof., 37
Dowling, Andrew, 97
Dowling, Andrew, Mrs., 103
Dowling, Angus, Rev., 104
Dowling, H. B., 104
Dowling, Hanford, 34
Dowling, John W., 25
Dowling, Louis, 89
Dowling, N. C., Mrs., 33
Dowling, Noel, 104
Dowling, Sarah D., Mrs., 104
Dowling, Shelley D., 82
Dowling, T. L., Mrs., 37
Dozier, Mrs., 52
Dozier, Annie, 92
Dozier, E. M., 89
Dozier, J. E., 89
Dozier, L. P., Dr., 88, 92

Dozier, W. M., 68, 89
Drake, Mrs., 63
Drakeford, A. H., Mrs., 53
Drewry, Hattie, 114
Drewry, J. W., 114
Drewry, J. W., Dr., 37
Drewry, James, 52
Drewry, James A., 113
Drewry, John, 114
Drewry, John, Mrs., 114
Drewry, John W., 52
Drewry, John W., Dr., 52, 113
Drewry, Lillie, 90
Drewry, Stella, 114
Driggers, Lizzie, Mrs., 76
Dubose, Margaret E., 87
Duffell, J. M., 30
Duncan, B. J., Maj., 15
Duncan, C. R., Dr., 21
Dunn, Louise, 60
Dunnaway, W. C., Mrs., 115
Durham, Mrs., 67
Durham, Alonzo, 25
Durham, Alonzo, Mrs., 51
Durham, James H., 25
Durham, Jeff, 25
Durham, Mary, 25
Dyches, Ann, Mrs., 20
Dyches, Z. W., 20
Dykes, Bob, 43
Dykes, James, 10
Edmonds, Asbury, 58
Edmonds, Helena, 58
Edmonds, Richard, 58
Edmonds, W. H., 58
Edmonson, E. L., 81
Edmonson, John, 81
Edmonson, John M., 69
Edmonson, John M., Mrs., 18
Edmonson, R. Q., 69, 97
Edmonson, R. Q., Mrs., 7, 82
Edmonson, Richard Q., Jr., 81
Edwards, M. H., 107
Efurd, John W., 109
Efurd, T. R., 79
Efurd, W. M., 20
Efurd, William, 21
Eley, Mary, Mrs., 41
Eley, Will, 41
Ellis, Mrs., 104
Ellison, Mrs., 47
Ely, Rebecca, 107
Emerson, B. F., 15
Emory, Ambrose M., 76

Emory, Gideon, 77
English, W. S., 101
English, W. S., Mrs., 91
Engram, Carltie, 67
Engram, Harry, 67
Engram, J. E., 82
Engram, John R., 66
Engram, Laila, 67
Engram, see Ingram
Espy, G. B., 98
Espy, J. S., 86, 89
Espy, J. Seaborn, Mrs., 98
Espy, John R., 89
Espy, T. M., Mrs., 42
Espy, W. C., 9
Estes, C. E., Mrs., 80
Ethridge, Dr., 37
Ethridge, Corrine, 37
Etheridge, E. A., Miss, 52
Evans, A. A., 53
Evans, A. A., Judge, 99
Evans, A. A., Mrs., 104
Evans, James, 53
Evans, James H., 98
Evans, John Q., 99
Evans, Thomas, 53
Farmer, Miss, 42
Farrior, J. B., Mrs., 99
Farrior, Lou, 47
Faulk, A. W., Mrs., 13
Faulk, J. H., 84
Faulkner, Charles, 53
Faust, B. F., Mrs., 67
Feagin, Daniel, 44
Feagin, Ike, Col., 44
Feagin, Ike, Judge, 75
Federick, Lizzie, Mrs., 96
Fenn, C. W., 45
Fenn, Cullis, 45
Fenn, Cullus, 56
Fenn, J. E., 45
Fenn, James E., 1
Ferrell, G. A., 30
Ferrell, George A., Mrs., 52
Ferrell, T. H., Mrs., 100
Ferrell, Thomas H., 10
Fields, Mary Emma, Mrs., 85
Fields, R. I., Mrs., 4
Fillengin, Julia, Mrs., 71
Fillingame, Jess, 28
Fisher, C. B., 108
Fitzgerald, Mary, Mrs., 65
Fitzaptrick, E. H., Mrs., 21
Flanders, J. C., Col., 61

Flewellen, Mrs., 114
Flewellen, A., Capt., 76
Flewellen, A. H., Mrs., 68
Flewellen, G. H., 68
Flewellen, J. T., 76
Flewellen, James T., 68
Flewellen, Jim, 76
Flewellen, Junius, Mrs., 8
Flewellen, W. W., 68, 70, 76
Flewellen, Willie Mae, 76
Florence, H. B., 69
Florence, Pete, 69
Florence, Pete (P. E.), 93
Florence, W. A., Dr., 69
Flournoy, J. T., Mrs., 33
Flournoy, S. J., Capt., 46
Flournoy, Sallie, 46
Flowers, D. W., 115
Flowers, Harrell, 111
Flowers, J. H. Mrs., 81
Flowers, John, 115
Flowers, John J., 112
Flowers, R. W., Dr., 18
Flowers, R. W., Mrs., 6
Flowers, W. H., 112
Flowers, W. H., Mrs., 81
Flowers, Wright, 3
Floyd, A. J., 18
Floyd, Mollie, Mrs., 81
Floyd, Page, 99
Floyd, (Page), Mrs., 99
Floyd, Pilot, 77
Folsom, Elizabeth, 100
Folsom, James, 100
Folsom, R. S., Mrs., 88
Folsom, Wash, 100
Forney, William H., Gen., 28
Foster, A. B., 68
Foster, J. W., Mrs., 18
Foster, John A., 68
Foster, John M., 21
Foster, Mary, Mrs., 61, 86
Foster, Webb, Judge, 68
Foy, Fred, 90
Foy, J. P., Mrs., 52
Foy, John P., Mrs., 114
Foy, Levy, 90
Foy, Mary, Mrs., 56
Foy, Nellie B., 90
Foy, S. R., 7
Foy, William, Mrs., 90
Franklin, John N., Mrs., 71
Frazer, Judge, 64
Frazer, C. C., 64
Frazer, F. J., 64

Frazer, Martha, 38
Frazer, N. H., Col., 64
Frazer, Thomas G., 38
Fredrickson, F. M., 27
Freeman, Mollie, Mrs., 2
Freeman, T. R., Mrs., 8
Freidman, J., Mrs., 80, 102
Fry, W. A., 3
Fryer, Dr., 45
Fryer, J. B., 42, 116
Fryer, Lucinda, 45
Fryer, Lucinda, Mrs., 22
Fryer, R. D., 45
Fuller, Hiram, Col., 29
Fuller, J. C., 50
Fuller, Julia, 29
Fulmore, Andrew C., 26
Fuquary, George, 33
Fuquay, Randolph, 44
Fuquay Richmond, Mrs., 106
Furgurson, Sophia, 73
Fussell, John, 65
Gallavotti, S., 11
Galloway, A. J., 9
Gamsnell, Martha J., Mrs., 86
Garland, E. H., 27
Garland, J. B., 27
Garland, Mary, Mrs., 27
Garner, Jesse B., Mrs., 38
Garrett, Miss, 18
Garrett, James, 75
Garrett, Sam M., 75
Gaston, Amanda, Mrs., 84
Gaston, J. B., 84
Gaston, Zell, Judge, 84
Gay, F. M., 50
Gay, G. B., Mrs., 106
Gay, W. E., 105
George, Charles, 46
George, J. M., 55
George, J. F., Mrs., 46
Gibbons, Eugene, 95
Gibbons, J. W. T., 28
Gibbons, Stephen T., 28
Gibhard, Miss, 26
Gibson J. B., Mrs., 110
Gilchrist, Daniel, 48
Gilchrist, Eliza, Mrs., 107
Gilchrist, James G., Col., 79
Gillam, Harry J., 107
Gillis Malcolm, 72
Gillis, Victoria, Mrs., 72
Givens, B. D., 86
Givens, Thomas W., Mrs., 8
Glass, John D., 3

Glass, L. D., 69
Glass, Nancy, Mrs., 69
Glenn, A. J. S., 53
Glenn, H. C., Mrs., 94
Glenn, Henry C., 94
Glenn, J. M., Rev., 69
Glenn, J. W., Rev., 69
Glenn, Sarah, 59
Glover, Mrs., 8
Glover, E., 14
Glover, E. E., 14
Glover, E. M., 14
Glover, Ed., 8
Glover, John, 35
Glover, Willie, Mrs., 21
Godfrey, Laura, 5
Godfrey, Enoch, 5
Godwin, J. L., Mrs., 85
Godwin, J. S., 110
Godwin, John D., 110
Godwin, Mary, 22
Godwin, Mary, Mrs., 110
Godwin, Rance, 28
Golden, Caleb, 49
Goldsmith, Bettie, 60
Goldsmith, Dan, Dr., 78
Goodwin, Mrs., 57
Goodwin, A., Dr., 96
Goodwin, Albert, Dr., 75
Goodwin, F. L., Miss, 76
Goodwin, Mamie, 76
Goodwin, S. A., Dr., 96
Goodwin, Sam, Rev., 76
Gorden, Augusta, 96
Gorsuch, Lucy, 48
Grace, E. E., 41
Graddy, Heywood, 67
Graddy, William, 82
Graham, E. A., 113
Graham, M. B. Mrs., 5
Graham, W. H., 50
Grant, George, 55
Grant, J. M., Mrs., 48
Grant, James W., 54
Grant, Joe, Mrs., 111
Graves, Mrs. 34
Graves, J. R., Rev., 22
Graves, Lottie, 94
Graves, Parish, 94
Graves, W. Z., 94
Gray, Mollie, 71
Green, Aaron, Mrs., 110
Green, A. S., Mrs., 57

Green, Emeline, Mrs., 43
Green, J. A., Mrs., 93
Green, M. B., Judge, 8
Green, T. C., 70
Green, T. G., 43
Green, V. B., 53
Green W. J., 57
Green, Willian, 109
Greenwood, Mr., 40
Gregory, Rev., 45
Gregory, E. H., Mrs., 45
Gregory, W. F., Mrs., 31
Griffin, Bennie, 75
Griffin, Ethel, 75
Griffin, Ida, 98
Griffin, J. E., 75
Griggs, Mrs., 76
Grisman, James, 68
Grissitt, Daniel, Mrs., 105
Grissett, Daniel M., 19
Grubbs, Dr., 32
Grubbs, Mrs., 14, 45
Grubbs, Britt, 45
Grubbs, Green, Mrs., 32
Grubbs, J. T., Mrs., 94
Grubbs, James W., 14
Grubbs, Mary, 76
Guerry, Jim, Judge, 42
Guerry, LeGrand, 42
Guerry, LeGrand, Capt., 74
Guerry, Sam, 42
Guerry, T. L., Col., 42
Guice, B. L., Mrs., 75
Guice, C. W., 34
Guice, J. G., Mrs., 52
Guice, Stella D., Mrs., 114
Guice, Susie, Mrs., 83
Guilford, J. C., Capt., 42
Guilford, W. E., Mrs., 76
Gunn, William C., 26
Hagler, C. W., 17
Hagood, Anna B., 109
Hagood, J. J., Mrs., 109
Hales, Julia, Mrs., 77
Hall, Hewlett A., 100
Hall, Lizzie, Mrs., 77
Hall, R. G., 1
Hall, William, 77
Hamilton, W. G., 91
Hance, Miss, 72
Hancock, G. W., 115
Hanson, C. C., Mrs., 63
Hardaway, Robert, Col., 67, **68**

Hardaway, Sallie, 68
Hardeman, Thomas, Mrs., 12
Harding, Horace, Col., 68
Hargrove, Julie, Mr., 33
Harp, J. W., Mrs., 46
Harrell, Elisha, 5
Harrell, Hol., 35
Harrell, J. M., 106
Harrell, Liza, 112
Harrell, Sarah E., 5
Harrell, W. H., 48
Harrell, W. J. C., 106
Harrington, Argent, Mrs., 64
Harris, A. B., 20
Harrison, Henry, 46
Harrison, Mamie, 113
Harrison, Thomas, 46
Harrison, Thomas H., 23
Hart, Mrs., 85
Hart, Annie, Mrs., 27
Hart, B. Frank, 100
Hart, Beall, 100
Hart, C. B., 65
Hart, Charles, 100
Hart, Frank, Mrs., 7
Hart, H. C., 65
Hart, Harrison, 65
Hart, Lucy, Mrs., 100
Hartung, F. J., 25
Hartung, Joe, 25
Hartung, John, 25
Hartzog, Daniel, 30
Hartzog, George, Mrs., 35
Hartzog, George W., 87
Hartzog, Henry, 82
Hartzog, Rebecca, Mrs., 7
Hartzog, Wiley, 24
Hartzog, Wyley, 82
Harwell, Irene, 97
Hatcher, L. D., 48
Hatfield, Forrest D., Mrs., 73
Hatfield, James, 50
Hawkins, Hon., 35
Hawkins, A. N., 104
Hawkins, Eugene H., Rev., 91
Hawkins, Hiram, 40
Hawkins, Hiram, Mrs., 35
Hawkins, J. F., Mrs., 61
Hawkins, Lizzie, 104
Hawkins, T. A. J., 104
Hawkins, V. P., Dr., 91
Hawkins, W. W., Mrs., 69
Hawley, N. L., 76

Hayes, Charles, B., 49
Heath, Miles, 86
Helms, J. M., Mrs., 19
Helms, Gilbert, 44
Helms, Joel, 110
Helms, John, 10
Helms, T. C., 94
Helms, Wade, Mrs., 2
Henderson, James, 55
Henderson, Mary E. Mrs., 86
Henderson, R. M., 86
Hendley, R. M., 56
Hendley, W. J., Mrs., 56
Hendricks, Mrs., 85
Hendrix, Miss, 71
Hendrix, George W., 77
Henley, James Z., 69
Henry, Beverly M., 99
Henry, Martha F., Mrs., 99
Hentley, Will, 31
Herman, W. F., Mrs., 112
Herndon, Benjamin, 5
Herndon, Huldah, Mrs., 5
Heron, D. J., 82
Heron, E. M., Dr., 82
Herring, Seth, 21
Herron, E. M., Dr., 14
Hickey, J. C., Mrs., 74
Hickman, John A., Dr., 102
Hightower, Thomas A. A., 44
Hildreth, Mrs., 7
Hildreth, T. Z., Rev., 7
Hill, B. H., Jr., 105
Hill, B. H., Jr., Mrs., 2
Hill, B. H., Sr., Mrs., 105
Hill, C. D., 105
Hill, James J., Mrs., 89
Hill, Jashua, 15
Hill, W. A., Mrs., 39, 99
Hilliard, Jack, 2
Hillman, Joseph, 6
Hinson, James, 102
Hirsh, Herman, 51
Hobdy, Addie, 115
Hobdy, Anne, 97
Hobdy, Bufford, 97
Hobdy, E. H., 51
Hobdy, Harrel, Mrs., 14
Hobdy, Ila, 104
Hobdy, Jenny, 97
Hobdy, John, 104
Hobdy, Marie, 97
Hobdy, R. L., Capt., 43, 51

Hobdy, R. L., Mrs., 97
Hobdy, Robert, 97
Hoge, Moses D., 63
Hogue, Caroline R., Mrs., 12
Hogue, Fred, 111
Hogue, J. R., Col., 111
Holder, G. G., 113
Holder, Paul, 113
Holland, William, 79
Hollingsworth, J. H., 79
Hollis, M. J., 1
Holmes, Amanda, Mrs., 55
Holmes, Dallas, 106
Holmes, H. S., 55
Holmes, James, 58
Holmes, John, 55
Holmes, S. J., Mrs., 58
Holt, P. R., Dr., 113
Holt, S. A., Dr., 42, 113
Holt, S. A., Mrs., 33
Holt, Syd, 42
Hood, Arthur, Col., 81
Hood, E. C., Mrs., 38
Hoole, Bertram J., 80
Hoole, Victoria, 80
Hooper, Charlotte I., Mrs., 104
Hooper, George B., 104
Hooper, George W., 104
Horn, James, Mrs., 104
Hortman, Belle, 56
Hortman, Emma, 85
Hortman, H., Mrs., 81
Hortman, J. G., 85
Hortman, J. W., 85
Hortman, James, 78
Hortman, John F., 56
Hortman, Lizzie D., Mrs., 78
Hortman, W. H., 85
Houston, R. L., Mrs., 33
Howard, Mrs., 39
Howard, T. W., Mrs., 83
Howell, G. H., 82
Howerton, Jennie, 54
Howerton, T. J., 54
Hubbard, W. D., Rev., 71
Hudgens, L. A., Mrs., 91
Hudspeth, Dora, Mrs., 105
Hudspeth, Gus, Mrs., 40
Hudspeth, Mary, 83
Hudspeth, R. T., 70
Hudson, Mrs., 39
Hudson, E. A., 12, 91
Hudson, Nan, 12
Hudson, Sarah, Mrs., 91

Huff, Warren, Mrs., 76
Hughes, Henrietta, 84
Hughes, John, 84
Hulsey, Mrs., 42
Hunt, L. A., 31
Hunt, W. G., 109
Hunter, Geraldine, 31
Hunter, H. M., Dr., 31
Hunter, James L., 40
Hunter, John Lingard, Gen., 73
Hurst, James, Mrs., 16
Hurst, James F., Mrs., 116
Hurt, Louise, Mrs., 89
Hutchinson, J. P., Mrs., 39
Hutto, W. J., 40
Hyatt, Meltrose, 33
Hyatt, Mollie, 96
Hyatt, N. H., 33
Ingram, Oliver, 82
Ingram, see Engram
Irby, C. C., 63
Irby, Hilliard J., Col., 63
Irby, L. E., 12, 63, 101
Irby, T. J., Mrs., 46
Irby, Virginia, Mrs., 112
Ixes, Sarah B., Mrs., 75
Jacobs, E., 15
Jacobs, John, 31
Jackson, Bishop, 27
Jackson, H. M., 67
Jackson, H. M., Mrs., 27
Jackson, Henry M., 75
Jackson, James, Capt., 39
Jackson, Jim, 39
Jackson, John, 31
Jackson, S. K., Dr., 67
James, Andrew, Mrs., 72
James, B. B., Mrs., 100
James, Benjamin, 35
James, Benjamin S., Dr., 35
James, Elizabeth, Mrs., 71
James, Fannie, 35
James, George S., 35
James, J. A., 88
James, J. J., Mrs., 89
James, J. Berry, 72
James, John, 26
James, John Stobo, 35
James, Mamie, 116
James, W. A., 72
Jelks, W. D., 38
Jelks, W. D., Mrs., 63
Jenkins, E. L., Capt., 54
Jenkins, S. F., Mrs., 69

Jennings, Annie, 82
Jennings, B. H., 35
Jennings, Carrie, Mrs., 45
Jernigan, L. A., Mrs., 81
Jernigan, William, Mrs., 44
Jessup, Eloise Buford, Mrs., 17
Jimmerson, W. M., 110
Johnson, A. D., Mrs., 60
Johnson, Alex, 12
Johnson, Alex, Mrs., 44
Johnson, Ann, Mrs., 77
Johnson, Berry, Mrs., 87
Johnson, C. G., 68
Johnson, Ed M., Mrs., 106
Johnson, Edward, 40
Johnson, Eldridge, 86
Johnson, F. M., 2
Johnson, G. B., 86
Johnson, J. B., Mrs., 78
Johnson, Jack, 6
Johnson, Jane, Mrs., 15
Johnson, John, 84
Johnson, Joseph E., 50
Johnson, Lee, 64
Johnson, Richard, 84
Johnson, Sidney, 2
Johnson, T. L., 84
Johnson, Will, Mrs., 96
Johnston, C. E., Mrs., 67
Johnston, L. F., 28
Jones, A. P., Mrs., 20
Jones, Ben, 22
Jones, Harrison, 20
Jones, Jason, Mrs., 59
Jones, Joseph, 76, 92
Jones, Mattie, Mrs., 76
Jones, Primus, 20
Jones, R. S., 92
Jones, Reuben, 20
Jones, Sallie, 45
Jones, Susan, Mrs., 41
Jones, T. F., 22
Jordan, Rev., 12
Jordan, A. B., 25
Jordan, Adrian P., 25
Jordan, Carrie Lou, 78
Jordan, Earnest, 78
Jordan, Emma, 78
Jordan, George, Mrs., 78
Jordan, George M., 69
Jordan, H. C., 25
Jordan, H. E., Mrs., 25
Jordan, H. L., 69
Jordan, J. H., 30

Jordan, J. S., Rev., 25
Jordan, Junius, 25
Jordan, Junius, Mrs., 12
Jordan, Junius, Rev., 24
Jordan, Lorenzo, 65
Jordan, Mary, Mrs., 44
Jordan, Sarah A., Mrs., 114
Joseph, W. F., Capt., 51
Joyner, Abednego, 50
Joyner, B. T., 50
Joyner, Meshach, 50
Joyner, Shadrach, 50
Juhan, Charles, 83
Juhan, Louis, 83
Juhan, W. A., Mrs., 83
Juhan, W. J., 83
Juhan, William, 83
Kaigler, B. R., 7
Kaigler, E. L., 83
Kaigler, H. M., Dr., 59
Kaigler, H. M., Mrs., 57
Kaigler, J. J., Capt., 21
Kaigler, Mary A., 44
Kates, N. E., Miss, 87
Kaufman, Mrs., 13
Kay, Jesse, 82
Keener, J. O., Dr., 72
Keesee, William, Mrs., 102
Keils, Elias M., Judge, 18
Keitt, Anna C., 63
Kendall, J. T., Mrs., 69, 83
Kendall, John, 106
Kenderick, J. W., 35
Kendrick, N. S., Mrs., 27
Kennedy, Annie, 14
Kennedy, Fletcher, 51
Kennedy, Sanford, Mrs., 115
Kennedy, W. L., 14
Kennedy, W. L., Mrs., 116
Kenneworth, Herman, Capt., 6
Key, D. M., Judge, 74
Key, H. E., 75
Key, Judson, 75
Keyton, J. T., 9
Keyton, N. K., Mrs., 9
Kilby, Mrs., 72
Killebrew, M. N., 69
Kimball, A. M., 2
King, E. N., 114
King, E. R., 37
King, Mary, Mrs., 91
King, Porter, Mrs., 71
King, Sarah, Mrs., 78
King, William, 78

Kirkpatrick, Mrs., 77
Knight, G. W., Mrs., 34
Knowles, F. M., 49
Knox, Cephas J., 82
Knox, John B., 64
Knox, Sue, 64
Kolb, Reuben, 18
Koonce, Bessie, 53
Koonce, Jeff, 97
Koonce, Mary, 74
LaHattie, Albert, 82
LaHattie, C. B., Rev., 82
LaHattie, C. O., 82
LaHattie, Lucile, 82
LaHattie, M. T., 82
LaHattie, Mittie E., 82
Lampley, Deila, 70
Lampley, Harmon H., Mrs., 111
Land, Floyd, 30
Land, Mary, 30
Landauer, Sigmund, 69
Laney, N. L., Mrs., 104
Laney, Noah S., 101
Lang, James, Capt., 79
Langford, Ellen, Mrs., 115
Langston, Ada, Mrs., 95
Lanier, Cyntha, Mrs., 88
Lanier, J. M., 88
Laseter, Earnest, 95
Laseter, M. E., Mrs., 45
Lassiter, Jane, Mrs., 20
Law, Fleming, 46
Lee, Dr., 7
Lee, A. V., Capt., 36
Lee, C. W., Dr., 36
Lee, Edna, 98
Lee, Frank, 96
Lee, I. J., Col., 96
Lee, Jeffie, 98
Lee, Lovard, Maj., 44
Lee, M. J., Miss, 108
Lee, Needham, 98
Lee, Needham, Mrs., 22
Lee, R. B., 23
Lee, R. B., Mrs., 23
Lee, Robert, 98
Lee, Robert, Mrs., 18
Lee, Robert B., 98
Lee, Sallie, Mrs., 115
Lee, Timothy, 72
Lee, W. B., 98
Leeds, William R., 32
LeGrand, M. P., Mrs., 10
Leham, Abe, Mrs., 84

Leonard, Eliza C., 86
Lester, James W., 4
Lewis, A. J., 81
Lewis, Annie, 62
Lewis, G. A., 81
Lewis, Hanse, 36
Lewis, Hanson, 41
Lewis, Harrison, 80
Lewis, J. N., Mrs., 96
Lewis, James, 21
Lewis, John, 36, 87
Lewis, John R., 80
Lewis, L. J., Mrs., 83
Lewis, Quinn, 20, 81
Lewis, Rose, 20
Lewis, Straton, 81
Lewis, Susan A., 116
Lewis, W. A., 41
Lewis, W. G., Mrs., 89
Lewy, Simon, 60
Lidden, C. C., Mrs., 108
Liebman, Isaac, 53
Lignoski, F. B., 59
Ligon, T. B., Dr., 16
Line, Margaret, 71
Lingo, E., 102
Link, William, Mrs., 52
Livesay, Quincey, 30
Lockard, A. T., 13
Lockhart, W. W., Mrs., 66
Logan, Kate, Mrs., 11
Locke, A. J., 83, 99, 103, 107
Locke, A. J., Mrs., 25
Locke, C., 106
Locke, R. D., 83, 103
Locke, Thomas S., 70
Locke, W. F., Mrs., 82
Lokey, B. F., Mrs., 5
Lomax, Carrie, Mrs., 84
Long, Ann, 14
Long, Anna, Mrs., 7
Long, B. F., 22
Long, Daisy Lee, 22
Long, E. T., Mrs., 36, 113
Long, G. T., 56
Long, J. H., 22
Long, Jackson E., 7
Long, Lemuel, 14
Long, N. W. E., 7
Long, Nannie D., Mrs., 89
Long, W. O., 22
Lore, Capt., 26
Lore, Dave, Mrs., 26
Loring, George B., 10

Lott, Taylor, 108
Lovelace, Susan E., 44
Loveless, E. L., Rev., 61
Loveless, W. F., Rev., 61
Lowenstein, Mrs., 13
Loyd, F. B., 47
Lucas, Garlington, 65
Lucas, Mollie E., Mrs., 6
Ludwig, Maggie, Mrs., 60
Ludwig, P. J., Mrs., 41
Lumsden, B. D., Mrs., 12
Lunsford, H. F., 84
Lunsford, John F., Mrs., 101
Mabry, Mrs., 63
Mabry, James W., Col., 28
Mabry, Seth, 88
Mabry, Seth, Mrs., 88
Mackenzie, Mrs., 77
MacKenzie, Anna V., 76
Mackenzie, George N., 76
Mackenzie, Lucie T. E., 76
Mackenzie, Mary M., 76
Magee, J. M., Mrs., 92
Mahone, Butler, 36
Mahone, William, Gen., 36
Mahone, William, Jr., 36
Mainor, J. B., Mrs., 8
Mallet, Lizzie, Mrs., 85
Mallory, L. P., 96
Mallory, Lester P., 75
Malone, Alva, 50
Malone, Thomas, 24
Manassas, L., Mrs., 13
Mancill, J. D., 38
Mangum, Annie W., 107
Mangum, Helen, 105
Mangum, Robert, 105
Mangum, T. F., Jr., 105
Mangum, T. F., Rev., 105
Mangum, Tom, 105
Mangum, W. W., 105
Mangum, W. W., Dr., 107
Mangum, W. W., Mrs., 107
Manley, Albert, 19
Manley, Benjamin, 19
Mann, Mrs., 19
Mann, Jube, 19
Margart, J. P., Rev., 82
Margart, S. F., 82
Margart, S. T., 82
Margart, S. T., Mrs., 8
Marks, John, 8
Martin, A. L., Mrs., 23, 116
Martin, C. A., Mrs., 57
Martin, Christian, Mrs., 89

Martin, D., Mrs., 10
Martin, Daniel, Capt., 13
Martin, E. Z., 108
Martin, Edgar Z., Mrs., 108
Martin, J. P., Dr., 10
Martin, John, 94
Martin, Lavinia, 35
Martin, M., 13
Martin, Murdock, 10
Martin, Queen J. O., 110
Martin, Queen J. O., Mrs., 110
Martin, Robert, Mrs., 106
Martin, Sandy, 10
Martin, Sandy, Mrs., 9
Martin, W. J., 70
Martin, Will, 89
Matthews, Stella, Mrs., 99
Matthison, Tip (Elias), 73
Mays, Georgia, 13
McAllister, J. T., 58
McAllister, John T., 58
McAllister, R. C., 58
McAllister, W. A., 58
McArthur, Mary A., Mrs., 59
McBryde, James, 32
McCall, Charles R., 60
McCall, Gilbert, 103
McCall, Gilbert, Mrs., 28
McCall, Hart, 47
McCarty, T. R., Mrs., 86
McComb, W. B., Mrs., 110
McCormick, Ross, 66
McCracken, M. E., Mrs., 20
McCrae, J. W., Mrs., 84
McCraney, Arabella, Mrs., 23
McCraney, Edith, Mrs., 19
McCraney, Fletcher, Mrs., 19, 46
McCraney, Jane, Mrs., 93
McCraney, Maggie, 79
McCraney, Norman, 19, 79
McCrary, E. D., 108
McCrary, Ed B., 108
McCrary, Nell, 108
McCurdy, Augustus R., Col., 43
McCurdy, Eula, 53
McDaniel, Nicie, Mrs., 68
McDonald, A. A., 44
McDonald, A. A., Mrs., 47
McDonald, A. C., 38
McDonald, Annie, Mrs., 36
McDonald, Christopher, 78
McDonald, Eliza, 67
McDonald, Harris, 37
McDonald, J. F., 16
McDonald, Jesse, 12

McDonald, John, 32
McDonald, Marshall, 35
McDonald, Mary, Mrs., 37
McDonald, Sarah D., 104
McDonnell, Annie, 59
McEachern, Daniel, 29
McEachern, John C., 97
McEachern, J. D., Mrs., 7
McEachern, M., 97
McEachern, William, 93
McFadden, Mary, 88
McGee, J. M., Mrs., 91
McGehee, Mrs., 4
McGehee, Alfred, 4
McGhee, John, 10
McGilt, Mrs., 36
McGilvary, Elizabeth, Mrs., 111
McGilvary, H. H., Mrs., 37
McGilvary, J. F., 111
McGilvary, J. F., Mrs., 104
McGilvary, M., Rev., 115
McGint, Laura, Mrs., 110
McGlaun, John F., 96
McGlaun, John F., Mrs., 96
McGough, H. B., 27
McGough, Hugh, 29
McGrady, Susan, 116
McInnis, Miles, 38
McInnis, Sarah A., Mrs., 38
McIntosh, J. G., 77
McIntyre, Johanna, Mrs., 83
McIntyre, Patrick, 83
McKay, Alex, 90
McKay, Alexander, 89
McKay, F., 94
McKay, Farquhar, 16, 57, 90
McKay, Phil, 16
McKay, William A., 12
McKee, D. J., 1
McKenzie, B. B. Capt., 107
McKenzie, Clara Belle, Mrs., 79
McKenzie, Mary Lou, 103
McKenzie, P. B., Mrs., 74
McKenzie, W. R., 79
McKinney, W. E., Mrs., 53
McKinnon, Mrs., 32
McKinnon, Alex., 5
McKinnon, Daniel, 47
McKinnon, John, 47
McKinnon, Katie, Mrs., 47
McKleroy, J. M., Mrs., 2
McKleroy, John M., Mrs., 91
McKleroy, W. H., 91
McLain, Daniel, 59

McLain, LeElla, 85
McLain, Lockland, Mrs., 85
McLaughlin, Charles I., Mrs., 25
McLaughlin, Duncan S., 56
McLaughlin, L. W., Mrs., 65
McLaughlin, L. W., Mrs., 65
McLean, Hugh, 104
McLean, Hughey, 102
McLean, L. D., 65
McLendon, Sallie, Mrs., 98
McLendon, W. B., 98
McLendon, W. B., Mrs., 52
McLeod, Alex., 9
McLeod, Archie, Mrs., 25
McLeod, Carrie, 85
McLeod, D. D., 74
McLeod, Daniel, 74
Mcleod, Daniel D., Maj., 65
Mcleod, Ed, 74
Mcleod, F., 85
McLeod, F. E., Mrs., 85
McLeod, H. J., 10, 85
McLeod, Jane, Mrs., 87
McLeod, John, 87
McLeod, L. C., 10
McLeod, Tudse, Mrs., 34
McLeod, W. E., Mrs., 40
McLeod, W. L., 85
McLeod, W. T., 10
McLeroy, Miss, 74
McLeroy, C. G., 56
McMurry, George, 81
McMurry, Katherine, Mrs., 81
McNab, Fanny, 34
McNab, J. C., 34
McNab, J. C., Capt., 71
McNab, John, 1, 90, 111
McNab, John, Capt., 110
McNab, John, Mrs., 110
McNab, John R., 20
McNab, John C., Capt., 6, 20
McNair, John, 16
McNeal, Daniel, Mrs., 92
McNeill, J. C., Dr., 14
McNeill, John, 14
McNeill, S. E., Mrs., 8
McRae, A. K., 25
McRae, Amma, 83
McRae, Colon, 61
McRae, Drucilla, Mrs., 61
McRae, Duncan, 78
McRae, Frank, 51
McRae, Jabez, 83
McRae, Jack, 37

McRae, Jane, 51
McRae, Jennie, 83
McRae, John, 83, 109
McRae, John L., Capt., 61
McRae, John McL., 83
McRae, Julia, 83
McRae, Kate, Mrs., 7
McRae, Kittie, Mrs., 51
McRae, Louie, 83
McRae, Mary, 51
McRae, Phil, 51
McRae, Tom, 21
McRae, W. H., Mrs., 23
McRae, W. N., 23
McSwain, Catherine, 88
McTyer, Mrs., 31
McTyer, Bessie, 75
McTyer, John, Mrs., 57
McTyer, Maggie, 75
McTyer, T. R., Mrs., 75
Meadows, Felix, 22
Meadows, J. E., 116
Meadows, Jule, 22
Meadows, Leila, Mrs., 116
Meek, Benj. F., Dr., 73
Menderson, Nathan, 105
Mercer, Charles G., 27
Mercer, J. W., Dr., 27, 52
Meridith, Tessie, 81
Meriwether, Chas. G., 10
Merrick, Annie, Mrs., 29
Merrick, John, Col., 29
Merritt, M. C., 48
Merritt, Marvin, 48
Merriwether, Bessie, 67
Messing, Rabbi, 101
Methvin, Anna, 90
Methvin, Bob, 90
Methvin, Clifford, 90
Methvin, Daniel J., 90
Methvin, Ralph, 90
Methvin, T. J., 90
Methvin, William, 90
Middlebrooks, John, Mrs., 104
Middlebrooks, Z. T., Mrs., 70
Miles, Mrs., 34
Miles, Abram, 34
Miles, W. J., Mrs., 101
Miller, A. J., 41
Miller, Hayne, 73
Miller, Irwing L., 73
Miller, James, 39
Miller, Joe, 41
Miller, John, Mrs., 56
Miller, Maude, 73

Miller, N. H., Mrs., 19
Miller, Nancy, Mrs., 41
Miller, Teresa, Mrs., 73
Miller, W. J., Mrs., 78
Miller, W. M., Mrs., 44
Milligan, Marcellus E., 60
Milligan, Robert, Mrs., 101
Mills, Bartow, 117
Mills, Enoch, 23, 117
Mills, George W., Rev., 4
Mills, Jennie, Mrs., 23
Mills, Kate E., 103
Mills, Sisler, 117
Milton, James, 60
Milton, John, 60
Milton, Lula, 60
Milton, May, 60
Milton, Victor M., 60
Milton, Walter, 60
Mitchell, A. C., Col., 6
Mitchell, A. C., Jr., 6
Mitchell, A. C., Mrs., 39, 52
Mitchell, Americus C., 6
Mitchell, A. C., 23, 39, 90
Mitchell, C. Ray, Dr., 99
Mitchell, E. S., Dr., 99
Mitchell, H. L., 101
Mitchell, James B., 7
Mitchell, James W., Dr., 99
Mitchell, Lillie, 70
Mitchell, Lillie D., Mrs., 114
Mitchell, Mac, 90
Mitchell, R. P., Rev., 59
Mitchell, T. S., Dr., 70
Mitchell, T. Rudledge, Dr., 99
Mitchell, Thomas S., Dr., 99
Mitchell, Thos. S., Dr., 59
Mitchell, W. A., Dr., 6, 7, 83
Mitchell, W. A., Mrs., 23
Mitchell, William C., 99
Mitchell, Willie S., Mrs., 99
Moberly, Thomas, 40
Monroe, J. T., Dr., 54
Monroe, W. O., 87
Montgomery, Mary, Mrs., 99
Moody, W. E., 50
Mooney, John A., 57
Mooney, Thomas, 57
Moonlight, Thos., Col., 64
Moor, J. G., 70
Moore, Mrs., 19
Moore, Charles, Mrs., 74
Moore, J. B., 112
Moore, James, 20

Moore, Jim, 76
Moore, John, 99
Moore, John M., 108
Moore, Levi, Rev., 71
Moore, Mary, 74
Moore, R. B., 71
Moore, S. A., Mrs., 85
Moore, Sarah, Mrs., 112
Moore, W. T., Mrs., 100
Moreland, S. F., Mrs., 54
Morgan, Annie, 12
Morgan, Cornelia G. W., Mrs., 30
Morgan, John T., 30
Morgan, Sarah, Mrs., 51
Morgan, Thomas, 33
Morrell, J. L., Mrs., 86
Morris, Dr., 70
Morris, Mrs., 42
Morris, George L., 48
Morris, J. T., Mrs., 58, 83
Morris, John, Mrs., 70
Morris, Josiah, 15
Morris, P. H., 62
Morris, Pat, 62
Morris, Seymour, 62
Morrison, Annie, Mrs., 46
Morrison, N., 36
Morrison, Neal McK., 36
Moses, Raphael J., 26
Mosley, Nancy, Mrs., 81
Moss, William, 86
Moulthrop, Albert, 78
Moulthrop, Albert, Sr., 78
Moulthrop, Robert, Jr., 78
Moulthrop, Robert, Sr., 78
Moultrie, J. L., 51
Muller, J. H., 108
Mulligan, Peter, 54
Mullins, S. Q., 22
Munn, Mrs., 58
Murphey, P. A., Mrs., 110
Naftel, E. T., Mrs., 100
Nance, B. E., 54
Nance, J. A., 54
Nance, R. F., 54
Nance, Z. F., 54
Nesbitt, S. H., Mrs., 106
Nettles, James, 71
Nettles, Kate, Mrs., 71, 110
Nevins, Page B., Mrs., 61
Nevins, William R., 61
Newton, Constantine, 12
Newton, E. C., Mrs., 34
Nix, Mrs., 42

Nix, David, 42
Nix, David, Mrs., 99, 103
Nix, David E., 42, 95
Nix, Eliza, Mrs., 93
Nix, G. Y., Mrs., 109
Nix, Gideon, 28, 42, 93
Nix, J. M., 42
Nix, Joe, 25
Nix, John S., Mrs., 115
Nix, W. H., 20, 42
Nobles, J. A., Mrs., 51
Norman, F. A., Mrs., 29
Norman, Fred, 66
Norman, James T., Col., 43
Northrup, Lucien B., Gen., 29
Norton, Colon, 109
Norton, Daniel, 55
Norton, James B., 115
Norton, L., 109
Norton, L., Mrs., 109
Norton, Margaret C., 115
Norton, Norman, 56
Norton, T. C., 94
Norton, Victor, 15
Norton, Wes, 116
Nowland, Mr., 88
Nowland, Butler, 88
Nowland, John, 88
Nowland, Robert, 88
Nuckols, Louisa A., 40
Oates, Mrs., 19
Oates, Cyrus, 12
Oates, W. C., 19
Oates, W. C., Mrs., 33
O'Brien, J. E., 69
O'Brien, Jno. Courtenay, 69
O'Brien, W. O., 13
O'Byrne, Patrick, 107
Odom, John, 50
Odum, Mrs., 41,
Ogletree, Mrs., 85
Ogletree, A., Dr., 25
Ogletree, A., Mrs., 57
Ogletree, Absalom, Dr., 52
Ogletree, Sam, 57
Ogletree, Samuel, 53
Ogletree, Seaborn, 57
Oliver, Clayton W., 28
Oliver, L. L., 49
Oliver, Lizzie J., Mrs., 28
Oliver, Lucy, 47
Oliver, Phil, 73
Oliver, T. W., Col., 91
O'Neal, Edwin, 2

O'Neal, George S., 54
Oppert, Gussie, 17
Oppert, H., 17
Oppert, Mattie, 17
Oppert, N. A., Mrs., 101
Ormond, Robert M., Mrs., 83
Orr, James, Mrs., 79
Otis, Mrs., 82
Pace, J. B., 27
Parish, Eddie, 111, 115
Parish, Ida, 34
Parish, J. E., 34, 111, 115
Parish, J. E., Sr., 34
Parish, Joseph, 115
Parish, Joseph, Mrs., 115
Parish, M. H., 34, 111
Parish, M. H., Mrs., 104
Parish, Martin H., 115
Parish, Rebecca, Mrs., 92
Parish, T. R., 34
Parker, Mrs., 42
Parker, Amos, 9
Parker, D. H., 66
Parker, E. A., 66
Parker, H. H., 66
Parker, H. Z., 12
Parker, J. D., Mrs., 62
Parker, J. W., Mrs., 38
Parker, Jane, 66
Parker, Joel, 10
Parker, Susan, Mrs., 10
Parkerson, D. C., 66
Parmer, Aaron, Mrs., 85
Parmer, Ann, Mrs., 75
Parmer, B. E. G., Mrs., 75
Parmer, Frank, Mrs., 78
Parmer, Jake, 43
Parmer, John, 43
Parmer, Mary, 98
Parrell, W. J. C., 110
Passmore, Lem, 22
Passmore, M. S., Mrs., 107
Passmore, Nettie, 36
Passmore, R. A., 78
Patterson, Angeline, 98
Patterson, F., 81
Patterson, Homer, 74
Patterson, Joe, Mrs., 111
Patterson, M. B., 51
Patterson, T. D., 98
Patterson, W. H., Rev., 81
Patterson, W. R., 81
Peach, Arthur, 105
Peach, G. W., 114

Peach, George W., 105
Peach, J. H., 114
Peach, John, 114
Peach, John H., 105
Peach, N. E., 114
Peacock, Mrs., 57
Peacock, Charles, 3
Peacock, Hattie, 17
Peacock, Jordan, Mrs., 11
Peacock, O. H., 17, 26
Peacock, O. H., Mrs., 96, 102
Peacock, T. M., 3
Peak, Alonza, 54
Peak, J. B., 68
Peak, L., Mrs., 107
Peak, Mary, 54
Peak, O. T., 68
Peak, R. D., 68
Peak, Rebecca, Mrs., 68
Pearson, George, 40
Peel, W. L., Mrs., 30
Peet, Margaret, 47
Pepper, R. P., Col., 38
Perkins, Mrs., 61
Perkins, Henry, 61
Perkins, J. P., 111
Perkins, James W., 30
Perkins, John D., 24
Perry, Louise T., 108
Perry, M. F., Maj., 85
Perryman, D. A., 83
Perryman, Mary A., Mrs., 83
Peters, Agnes, 5
Peters, Alice, Mrs., 5
Peters, Francis L., 86
Peters, W. T., 5, 13
Petry, Clifford A., 96
Petry, Frank. 96
Petry, Lottie, 96
Petry, Louis, 96
Petry, Mina, 96
Petry, William, 33, 98
Petry, William, Mrs., 66
Petry, William M., 96
Petty, Allen, Dr., 15
Petty, B. F., Mrs., 18
Petty, Chris, 31
Petty, Dick, 93
Petty, Ed, 93
Petty, J. V., 55
Petty, Jennie Ellison, 45
Petty, Katie, 32
Petty, N. A., Mrs., 15
Petty, Narcissa, Mrs., 93

Petty, Robert, Mrs., 105, 114
Petty, Walter, 71
Petty, Will, 55
Phelps, D., Mrs., 38
Phelps, Mary, 34
Phelps, Robert, 34
Phillips, Florence, Mrs., 4
Phillips, Isham, 28
Phillips, Jehu, 68
Phillips, J. W., Mrs., 34
Philips, John M., 69
Phillips, Monroe N., 4
Phillips, R., 34
Phillips, Sussie, Mrs., 46
Phillips, T. J., Capt., 69
Pierce, F. B., Mrs., 116
Pierce, J. R., 92
Pierce, Phil, 90
Pierce, Phil, Sr., 90
Pilcher, Swin, 74
Pinkston, J. E., Mrs., 76
Pippin, Dallas, 83
Pippin, George, 83
Pippin, Gordon, 83
Pippin, J. W., 83
Pippin, Weeks, 83
Pipkin, Haywood, 23
Pitts, Fred, 71
Pitts, J. E., Mrs., 50
Pitts, J. L., 51
Pitts, J. L., Mrs., 56
Pitts, R. M., 70
Pitts, R. N., Mrs., 94
Pitts, T. F., 51
Pitts, W. M., 51
Pitts, Whitfield, 51
Plumb, Preston B., 13
Pomeroy, F. A., Mrs., 54
Pomeroy, Maggie, 54
Ponder, John, 79
Ponder, Maggie, Mrs., 79
Pope, Alexander, Dr., 39
Porter, J. H., 49
Poston, Bates, 108
Poston, James, 108
Poston, John H., Mrs., 108
Poston, Johnnie, 108
Poston, Russie, 108
Poston, Stella, 108
Pou, Walter L., 40
Pournelle, Geo., R. Rev., 62
Powell, John, 60
Powell, Joseph S., 8
Powell, Mary, 60

Powell, R. D., 13
Powell, Seney, Mrs., 13
Powell, Sid, 8
Powers, Mary, Mrs., 76
Prechaska, George B., 27
Price, Aaron, 106
Price, Andrew, 2
Price, Benny, 43
Price, Burrell, 1
Price, Eliza J., Mrs., 59
Price, George C., 26
Price, H. B., Maj., 32
Price, H. W. B., Maj., 100, 116
Price, H. W. B. Mrs., 16, 73
Price, Jemsey, 43
Price, John, 2
Price, John E., Dr., 58
Price, R. J., 6
Price, Sam, 106
Price, Smitha, Mrs., 17
Price, William E., Mrs., 50
Priest, Eb, 64
Prince, J. A., Mrs., 69
Prince, W. L., Gen., 26
Proctor, John, Mrs., 62
Pruett, Mrs., 14
Pruett, Anna, Mrs., 5
Pruett, Louisa F., 42
Pruett, Oscar, 21
Pruett, S. G., 21, 86
Pruett, W. H., 86
Pruett, W. H., Judge, 21, 42
Pruett, W. H., Maj., 5, 14
Pruden, J. H., 62
Pruden, Theo., 62
Pugh, James L., 71
Pugh, James L., Mrs., 80
Pynchon, Louis C., Dr., 47
Queen, Frank J., 61
Quillin, E. R., 9
Quillin, Edgar R., 45, 47, 48
Quillin, M. M., 9
Quillin, Maggie, 9
Raleigh, A. A., 35
Raleigh, Fannie, Mrs., 77, 80
Raleigh, J. A., 38
Raleigh, Sallie K., 35
Raley, G., 14
Raley, G., Mrs., 47
Ramser, Dozier, 92
Ramser, Jacob, Mrs., 52
Ramser, Julian, 92
Ramser, Laura V., 92
Ramser, Mary, 92

Ramser, Mary, Mrs., 89
Ramser, T. J., Mrs., 89
Ramser, Thomas, 92
Ramsey, Seab, 6
Randall, E. T., 113
Randall, E. Troupe, 97
Randolph, James H., Dr., 19
Rau, Ed J., 101
Rau, Luna, Mrs., 101
Ray, Mrs., 90
Ray, Fannie, Mrs., 91
Ray, Hannah, Mrs., 84
Reaves, Thomas, Mrs., 3
Redd, C. A., Capt., 11
Redd, L. D., 11
Redd, W. A., 11
Redding, A. M., 73
Redding, Martha, Mrs., 50
Reed, Jennie D., Mrs., 8
Reed, Thomas, 74
Reed, Wyat, 23
Reeder, Susan S. E., 96
Reeder, W. N., 96
Reese, C. P., 87
Reese, J. W., 87
Reeves, Charlie, 111
Reeves, D. S., 78
Reeves, Daniel, 52
Reeves, David, 111
Reeves, Flora M., Mrs., 111
Reeves, Florine, 100
Reeves, J. H., 90
Reeves, J. W., 102
Reeves, Jeremiah, Rev., 112
Reeves, John, Dr., 111
Reeves, Junie, 52
Reeves, Lillian, 100
Reeves, Lizzie, Mrs., 90
Reeves, S. E., Mrs., 102
Reeves, T. J., 68
Reeves, W. E., 102
Reeves, W. N., Jr., 100
Reeves, W. N., Mrs., 111
Reeves, W. N., Rev., 111, 112
Reeves, William N., Dr., 111
Reid, Mrs., 109
Reid, Hines, 40
Respess, John R., 33
Reynolds, A. L., 14
Reynolds, Charlotte, 72
Reynolds, J. B., 93
Reynolds, John A., Dr., 16
Reynolds, R. G., Mrs., 57
Reynolds, Strada, 14
Reynolds, Thos. J., Mrs., 6

Rhodes, C., 3
Rhodes, Chauncey, 36, 113
Rhodes, Elizabeth, Mrs., 113
Rhodes, Jamie, 36
Rhodes, Jamie D., 113
Rhodes, John U., Lieut., 3
Rhodes, W. J., 56
Rhody, Annie, 88
Rhody, Barney, 88
Rhody, Emma, 88
Rhody, James, 88
Rhody, Maggie, 88
Rhody, Mary, Mrs., 88
Rhody, Maude, 88
Rhody, Theressa, 88
Rhynehold, Mr., 5
Rice, S. T., 39
Rich, Emanuel, 52
Rich, G. A., 87
Rich, L. F., 87
Richards, A. L., Mrs., 110
Richards, Ada, 2
Richards, Dallas, 2
Richards, G. W., 7
Richards, Giles, 96
Richards, James, 24
Richards, James, Mrs., 34
Richards, R. J., Sr., 34
Richardson, Judge, 12
Richardson, A. A., 75
Richardson, B. H., Col., 41
Richardson, Israel, 75
Richardson, John, 75
Richardson, W. L., Mrs., 105
Richardson, William, Mrs., 1:
Ricks, Miss, 11
Ricks, Leila, 25
Ridley, Mary, Mrs., 39
Riley, Daniel, Rev., 51
Ridley, Lucinda, Mrs., 51
Rish, R. F., 5
Roach, Ed., 28
Roach, Samuel, 28
Roberts, C. F., 112
Roberts, C. L., 112
Roberts, Clarence P., 5
Roberts, E. H., 103
Roberts, Ed, 5
Roberts, G. A., Capt., 14
Roberts, Henry, 64
Roberts, J. R., 112
Roberts, Jim, Mrs., 27
Roberts, Mac, 5
Roberts, Mary, Mrs., 90

Roberts, N. W., Mrs., 102
Roberts, Noah W., 5
Roberts, Ola, 112
Roberts, Oliver T., 5
Roberts, Will H., 5
Roberson, George, 109
Robertson, S. G., Dr., 4, 71, 106, 114
Robertson, Sarah, Mrs., 4
Robinson, C. C., 102
Robinson, C. C., Dr., 96
Robinson, Charles C., 57
Robinson, Cornelia, 57, 102
Robinson, Fred, 57
Robinson, Hugh, 57
Robinson, Lizzie, Mrs., 40
Robinson, Roby, 57
Robinson, Van, Mrs., 77
Robinson, W. F., Capt., 57
Robson, Dell, 73
Robson, Frank, 87
Roddenberry, R. S., 9, 17
Roddenbery, R. S., Mrs., 25
Rogers, Harrison, Mrs., 82
Rogers, J. G., 70
Rogers, James, Mrs., 114
Rogers, Reuben, 72
Rollins, Prof., 96
Rollins, Dock, Mrs., 7
Rollins, Elizabeth, Mrs., 112
Rollins, Fannie, Mrs., 7
Rollins, G. W., 36, 112
Rollins, J. W., 7
Rollins, J. W., Mrs., 96
Rollins, John D., 70
Romaine, Charles N., 30
Roney, Thomas, Mrs., 108
Roquemore, E. W., Mrs., 8
Roquemore, J. W., 8, 41
Roquemore, John D., 11
Roquemore, John D., Col., 79
Roquemore, John Will, 22
Roquemore, M. C., Mrs., 115
Roquemore, Mary L., Mrs., 40
Roquemore, May, 11
Ross, Ada, 57
Ross, C. R., 44
Ross, Charles R., 26
Ross, Clara, 26, 66
Ross, Clifford, 26
Ross, E. H., Mrs., 108
Ross, Edward H., 26
Ross, Florence K., Mrs., 44
Ross, J. L., 57

Ross, James, 13, 25
Ross, James L., 26
Ross, William J., 13
Rowland, James, 30
Rowland, Robert, 30
Rulterford, Foy, 42
Rulterford, Jessie, 42
Rutherford, see Rulterford
Rutland, John Q., 9
Rutland, Martha Jane, 9
Rutland, W. W., 9
Ryals, J. W., 41
Ryals, James, 38
Ryals, Richard, 38
Ryder, W. L., Dr., 53
Russell, H. C., Judge, 44
Russell, Mary, 53
Russell, W. H., Mrs., 28
Sams, J. K., Mrs., 80, 102
Sanders, Pres., 107
Sanders, H. V., 109
Sanders, J. R., 53
Sanders, J. R., Mrs., 107
Sanders, Jack, 53
Sanders, Moses, Mrs., 5
Sanders, Pess, Mrs., 67
Sanders, Peter, Mrs., 109
Sanders, Rufus, 47
Sandifer, Edna, Mrs., 85
Sandifer, Lou, Mrs., 85
Sanford, Emma, 102
Sapp, J. E., 65
Sapp, Meta, 65
Sauls, John, 51
Sauls, Lawrence, 51
Saunders, E. A., Mrs., 50
Saunders, J. R., 85
Sauter, Fred, 24
Sawyer, Anson, 53
Sawyer, Martha, Mrs., 100
Sawyer, W. W., 53
Sawyer, W. W., Mrs., 53
Scaife, Paul B., 59
Scarborough, D. M., Mrs., 92
Scarbrough, Henry, 41
Schloss, Mrs., 105
Schloss, Hugo, 105
Schmaeling, Phil, Mrs., 60
Scoot, Susie, Mrs., 91
Scott, Celia, Mrs., 58
Scott, Crawford, 105
Scott, George, 105
Scott, Lucy, 105
Scott, Manning, 58

Scott, Mary, Mrs., 105
Scott, Windfield, 105
Screws, Benjamin H., 111
Screws, W. W., Maj., 94, 111
Scroggins, Jim, 112
Seabon, William, 16
Seaborn, Joe, 95
Seaborn, William, 95
Seals, D. M., Mrs., 59
Seals, Morgan, Col., 59
Searcy, Mr., 61
Searcy, Christian A., Mrs., 92
Searcy, E. J., 11
Searcy, Ed, 92
Searcy, G. A., Mrs., 112, 113
Searcy, J. B., 11, 92
Searcy, Jesse B., Mrs., 61
Searcy, Joe, Mrs., 98
Searcy, Ollen, 51
Searcy, Quin, 11
Searcy, William, 87
Sears, Mr., 40
Seay, Ben, 26
Semple, Henry C., Maj., 29
Sessions, Donald, 55
Sessions, H. M., Mrs., 37
Sessions, L., Dr., 50
Sessions, Louis, Dr., 55
Shanks, Alsaza, 69
Sharp, Mrs., 57
Sheally, Chas. W., 67
Sheally, Chas. W., Mrs., 67
Sheally, John W., 67
Sheehan, D. T., 74, 95
Sheehan, D. T., Mrs., 74
Sheehan, Dan, Mrs., 97
Sheehan, E. S., 95
Sheehan, Merrill A., 95
Sheehan, R. E., 95
Sheehan, S. E., Mrs., 6
Sheehan, W. T., 60
Sheets, W. T., Mrs., 25
Shehane, W. T., Mrs., 88
Shehane, Will, 88
Shelton, J. B., Rev., 64
Shelton, John Bass, Mrs., 64
Sheppard, Thomas, 12
Sheppard, Thomas, Mrs., 12
Sherry, James, 77
Shirah, Silas, 58
Shirley, Ap, 66
Shorter, Carrie A., 21
Shorter, H. R., Maj., 37
Shorter, Henry R., Jr., 63

Shorter, Henry R., Maj., 63
Shorter, James B., 84
Shorter, Louise, 37
Shorter, Marietta, Mrs., 59
Shorter, Mary B., 40
Shorter, Reuben C., 21, 40
Shorter, Reuben C., Dr., 63
Shorter, Reuben C., Mrs., 63
Shropshire, R. D., Mrs., 81
Shropshire, William, 81
Silvas, Joseph, 10
Simmons, E. G., Col., 13
Simmons, J. W., 90
Simmons, John W., 98
Simms, Henry, 17
Simms, Mary, 24
Simonton, Mrs., 34, 93, 106
Simonton, J. H., 33
Simonton, J. R., 33
Simonton, R. H., Mrs., 25
Simpson, Lee, Dr., 103
Simpson, W. T., Jr., 102
Simpson, William T., 102, 113
Sims, S. A., 20
Singer, John G., 89
Singleton, S. S., 7, 94
Sinner, Fred G., Col., 30
Skillman, C. C., Mrs., 7, 100, 11
Skipper, Arthur, 50
Skipper, J. L., Mrs. 11
Slosson, Bena, Mrs., 46
Smart, Gussie, Mrs., 72
Smart, Press, 72
Smart, T. L., 94
Smart, W. A., Dr., 94
Smith, A. G., Capt., 53
Smith, A. J., Mrs., 77
Smith, Alice, Mrs., 41
Smith, C. J., Mrs., 77
Smith, E. A., Mrs., 73
Smith, E. P., 103
Smith, E. Q., Mrs., 68
Smith, Guy, 81
Smith, Howard, 53
Smith, J. B., Dr., 16
Smith, J. F., Rev., 72
Smith, J. G., 110
Smith, John, 42
Smith, M. F., Mrs., 105
Smith, Mary, Mrs., 18
Smith, Milledge, 52
Smith, Milton A., Col., 71
Smith, R. F., 51
Smith, R. G., Mrs., 104

Smith, R. S., Mrs., 78
Smith, W. Green, 30
Smith, Walter, 53
Smith, Wicher, 53
Smith, Willie, 93
Smith, Y. E., Mrs., 72
Smitha, William, 31
Smoot, J. W., 1
Snead, B. F., 41
Snead, Daniel, 41
Snead, Frank, 103, 110
Snead, Mark, 110
Snead, S. J., 41
Snipes, W. H., 21
Snow, Mr., 34
Solomon, J. W., Rev., 87
Solomon, John Wesley, Rev., 82
Solomon, Marcus L., 67
Solomon, R. A., 61
Solomon, Sam H., Mrs., 59
Southland, Jinnie, 67
Spann, Mamie, 2
Sparks, Angie, 40
Sparrow, F. S., 81
Sparrow, J. W., 105
Sparrow, W. J., 81
Sparrow, William Abbey, 105
Speight, J. W., Mrs., 18
Spence, William, 84
Spencer, C. H., 23
Spencer, Perry, 17
Spivey, H. J., 80
Spradley, James, 22
Spurlock, J. M., 79
Spurlock, Marian, Mrs., 79
Spurlock, O. O., 79
Spurlock, Orbie, 8
Spurlock, Solomon, 79
Stacey, J. W., Mrs., 98
Stallings, J. D., Rev., 77
Stallsworth, John L., 5
Stallsworth, N. J., 5
Stalnaker, L. T., Mrs., 35
Stanford, Samuel M., 91
Stantifer, W. H., Mrs., 9
Stantifer, see Sandifer
Stapleton, J. F., Mrs., 92
Stephens, Albert, Mrs., 54
Stephens, Calvin J., 75
Stephens, D. D., 14, 100
Stephens, Eliza, Mrs., 50
Stephens, Eunice, 35
Stephens, Kate, Mrs., 75
Stephens, N. K., 95

Stephens, Nancy, Mrs., 47, 100
Stephens, Nellie, 68
Stephens, R. H., 35, 68
Stern, Ben, 80
Stern, David G., 101
Stern, Henry, 80
Stern, J., 80
Stern, J., Mrs., 102
Stern, Leigman, 102
Stern, Mina, Mrs., 80
Stern, Minna, Mrs., 101
Stern, Seigman, 80
Stern, Silas, 80, 102
Stern, York, 102
Stevens, B. M., 32
Stevens, Bob, 102
Stevens, Callie, 59
Stevens, Charles A., 91, 102
Stevens, Charlie, 102
Stevens, Edward, 102
Stevens, Eli, 97
Stevens, Frank, 102
Stevens, Frank W., Mrs., 91
Stevens, Nellie, 102
Steverson, Charley, 22
Steverson, Civil, Mrs., 22
Stewart, Mrs., 87
Stewart, C. F., 21
Stewart, Charles, Sr., 87
Stewart, Hamp, Mrs., 96
Stewart, J. B., Mrs., 84
Stewart, Jane, 21
Stewart, W. B., Dr., 20
Stokes, R. E., Mrs., 7
Stokes, Viney, 10
Stokes, W. P., 23
Stone, George W., 29
Stout, Rev., 45
Stout, T. H., Mrs., 45
Stout, T. H., Rev., 70
Stovall, G. W., 10
Stovall, G. W., Mrs., 8
Stovall, George, 91
Stovall, J. H., Dr., 91
Stovall, Thomas, 91
Stow, Anthony, Mrs., 60
Stow, Ed, 60, 74
Stow, Kate, 60
Strauss, F., 26
Strauss, Meyer, 26
Strickland, C. H., 47
Strickland, F. J., Mrs., 24
Strickland, H., 47
Strickland, M. M., 56

Strickland, M. M., Mrs., 43
Strickland, Sidney, 11
Strong, William, Capt., 51
Sullivan, S. M., 40
Sutlive, Mrs., 57
Sutlive, Annie G., 55
Sutlive, E. J., Mrs., 55
Sutlive, M. G., Mrs., 113
Sutlive, W. G., 55
Sutton, B. H., 92
Sutton, B. H., Mrs., 95
Sutton, Margaret, Mrs., 92
Swanson, Thomas, Capt., 6
Swanson, W. C., 6
Swift, George P., 49
Sylvester, Allethia T., 84
Sylvester, Anna, 58
Sylvester, Edgar F., 85
Sylvester, Frances, 4
Sylvester, (Jos. A.), Mrs., 2
Sylvester, T. R., 85
Sylvester, Taylor, 85
Sylvester, Thos. R., 85
Sylvester, William O., 85
Talley, J. W., 98
Tansey, James, 54, 68
Tansey, James, Mrs., 39
Tanton, William C., 96
Tarver, Calista M., 108
Tarver, Charles, 56
Tatum, R. P., Mrs., 8
Taylor, Cal, 53
Taylor, Elizabeth, Mrs., 101
Taylor, James, 101
Taylor, John, 94
Taylor, S. A., Dr., 99
Taylor, Tom, 80
Teague, Angus, 49
Teague, E. V., Mrs., 49
Teague, Elijah, Judge, 59
Teague, L. L., 74
Teu, John, Mrs., 65
Tew, Martha, Mrs., 33
Tharp, Emily T., Mrs., 83
Tharp, V. D., 83, 106
Thiesen, Chris, Mrs., 99
Thomas, Mr., 116
Thomas, Mrs., 1
Thomas, Alex H., 23
Thomas, Alvin, 42
Thomas, Beauregard, 28
Thomas, Carlton, 97
Thomas, Carter, 20, 103

Thomas, Charley, Mrs., 113
Thomas, D. K., 20
Thomas, David K., 72
Thomas, Egletine B., Mrs., 112
Thomas, Estell, 113
Thomas, George H., 50
Thomas, Hassie, 113
Thomas, Hubbard, 10
Thomas, J. C., Jr., 103
Thomas, J. O., Jr., Mrs., 107
Thomas, John C., 9, 112
Thomas, John C., Jr., 10
Thomas, John W., 30
Thomas, M. V., Mrs., 112
Thomas, Mattie, 10
Thomas, Nancy, Mrs., 55
Thomas, P. L., Elder, 1
Thomas, W. H., 20, 23, 104
Thomasson, Dr., 42
Thomasson, J. R., Dr., 37
Thompson, Mrs., 105
Thompson, Rev., 45
Thompson, A. A., Col., 57
Thompson, A. B., 57
Thompson, Annie, 57
Thompson, Charles N., 72
Thompson, Coy, 57
Thompson, Geo. H., Mrs., 11
Thompson, Geo. W., Mrs. 71
Thompson, Georgia E., 72
Thompson, I. K., 57
Thompson, Mattie L., Mrs., 86
Thompson, N. F., Mrs., 61
Thompson, Robert, 72
Thompson, Sallie E., Mrs., 71
Thompson, Shade, Mrs., 79
Thompson, William, 71
Thornton, Dozier, 4, 11
Thornton, Fred, 4
Thornton, H. G., 4
Thornton, H. C., Mrs., 80
Thornton, J. M., Jr., 4
Thornton, John J., 49
Thornton, John M., 11
Thornton, John M., Col., 4
Thornton, Mary, 98
Thornton, Mollie, 4
Thornton, N., 11
Thornton, Nat, 4
Thornton, R. D., 26
Thornton, W. C., Mrs., 6
Thornton, William, Mrs., 11
Threatt, J. M., 57

Thrower, T. Emmett, Mrs., 108
Tibbetts, Wm. F., Mrs., 90
Tiller, Dan, Mrs., 80
Tiller, H. F., 98
Tillman, John, 97
Tillman, R. M., Mrs., 60
Timmier, T. J., 57
Timmons, Dr., 48
Timmons, R. A., Mrs., 48
Tindall, John, 51
Tomberlin, Alex, 37
Tomberlin, D. J., 1
Tomberlin, Dave J., 41
Tomberlin, Emma, 112
Tomberlin, R. Alex, 41
Tompkins, H. B., 97
Tompkins, Henry, 97
Tompkins, Lawrence, 97
Toney, Sarah A., Mrs., 33
Toney, Sterling, 33
Toney, T. W., 33
Toney, Washington, Col., 33, 46
Toney, Washington, Mrs., 46
Toole, John, 81
Tosh, James T., Capt., 30
Townsend, G. W., Mrs., 64
Traylor, Edward, 30
Traylor, William, 30
Treutlen, Celeste, 58
Tripp, C. H., Mrs., 92
Trofford, Mrs., 114
Troy, Daniel S., Col., 41
Troy, D. S., Col., 36
Tullis, Mrs., 2
Tullis, E. T., Mrs., 58
Tully, P. J., 80
Tully, William, Mrs., 10
Turner, Dr., 45
Turner, Mrs., 26
Turner, A. Dr., 73
Turner, Alley, 73
Turner, Jerre, 73
Turner, Richard, 100
Tye, M. M., Capt., 38
Tye, M. M., Mrs., 11
Tyler, Adam, Mrs., 97
Tyler, Dan, Mrs., 80
Tyre, J. T., 3
Urquhart, Henry, Dr., 90
Valentine, Charles, 28
Valentine, I. M., Mrs., 16
Vandiver, W. F., 86
Van Hoose, Mrs., 100
Van Hoose, Asa, Rev., 100

Van Hoose, Azor, Rev., 98
Van Houton, Prof., 1
Van Pelt, Sara, Mrs., 54
Vaughan, George, Mrs., 66
Veal, A. J., 38
Veal, Charley, 38
Veal, Jessie, 62
Veal, John, 96
Veal, Willia, 116
Venable, Henry W., 4
Venable, Sallie M., Mrs., 37
Venable, William H., 37
Ventress, James, 16
Ventress, Rena, 55
Ventress, T. H., 30, 55
Ventress, T. R., Mrs., 48
Verner, M. J., Mrs., 39
Vickers, Hatcher, Sr., 18
Vigal, Emmett, 63
Vigal, Will H., 63
Vining, Bob, 107
Vining, Elizabeth, Mrs., 107
Vining, Lizzie, Mrs., 79
Vinson, Charley, 47
Vinson, N. W., 33, 47, 93
Vinson, Vivie, 33
Waddell, deB., Rev., 104
Waddell, Dillie, 53
Waddell, Haynes, 104
Waddell, James F., Maj. 19
Waddell, James R., 104
Waddell, Mary F., Mrs., 104
Walker, Capt., 27
Walker, B. W., Mrs., 64
Walker, Daniel J., Mrs., 72
Walker, Hugh A., 26
Walker, Jason, 52
Walker, Jeremiah, 33
Walker, Lena, Mrs., 54
Walker, Minnie, 2
Walker, Nathan, 65
Walker, R. C., 25
Walker, Wyatt B., 25
Wallace, Allen, 78
Walls, Mary A., Mrs., 29
Walsh, Will, 31
Ward, Alfred G., 59
Ward, C., 12
Ward, E. D., 17
Ward, Lizzie, 17
Wardsworth, James, Mrs., 41
Ware, Henry, Mrs., 65
Ware, Lou, 96
Ware, Louise, Mrs., 96

Warr, Adam, 53
Warr, Elizabeth, Mrs., 106
Warr, Ezekiel, 106
Warr, G. W., 106
Warr, George, 106
Warr, J. E., Jr., Mrs., 44
Warr, James, 109
Warren, E. W., Dr., 27
Warren, Sophornia, Mrs., 33
Warren, T. E., 32
Warren, Thomas E., 33, 37
Watford, Barney B., 52
Watford, W. T., 50
Watkins, Mrs., 17
Watkins, Frank, 1
Watkins, Frank, Mrs., 20
Watkins, Henry, 15
Watkins, J. T., 15
Watkins, West, 17
Watson, Addie M., 110
Watson, E. C., Mrs., 60
Watson, Gerta, 60
Watson, James, 41
Watson, M. A., Mrs., 28
Watson, P. P., Mrs., 110
Watson, Penn P., 110
Watterson, Harvey M., 11
Watts, Thomas H., 20
Way, H. H., Mrs., 25
Weathers, Thomas, 24
Weaver, Mrs., 101
Weedon, H. M., Mrs., 15
Wellborn, Mrs., 27
Wellborn, C. B., Mrs., 46
Wells, Annie, Mrs., 9
Wells, C. C., Mrs., 1
Wells, Isaac, 111
Wells, Louis, 9
Wells, O. A., 97
Wells, O. S., 67
West, Almar, 104
West, Amos, 66, 89
West, Andrew, 66
West, Anson, Rev., 66, 89
West, Cornelius, 104
West, J. C., Mrs., 70, 91
West, Lizzie, Mrs., 99, 104
West, W. M., 104
West, William, 66, 89
Westbrook, Mrs., 87
Weston, Mrs., 43
Weston, Henry, 43
Wharton, M. B., Dr., 108
Whigham, T. G., 18

Whitaker, Nathan, 114
Whitaker, Nathan, Mrs., 62
White, Hillard, 16
White, J. M., 47
White, John C., 16, 116
White, P. W., 47
White, S. D., Mrs., 103
White, Susan A., Mrs., 116
White, W. J., 55
White, W. S., 47
White, Walter S., Mrs., 97
Whitehurst, Jesse, 4
Whitlock, George, 29
Whitlock, J. H., 29, 75
Whitlock, Mary, Mrs., 29
Whitney, Frank, Mrs., 80
Whittington, Obadiah, 17
Whittington, Ollin, Mrs., 32
Wilde, G. H., Mrs., 59
Wilhem, W. M., 90
Wilkerson, Jehus, 37
Wilkerson, Levi, Mrs., 32
Wilkerson, W. F., Mrs., 8
Wilkinson, Bunyan, 65
Wilkinson, Donie, Mrs., 65
Wilks, R. F., 43
Willford, L. E., Mrs., 90
Williams, Amma, 83
Williams, Buckner, 36
Williams, G. G., 3
Williams, George, 87
Williams, J. F., 113
Williams, J. N., 7
Williams, J. N., Mrs., 94
Williams, J. S., Mrs., 14
Williams, J. W., 87
Williams, John C., 36, 91, 95
Williams, M. F., Miss, 63
Williams, Martha, Mrs., 81
Williams, Martha Jane, Mrs., 87
Williams, Morgan, 36
Williams, N. T., 36
Williams, Nan, Mrs., 45
Williams, Nat, 113
Williams, Nathan, 87, 113
Williams, Osborne J., 19
Williams, Richard, 7
Williams, Richard, Capt., 15
Williams, Rinaldo, Mrs., 104
Williams, Robert, Dr., 31
Williams, Sarah, Mrs., 87
Williams, Savannah, 87
Williams, Sophia, Mrs., 19
Williams, W. H., 36

Williams, Walker, 77
Williams, Walker G., 77
Williams, Z. W., Dr., 31
Williamson, F. R. M., 3
Williamson, H. J., 68
Williamson, Henry E., Mrs., 25
Willis, C. C., Dr., 4
Willis, John W., 53
Wilson, E. B., 58
Wilson, Elizabeth, Mrs., 57
Wilson, H. M., Mrs., 9
Wilson, Lorenzo M., 16
Windham, John, Mrs., 14
Winn, J. J., Mrs., 88
Winslett, Joe, 107
Winslett, Rebecca, Mrs., 107
Wood, Mrs., 63
Wood, Benjamin, 110
Wood, F. S., 45
Wood, Fern M., Mrs., 117
Wood, Francis E., Mrs., 110
Wood, J. C., 110
Wood, J. C., Mrs., 113
Wood, Margaret, Mrs., 8
Wood, Mary V., Mrs., 86
Wood, N. H., Capt., 56
Wood, P., Judge, 88
Wood, S. P., 110
Wood, W. M., 110
Wood, William, 94
Woodall, L. A., Mrs., 3
Woodham, A. J., Mrs., 71
Woodham, Bill, 71
Woodham, Jim, 71
Woodham, Rube, 71
Woodruff, M. C., Mrs., 74
Woods, R. J., 2
Woods, S. A., 2
Woodson, John V., 5
Woolfolk, John C., 5
Woolfolk, Thomas, 30
Wooten, C. H., Col., 2
Word, R. C., Dr., 3
Worthy, O., Mrs., 77, 80, 86
Wright, Alex, 16
Wright, Calvin, 24
Wright, Clara, 29
Wright, Claud, 116
Wright, J. A., 9
Wright, J. H., 116
Wright, J. W., Mrs., 68
Wright, Jane Goodrum, 38
Wright, John W., Mrs., 67

Wright, R. G., Maj., 38
Wright, R. G., Mrs., 32
Wright, S. J., 116
Wright, Thomas C., 1
Wright, W. F., Dr., 1, 116
Wright, W. F., Mrs., 35
Wright, Winn, 116
Wyatt, Violetta, Mrs., 80
Yeates, James, Rev., 46
Yerby, John D., 77
Young, Dr., 93
Young, E. B., Col., 102
Young, Edward B., 89
Young, J. W., Mrs., 102
Young, Marie, 83
Zorn, D. H., Capt., 69
Zorn, George, Mrs., 98
Zuber, T. W., Mrs., 67

www.ingramcontent.com/pod-product-compliance
Lightning Source LLC
Chambersburg PA
CBHW020655300426
44112CB00007B/391